# The Only Guides You'll Ever Need!

THIS SERIES IS YOUR TRUSTED GUIDE through all of life's stages and situations. Want to learn how to surf the Internet or care for your new dog? Or maybe you'd like to become a wine connoisseur or an expert gardener? The solution is simple: Just pick up a K.I.S.S. Guide and turn to the first page...

Expert authors will walk you through the subject from start to finish, using simple blocks of knowledge to build your skills one step at a time. Build upon these learning blocks and by the end of the book, you'll be an expert yourself! Or, if you are familiar with the topic but want to learn more, it's easy to dive in and pick up where you left off.

The K.I.S.S. Guides deliver what they promise: simple access to all the information you'll need on one subject. Other titles you might want to check out include: Playing Guitar, Weight Loss, Gardening, Microsoft Windows Me, Astrology, and many more.

# GUIDE TO

# Gambling

## JOHN MARCHEL

Foreword by Lance Humble Ph.D
Author of *The World's Greatest Blackjack Book*

A Dorling Kindersley Book

LONDON, NEW YORK, MUNICH,
MELBOURNE, DELHI

**DK Publishing, Inc.**
**Senior Editor** Jennifer Williams
**Editor** Matthew X. Kieman
**Copyeditors** JoAnna Kremer and Miccinello Associates Editorial Consultants
**Category Publisher** LaVonne Carlson


**Dorling Kindersley Limited**
**Project Editors** Caroline Hunt, Julian Gray, David Tombesi-Walton
**Art Editors** Justin Clow, Simon Murrell
**Design Assistant** Martin Dieguez


**Managing Editor** Maxine Lewis
**Managing Art Editor** Heather M^cCarry


**Picture Research** Samantha Nunn
**Production** Heather Hughes
**Category Publisher** Mary Thompson

Published in the United States by
DK Publishing, Inc.
375 Hudson Street
New York, New York 10014

**Library of Congress Cataloging-in-Publication Data**

Marchel, John.
K.I.S.S. guide to gambling / author, John Marchel. – 1st American ed.
p. cm. – (Keep it simple series)
Includes bibliographical references and index.
ISBN 0-7894-8051-4 (alk. paper)
1. Gambling. 2. Games. I. Title: KISS guide to gambling. II. Title. III. Series.
GV1301 .M265 2001
795–dc21

2001001479

Color reproduction by Colourscan
Printed and bound by MOHN media and Mohndruck GmbH, Germany

See our complete product line at
**www.dk.com**

# Contents at a Glance

# CONTENTS

## PART ONE  Things to Know

### CHAPTER 1  Before You Begin to Play                     22

### CHAPTER 2  The Little Extras                             36

# PART THREE  Machine Games

# APPENDICES

# Foreword

GAMBLING IS ONE of the oldest forms of entertainment. The excitement of risking something of value with a hope of gain seems to be an instinctive magnetic force. If you've ever had an inkling to gamble, this K.I.S.S. guide will help make your foray into gambling more fun and more profitable or at least more fun and less costly, depending on how much time you decide to devote to studying your favorite game or sport. Today, playing in a casino, making a bet on a sporting event, or even buying a lottery ticket have all become very easy. Casinos, racetracks, and lotteries can be found virtually in almost every corner of the world.

Its fun and exciting to just gamble. However, it's much more exciting to gamble and win. Gambling is easy – all you need is some money. Winning, however, is more difficult. Winning requires a certain attitude, knowledge, and specific skills. The K.I.S.S. Guide to Gambling is about playing and winning. Whether you are getting ready to visit a casino, or going on a cruise vacation or even going to a bingo hall for the first time, I encourage you to take the time to read this book. John Marchel has written this fun and exciting book to help you become more successful playing the lottery, picking the horses, or getting more wins in a casino.

Before you venture into this exciting world of gambling, you need to learn certain skills such as money management, odds interpretation, establishing winning goals, or finding the best casinos. How can you learn such skills? There are classes, hundreds of how-to books, or perhaps you can get a friend or relative to teach you. However, some of these methods take too long, cost too much, or may just not be practical for you.

The approach that John uses in this fun book is simple: he starts with the basics and builds on them one step at a time. John has laid out each chapter assuming you have never gambled, been to a casino, racetrack, or bingo hall. He leads you step-by-step on the road to gaining the skills and confidence of a successful player. He does this by presenting the material in a simple, practical, and entertaining way that allows you, the reader, to understand and easily absorb all the information. John can not guarantee to make you a winner; however, he does offer an expert's experience and shares what he has learned over the years of playing and teaching others to gamble. His book will give you the knowledge to help keep your losses to a minimum while allowing you a better-than-average chance of being a winner.

Remember, John Marchel has gambled successfully for the past 25 years. I encourage you to take the time to read his book in detail so that you can benefit from his experience and know-how. John has created a masterpiece. This is truly a remarkable book and perhaps the best all-around guide ever produced on gambling. I recommend it to you highly and without reservation.

Sincerely and with best wishes,

LANCE HUMBLE PH.D

# Introduction

IN WHATEVER PART OF THE WORLD you travel, there probably is a lottery, casino, or racetrack waiting for you to explore. People have gambled for thousands of years, and today people gamble more than ever before. It's fun and exciting to pick your favorite numbers and imagine what you would do with a $10 million lottery win.

It's a good feeling when you first look at your cards and see a blackjack. Your spirits soar when the horse you picked is coming down the home stretch four lengths ahead of the field. Winning at gambling brings a thrill like no other. On the other hand, losing can drive you into a deep hole in many ways. It simply boils down to one of my favorite sayings, "Winning is skill and losing is bad luck."

My goal in writing this book is to show you what games are available, how to play them, and, most of all, how to play them skillfully. I believe there is no such thing as a bad player, only untrained ones. I do offer one caution: This book is not designed to encourage you to quit your day job and take up gambling as a profession. It's extremely difficult to be a professional gambler.

All games have built-in advantages for the house. This house advantage, or edge, along with a never-ending source of house funds, makes gambling a very tough sport for any player. On the other hand, players can and do win. You too can win, and win often, when you play correctly. I'll not only show you how to play correctly, but also tell you where you can play; and I'll even suggest when you shouldn't play. In addition, I'll show you how to manage your funds, an important part of successful gaming.

Just remember, there are some good games and some not-so-good games. By not-so-good games, I mean those with odds that are much too high and should be avoided. There are other games with bets that give the house a less then 1-percent advantage, and you should know and play these. I encourage you to read this book all the way through first, then go back and review the chapters that interest you the most. Read and study them in detail. The information is designed to show, in simple steps, how to play, and how to play successfully. By the time you've finished this guide, you should be able to gamble at any track or in any casino in the world.

I also want you to enjoy the fun that can accompany gambling. Take all the complimentary benefits that the new mega-casinos offer. See the shows and star entertainers. Try the gourmet meals, take in all the amenities that have become standard at today's modern mega-casinos. The games you learn and play should be one part of your overall entertainment outlook. Enjoy it all, and most of all have fun doing it.

*John Marchel*

JOHN MARCHEL

# What's Inside?

*THE INFORMATION in the K.I.S.S. GUIDE TO GAMBLING is arranged so that you gain an insight into the history and background of the subject as a whole before embarking on the rules and strategies of the individual games.*

## PART ONE

In Part One I'll give you information about early gambling, the types of games available and how to have fun while playing. I'll also show you what it takes to become a better player and most of all how to manage your funds effectively.

## PART TWO

In Part Two I'll teach you to play table games like blackjack, craps, baccarat, roulette, poker, and some of the newer games. You'll learn the basics along with some sound strategy techniques needed to win at these games.

## PART THREE

Part Three discusses machine games like slot machines, video poker, keno, bingo, and lotteries. Don't leave it all to chance. I'll show you how to improve your likelihood of winning at these games by using some simple but effective techniques.

## PART FOUR

In Part Four I'll introduce you to horse and dog racing along with wagering on sporting events. Like other games these involve techniques and strategies. I'll show you how to predict a winner at a racetrack or sporting event.

## PART FIVE

In Part Five you'll discover all the places where you can gamble today. I'll tell you about Las Vegas and other places in the US that have gambling and you'll get a good insight into the other countries that offer gaming. I'll also touch on Internet gambling and pleasures of gambling cruises.

# The Extras

THROUGHOUT THE BOOK, *you'll notice a number of boxes and symbols. They are there to emphasize certain points I want you to pay special attention to, because they are important to your understanding and improvement. You'll find:*

## Very Important Point

This symbol points out a topic I believe deserves careful attention. You really need to know this information before continuing.

## Complete No-No

This is a warning, something I want to advise you not to do or to be aware of.

## Getting Technical

When the information is about to get a bit technical, I'll let you know so that you can read carefully.

## Inside Scoop

These are special suggestions that come from my own personal experience. I want to share them with you because they helped me when I was learning the game.

You'll also find some little boxes that include information I think is important, useful, or just plain fun.

### Trivia...

*These are simply fun facts that will give you an extra appreciation for the history and uniqueness of this great pastime.*

### DEFINITION

*Here I'll **define** words and terms for you in an easy-to-understand style. You'll also find a glossary at the back of the book with all the gambling lingo.*

### INTERNET

**www.dk.com**

*I think the Internet is a great resource for gamblers, so I've scouted out some web sites that will add to your enjoyment and understanding of the games.*

# PART ONE

YOU'LL HAVE MORE FUN ONCE YOU KNOW THE BASICS

# THINGS TO KNOW

**M**OST PEOPLE WOULDN'T THINK OF GOING OUT on the tennis court or golf course without first taking some lessons. Well, it should also be true for gambling. You need to *take some lessons* before you begin to gamble. That is what this book is all about: The A to Z of how the games are played, along with the who, what, when, and why of gambling.

Keep this in mind: Casinos make their fortunes primarily because players lack sensible gaming knowledge and sound *money-management* techniques. These two simple elements allow the gaming industry to grow and thrive year after year. This book will give you the *knowledge*. Later you'll need to get some experience, but for now let's acquire some basics; and I promise I'll keep it simple.

# Chapter 1

# Before You Begin to Play

GAMBLING CAN BE FUN and frustrating; sometimes, it can be both at the same time. So, just what is this activity that has fascinated us for thousands of years? Here's one definition of gambling: speculating on an event that is uncertain and that involves placing at risk a possession in the hope of achieving more or a better possession. Getting married, having a child, starting a new job, and investing on the stock market could all be considered gambling. But for the purposes of this book, gambling is taken to mean the wagering of funds on events practiced in casinos and elsewhere, including sports betting and lottery-type games.

## In this chapter...

✔ In the beginning there was gambling

✔ Gambling here and there

✔ Types of games

✔ A little about probabilities

✔ What to do first

GAMBLING HAS BEEN WITH US IN MANY FORMS FOR MANY, MANY YEARS

# In the beginning there was gambling

THE WORD GAMBLE
*derives from the Anglo-Saxon word
gamenian, which means "to sport
or play." Gambling is one of the
few social activities that occurs
in nearly all cultures and, more
importantly, has occurred in almost
every period of time throughout
history. In fact, when we look back
over thousands of years, we
find gambling in all the great
civilizations, and at every social
level. The Egyptians, ancient
Chinese, Indians, Romans, Greeks,
Hebrews, and North and South
American Indian tribes all practiced some form of gambling in their societies.
They gambled for fun, for riches, and sometimes even as a
peaceful way to end disputes. In fact, it appears that the Inuit
are the only people not to include some form of gambling in
their society. All in all, then, there is no doubt that people have
gambled a lot throughout the ages, and still do today.*

■ **The ancient Aztecs** *gambled on a board game
called patolli, which was played with beans as dice on
a diagonal cross-shaped board. Players often wagered
vast treasures on the outcome.*

## What to gamble on

You can gamble on almost anything today. You can bet on who will
win the presidential election, the World Series, the World Cup of
soccer, golf or tennis matches, or any other sport. You can wager on
horse and dog races. You can gamble in casinos, which have a variety
of table games, machines, and wheels you can bet on. Many states
have lotteries; native American (Indian) casinos offer bingo and pull
tabs, along with a full array of casino-type games. You name it, you
can bet on it somewhere in the world.

## Types of gamblers

You'll see many different types of players at the track and at the casino. Generally speaking, you'll find some foolish types who will bet on anything and lose most of the time, but you'll also find some very good gamblers who will win a lot of bets. You might even see some expert gamblers who seem to win big bets all the time. The real question is this: What type of gambler or player do you want to be? Do you want to be an amateur, a knowledgeable player, or a professional? To be an amateur is easy: Just go into any casino and play any game, regardless of your knowledge, and hope Lady Luck looks fondly on you. To place yourself in the second category, that of knowledgeable player, you can read this book and become knowledgeable and be successful during your visits to racetracks and casinos. To take it a step further, you should study this book in depth, practice what's in it, and then go further, reading and practicing everything you can in regard to your game. (It also doesn't hurt if you have a bankroll that can carry you through some inevitable downturns.) After all that, you might just be starting down the road to becoming a professional gambler.

# Gambling here and there

TODAY, YOU NO LONGER *need to make a long journey to Las Vegas, Reno, or Atlantic City to gamble in a casino. Casinos, riverboats, and racetracks are now located in 33 US states from Arizona to Wisconsin, from New England to Southern California. It's been estimated that every American – except for those who reside in Alaska (because it's too big), Hawaii, Tennessee (because it has no casinos) and Utah – is now within 300 miles (500 km) of a casino. Only two states in the US, Hawaii and Utah, do not have any form of legalized gambling. Furthermore, in addition to casinos, 46 states and the District of Columbia all have some type of gambling, such as a lottery, horse racing, or dog racing. People of all ages are flocking to the biggest, wildest, and most outlandish type of entertainment available anywhere on the entire planet.*

## Gambling around the world

In addition to gambling in America, there are 139 countries (ranging from Aruba to Zanzibar) that have casinos, and there are 138 cruise ships around the world with casinos on board. Canadians can gamble at year-round, permanent casinos in Quebec (the first province to have casino gambling), Ontario, Nova Scotia, Manitoba, and Saskatchewan, and other casinos are in the works. The oldest casino in the world is in Baden-Baden,

Germany, where people have been gambling for more than 200 years. The most famous casino is in Monte Carlo, in Monaco. The games we're familiar with as part of today's gambling come from all over the world. For instance, the French take credit for inventing many of the casino games we play today, the "surrender" option in blackjack came from Asia, and baccarat is as popular in some South American countries as it is in Western Europe. In this book, I'll lead you through the enchanted land of gambling and show you the who, what, when, where, and why of it. And I promise to try to keep it simple!

■ **The Grand Casino in Monte Carlo** *is perhaps the most famous casino in the world. High- and low-rollers alike come from all over to try their luck.*

## Early gambling in America

The United States has had a long history of gambling. For example, the Virginia colony was financed by a lottery that was held in England in 1612, and the American Revolution was paid for largely by state lotteries. Later, states and towns followed this lead, and paid for roads and public works projects through the sale of lottery tickets.

> ### Trivia...
> *Soldiers in the American Revolution would flatten musket shot into cubes, and then use their bayonets to mark spots on them so that they would have dice to play with during those long nights at Valley Forge.*

But there's more . . . The first president of the United States, George Washington, had a string of horses that he raced in Alexandria and Annapolis. And it is well-documented that Thomas Jefferson frequently enjoyed a little gambling, regardless of such pressing issues as working on the Declaration of Independence.

It wasn't until later, though, that America's first true casino was opened. A Louisiana entrepreneur named John Davis established an opulent casino in New Orleans in 1827. Then, during the westward expansion of the 1800s, riverboat gamblers rode all the steamboats of America's river system. By 1850 there were approximately 6,000 gambling houses in New York City alone. Later, when tent towns were thrown up in the far west, gambling tables and roulette wheels were among the first pieces of furniture brought in.

PLAYING FARO AT A NEW YORK GAMBLING "HELL"

## Gambling today

Today, casino gambling is no longer seen as an evil pastime; rather, it is now viewed as a hobby that includes fine dining, great entertainment, and a respectable environment in which to have some fun. Even Las Vegas has transformed itself over the last 20 years, changing from a glitter and risk town for grown-ups into a family vacation destination. Throughout the rest of America, voters have approved casino gambling in 30 states, and American Indians consider casino gambling on their land to be something that offers substantial financial rewards for their people.

## GAMING IN THE UNITED STATES

| | |
|---|---|
| Commercial casinos | 11 states |
| Native American (Indian) casinos | 19 states |
| Horse racing, dog racing, or jai alai | 41 states |
| Charitable gaming (bingo, raffles, etc.) | 46 states |
| State lotteries | 37 states |

# Types of games

*WHEN IT COMES TO GAMBLING, there are two basic types of games: games of chance and games of skill. Knowing the differences between the two is very important to you, the player. One type of game depends totally on Lady Luck, and requires little skill on the part of the player; conversely, the other type depends a great deal on the skill of the player and very little on luck.*

Smart, knowledgeable, and professional players will only play in games that have a small house *edge*. Novice and uninformed players, on the other hand, will play in any and all games, unaware of the *house advantage* or edge. Just remember that the house must charge a price to be able to stay in business – but in some games that price can be unreasonable. So, you need to find those games and situations that allow for a house advantage of 2 percent or less.

## Games of chance

Games of chance include craps, roulette, slot machines, the Big 6 wheel (or wheel of fortune), keno, bingo, and lotteries. The key to determining why these are considered games of chance is this: The dice, wheel, and ball have no memory. In other words, what happened on the last throw of the dice or spin of the wheel has no bearing on what will happen next. Each event is independent and separate, with no relationship to the preceding or succeeding event.

■ **Dice don't remember,** *and neither does the ball as it bobbles about on the roulette wheel. Games of chance have no respect for history.*

*Games of chance depend totally on Lady Luck, not on any skill on the part of the player. The term used by scholars to describe games of chance is events of independent trials.*

## Games of skill

When we look at games of skill such as blackjack, baccarat, video poker, regular poker, sports, and horse racing, we discover that what happened before does affect what is going to happen next, making these events of dependent trials. For example, if all the aces have shown up in the first round in blackjack, we know that no more will turn up until the deck is reshuffled. Likewise, playing perfect strategy at poker (or even video poker) will greatly increase your chances of winning the hand, and becoming a handicapper at racing will give you the best chance of betting successfully at the track.

■ **Playing perfect strategy** *at games of skill such as video poker will increase your chance of winning.*

You need to have some basic understanding of what is going on when you play in today's modern mega-casinos or at the racetrack. It has been proven time and time again that most losses at gambling are the result of poor playing, faulty strategy, poor money management, and flawed systems on the part of the player. In other words, players often beat themselves. Players who hit when they should stand, call when they should fold, and continue to bet when they should walk away will consistently lose. There is an old gambler's saying: "The smarter you play, the more lucky you'll be."

*When it comes to gambling, knowledge is the key to winning. To overcome any shortcomings, you should know how to play the various games that are offered, and play them correctly.*

The naive visitor doesn't really know what he is facing when he enters a casino. He's often unaware of the house advantages on the table games and machines. Obtaining knowledge about gambling is the best way to ensure you have many successful visits to the casino.

# A little about probabilities

THE HEART OF GAMBLING *is probability. What is probability? It is the chance of achieving a particular outcome compared to all possible outcomes. This ratio is often called the law of averages. One important thing you should always remember is that the law of averages doesn't work for you during a 3-day visit to Monte Carlo. (It does work for the casino in the long run, though, because they play 365 days a year.) But understanding a little about the mathematics of probability will help you to determine which are good bets to make and which are bad. Casino management knows all about probabilities, and so do professional gamblers. You, as a gambler, should have at least a working knowledge of probabilities.*

## Probability 101

If you use a coin toss as a means of determining probability, you'll find that there are only two possible outcomes: heads or tails. Thus, you have a one in two chance of getting heads. Therefore, the probability of getting a head is ½, or 0.5. We can talk about probabilities in decimals or fractions, or we can say the odds of getting a head is 50–50, which is a ratio. How it is expressed doesn't matter, as long as you understand the chances, or the probability, of a specific event occurring. In blackjack, the probability of getting an ace and a 10-value card is 1 in 20 hands. When we look at

■ **When playing blackjack,** *you should know that there is a 1 in 20 chance of being dealt a blackjack (an ace and a 10-value card).*

roulette with a single zero, the probability over 100,000 spins will be about 49 percent red, 49 percent black, and 2 percent green. In other words, each game has a probability of a specific event happening, and you should know what the probabilities are.

*By studying each game, you will learn what the probabilities are. The main thing to remember, though, is that the probability of the event happening can be considerably different from what the casino will pay you. This is the price you pay for playing.*

## The cost of playing — odds versus edge

Modern gambling facilities earn their profits by charging the customer a fee or commission for the privilege of playing in their facility. This fee is known as the edge or house advantage, which is built into each and every wager made in the casino or at the racetrack. The formal term used in the gambling business for this commission is the vigorish, or vig.

One way of looking at this edge is by tossing a coin. In this hypothetical coin-toss game, let's say you bet $1 and hope to win on the side of heads, and lose to the casino if tails comes up. If tails does come up you lose $1, but if heads wins, you receive only 99¢. This 1¢ difference is the house edge, or vig, which the casino uses to make its profit.

■ **When is a coin toss** *not a 50–50 proposition? When you have to pay a vig to the casino after a win. That's how casinos make their money.*

## The real return

It is interesting to see what the real return is for the casinos on the specific games they offer. The real return is the actual amount players lose when they play against a casino. For example, in the chart opposite, you can see that the casino should win 0.80 percent (or 80¢) for every $100 played at blackjack against a skilled and knowledgeable player who uses basic strategy. When reviewing public records from Nevada casinos, however, we find that the casinos are winning 14 to 15 percent, or $14 to $15 per $100 played. This tells us that there are a lot of players who really don't know how to play blackjack. The same is true with craps: The house should win 60¢ per $100, but is actually winning $16. There is a saying that is common among gamblers: "If you want to get rich at gambling, buy a casino!"

## GAME ODDS VERSUS REAL RETURN

The house receives a lot more return than the game really offers. The reasons for this are simple: lack of skill at playing the game and poor money management techniques on the part of the player. Overcoming these two simple obstacles will greatly improve your win-rate when playing games in the casino. As you read this book, you'll learn how to play each game and how to manage your money, as well as how to get the most enjoyment out of playing.

| Game | House edge | Real return |
| --- | --- | --- |
| Baccarat (banker) | 1.17% | 17% |
| Baccarat (player) | 1.63% | 18% |
| Big 6 wheel | 11.1% to 24% | 37 to 44% |
| Blackjack | 0.80% | 14 to 15% |
| Caribbean stud poker | 5.26% | 23 to 26% |
| Craps (double odds) | 0.60% | 13 to 16% |
| Keno | 25% | 25 to 26% |
| Let It Ride | 3.5% | 19 to 22% |
| Pai Gow poker | 2.5% | 20 to 23% |
| Sports book | 4.5% | 15 to 18% |
| Roulette (double 0) | 5.6% | 25 % |
| Roulette (single 0) | 2.7% | 24% |
| Three-card poker | 3.4% | 15 to 25% |

# What to do first

READ THIS BOOK CAREFULLY *from cover to cover, and then go back and take a second look at any particular chapter or game that may catch your interest or that you would like to learn to play better. Study the text carefully to ensure complete understanding. Remember, when it comes to gambling, knowledge is the only sure way of winning consistently.*

## Read, read, read

If you buy a new car, you will want to read the owner's manual. If you are planning to plant in a garden, you want to get a good book on gardening. If you're planning to go to a casino, it stands to reason that you'll need a good book about gambling. Before you head to the casino, you should read everything you can about your favorite game. Note that there are magazines on sports betting, slots, blackjack, and casino games in general. You might want to start by reading some of the books listed in the Appendices at the back of this book.

■ **It makes sense** *to read up about the games you're going to play before you actually play them.*

## Use the Internet

Go to the web sites suggested throughout this book. Search the Internet using keywords about your game. Find and join chat rooms to get the latest information about your favorite game and where to play it. Your objective should be to study your game, practice it, and learn everything you can about it. This will make you a knowledgeable player, and one who is in complete control when it comes to gambling. As with anything, practice makes perfect.

## Early casino visits

Watch the game you're interested in prior to playing. This will help you gain some insight, such as where and when to place your bets and how to handle the dice or cards. You will also be able to determine if conferring with other players is allowed. (For example, in games such as craps and blackjack it's okay, but in Caribbean stud poker, it's not.) Feel free to ask the dealers questions. They have some limits on what they can tell you, but in general they will help a new player. Watch the table limits; it might seem obvious to you that you should check the minimum bet, but don't forget to also check for the table maximum. (For instance, if the table maximum is $3,000, don't expect to be paid $10,000 if you bet $100 playing Caribbean stud poker and are dealt a royal flush with 100:1 odds. You will only receive the maximum – $3,000.) Be sure to see and read everything while you are in the casino.

*Don't jump into a game with serious money just for the experience of playing. Learning at the table is one of the best ways to learn, but it is also the most expensive way.*

# Who are all those people?

When you enter a casino you will encounter the wide variety of house personnel required to run a large modern casino. You should know who they are and what they do. Some you will see in the gaming areas and others work behind the scenes, but it takes all of them to keep the place running effectively. First and foremost, don't be intimidated by dealers or pit bosses. They are paid to look at everyone as if they are a cheater. Because you are not a cheater, you have nothing to worry about. But this doesn't mean you should get cocky, either.

*Remember, casino management has the right to refuse service and ask you to leave their casino at any time and for any reason. And the courts have upheld that action, so don't even consider fighting it.*

(a) The dealer is the main person you'll come into contact with at the blackjack, craps, and roulette tables. The dealer makes change, takes and gives chips, and deals the cards, controls the dice, or spins the wheel. Normally, he or she deals for 40 minutes and breaks for 20 over an 8-hour period.

(b) The keno runner solicits and shuttles keno tickets from the casino area to the keno lounge and delivers results and payments to winning players.

(c) The change person is assigned to the slot area to provide change and, on big payouts, cash for award winners. Most new casino employees start out as change personnel.

(d) The floor man supervises a group of tables within the gambling pit. He or she can extend credit, give comps, settle disputes, and bar players. The floor man answers to the pit boss.

(e) The pit boss is the supervisor in charge of the entire pit area, including the blackjack tables, roulette, craps, and the Big 6 wheel games. He or she is the final authority in any dispute. The pit boss will also approve credit for high rollers and supervise all floor men.

■ **A roulette dealer** *removes all losing bets before paying all winning bets, watched closely by the floor man (right) and pit boss.*

*(f)* The shift supervisor takes full responsibility for all action in the casino during his 8-hour shift. He reports to the casino manager, oversees any big payoffs at the slots or keno, and ensures that enough staff are available for all the games.

*(g)* The casino manager is responsible for the entire casino operation. He's the key manager for all gaming, setting the tone of the casino and deciding what rules are used for the games, how many tables there are, and how the pits are laid out.

*(h)* The general manager is the head of the organization and may even be an owner. He makes the major decisions about everything. In large casino resorts, he's usually responsible for other areas in addition to the casino, such as the restaurant, the entertainment, and the hotel.

*(i)* The eye-in-the-sky are hidden cameras suspended in bubbles on the ceiling of the casino. With these videos, special surveillance staff observe and record all action throughout the casino floor, looking for cheating players, and sometimes even for cheating employees.

*(j)* An outside man, usually a former card counter or law enforcement officer, works undercover. He looks for cheats, dishonest employees, and card counters.

*(k)* The Gaming Commission is the official US state or government agency that issues licenses and governs all gaming and oversees enforcement of rules and regulations as applied to US casinos. The major exceptions to this rule are Native American (Indian) casinos. They have no formal oversight agency. Instead, the casino management oversees the games itself.

## Starting to play

As you gain know-how, you prepare yourself to venture into the real world of gambling. You'll want to start by playing in the mornings and early afternoons in the casinos – the table limits are lower and it's less crowded, allowing you more flexibility in choosing tables and machines. Consider playing the blackjack 25¢ machines. You can start off with a small stake on these machines and take all the time you need before you have to make a decision. Sit in the keno lounge and watch a few games. Find the sportsbook area or go to a racetrack and watch some horse racing to familiarize yourself with the payouts and how to read the racing form. By the time you go, you'll already have book knowledge, having read so much about gambling; now it's time to get the hands-on experience of participation.

**INTERNET**

www.gamblesearch.com
/casino.html

*"A Gamblesearch Edition" claims to have the best sports and gambling links anywhere on the Net. Their motto is, "If it's gambling, it's here."*

## Wagering for real

As you begin to wager on events and in casinos, you should start with small bets. Play at the $3 blackjack table, the 50¢ roulette wheel, the 5¢ video poker machines, or the $2 win-place-show bets at the racetrack. Remember, you are still learning and gaining real experience, and the objective here is not to pay a high price for it. As you gain hands-on experience and win some wagers, use those funds to move up in scale. Now you can afford to play at the $5 tables and the 25¢ or dollar machines. You do need your own bankroll to start with, but it's nice if the casino or racetrack can help finance some of your gambling ventures later on.

## A simple summary

✓ Gambling has been found in almost every civilization and at every social level throughout history, going back thousands of years. Today you can gamble on almost anything from cards and tennis to poker and horse racing.

✓ In the United States today, you can gamble in 48 of the 50 states. Some states have casinos and card rooms, others have horse and dog racing, and still others have lotteries. There are also 139 other countries and 138 cruise ships around the world that allow some type of gambling.

✓ There really are only two types of games: games of skill and games of chance. They are known as events of dependent or independent trials. Good players know the difference, and how to play each type of game correctly.

✓ As a player, you need to know a little about probability and the law of averages. In addition, knowing the house edge for any given game will have a positive impact on your win-rate.

✓ There is a lot to do when you are first learning to play. Read, use the Internet, ask lots of questions, and get to know who you will be playing against at a casino. Start slow and for low stakes, building your knowledge and skill along the way.

# Chapter 2

# The Little Extras

WHETHER YOU VISIT A CASINO REGULARLY or are a novice on your way to Atlantic City or Las Vegas for the first time, there are some important things you should know when it comes to gambling. Is there any cheating in the casinos? And what about those important comps that the house gives away all the time? Can you make a living at gambling? What do you need to know about taxes?

*In this chapter...*

✓ *The little things*

✓ *Comps: are they really free?*

✓ *Making a living*

✓ *Having fun*

✓ *Your government wants to hear from you*

THE GRANDNESS OF YOUR COMPS ARE DICTATED BY THE SIZE OF YOUR BANKROLL

# The little things

LEST WE FORGET, casinos, racetracks, and lotteries are all designed to remove players from their money. They might make it interesting and fun, but their true motive is pure profit. The profit can be for the stockholders, the state coffers, or the private owners; it really doesn't matter – they all want your money. You might agree that you get your money's worth in the fun and entertainment you receive in return for paying the casinos. However, your attitude should be as follows: If they are willing to offer you the chance to obtain some of their funds in exchange for the risk involved in gambling, you should make a point of trying to get their money, instead of vice versa.

## Cheating

Players always ask questions about cheating in casinos. Most experts will agree that casinos do not cheat. In fact, casino gambling is one of America's most heavily regulated industries. Today, casinos are owned and operated by some of the largest shareholder corporations in the world. These companies are not foolish enough to risk their gaming licenses by cheating. In the US, if a state's Gaming Commission were to find a casino cheating, they would close it down. And the truth is, when you watch how some people play the games, you begin to understand that casinos don't have to cheat. Most players beat themselves when they gamble.

*Why do dealers cheat? Well, they cheat for personal gain; they are not cheating for the house.*

Most experts generally agree that casino employees and dealers will sometimes cheat. They might cheat a customer, say for $300, by dealing **seconds** at a blackjack table, or by shorting the amount of a craps payout bet. Later, an accomplice will play at the same table, and the dealer will again cheat; but this time, the accomplice wins or gets a higher payout than is the required amount at the craps table. Later, after work, they meet and divide the winnings. Such occurrences are rare; however, if you even think that you are being cheated, move to another table, pit, or even another casino immediately. That will solve your problem.

> **DEFINITION**
>
> At cards, cheating dealers don't deal from the bottom of the deck, as they sometimes do in the movies. Rather, they deal the second card from the top. This is called dealing **seconds**. A dealer will do this because he has already peeked at the top card, and is saving it until the right moment to put it into play.

## Souvenirs

Everyone likes to take a souvenir home from a visit to an exciting place. The same is true when it comes to visiting a casino: Many folks will take home a casino chip as a reminder of a great visit. It costs the casino between 18 and 23¢ to obtain each chip from the manufacturer. You pay out $1, $5, or $25 per chip, depending on the value. Another fun and free souvenir is a change cup. There is a lady in the Midwest who has a large collection of change cups from different casinos around the country. In fact, there are collectors who buy, sell, and trade casino memorabilia all over the world: chips, change cups, ashtrays, stir sticks, match books, and so on. This could be the start of a new hobby for you!

■ **Why not hold on** *to that change cup? It's a free souvenir and might be the first item in a new collection.*

**INTERNET**

### www.ebay.com

*When you get to this site, look up "games," and then "gambling." The last time I looked, there were more than 350 gambling items for sale, ranging from a tin roulette wheel to casino collector spoons. If you want to collect casino memorabilia, e-Bay is a good place to start.*

*An alternative to taking a chip as a souvenir is to ask the pit boss for a deck of playing cards or a set of dice. These are free, and you can use them after you get home.*

# Comps: are they really free?

CASINOS GIVE AWAY comps – *everything from a free drink at the table or machine to rooms, food, and beverages (RFB). Sometimes, they'll even provide reimbursement for airline tickets, choice seats at a gourmet restaurant, or maybe a 5,000-square-foot (465 m²) suite with a butler. Most people think comps are for high rollers only; that's not true. Comps can be obtained by all players (particularly in the US), high roller or otherwise.*

**DEFINITION**

**Comp** *is short for complimentary. Casinos give services, rooms, food, and show tickets to players for free (or at very good discount rates) to entice them to come to their casino and gamble.*

■ **Make sure you pick up a comp card** *from every casino you visit. If the casino is prepared to give you things for free, why not take them up on their offer?*

# Getting comps

There are some things you will need to do to get comps, regardless of your betting level. When you first arrive at a casino, go to the guest service desk or cashier cage and ask for a VIP, slot club, or players' club card. (The card names might vary from casino to casino.) You'll want a card that will identify you as a player in that specific casino. Use the card every time you play, and get a card from every casino you visit. By using this card at table games and slot machines, you are being "rated" while you play. This means that the casino staff will evaluate you based on the amount you bet, which games you play, and the amount of time you spend on each game. When you reach specific levels in these categories, the house will grant you a comp. If you play machines, always put your card into the machine before you begin to play. Even 25¢ slot players can get comps, so don't think your level is too low. If you are playing table games, give your player card to the dealer when you first begin to play. If you want comps, it's important that you always use your card when gaming.

*Remember, a 25¢ slot player is playing at a rate of almost 600 spins per hour. That equates to $150 an hour! You should get a comp lunch or buffet at that rate. Always ask . . . and thou shalt receive!*

All casinos use a similar formula when determining comp eligibility:

average bet x decisions per hour x hours played x
house advantage

Let's say you are playing blackjack for $20 per hand, and you play for 4 hours. You can expect about 70 hands per hour. The house expects at least a 2 percent return from the average player. In other words, the house expects to make $112 from you. This is how it works out:

$20 x 70 rounds x 4 hours x 2% = $112

The casino normally returns about 40 percent in comps; in this case, they will authorize a comp for about $45, or dinner for two.

## Trivia...

*Las Vegas, the gambling capital of America, gives away about $2 million per day in comps. That's about $700 million per year from its $7-billion income. In other words, they are giving a little to get a lot.*

## STATS USED TO HELP DETERMINE COMPS

| Game | Decisions per hour | House advantage |
|---|---|---|
| Baccarat | 70 | 1.5% |
| Blackjack | 70 | 2% |
| Craps | 140 | 1.5% |
| Mini baccarat | 110 | 1.5% |
| Pai Gow poker | 25 | 2% |
| Roulette | 40 | 5.3% |
| Slot machines | 400–600 | 3–11% |

# Making a living

THERE IS AN OLD JOKE *that says that to end up with a million dollars at gambling, you need to start with two million dollars. In other words, to make a living as a professional gambler is extremely difficult. Most gambling professionals specialize in sports betting, which takes a lot of time and experience. Mason Malmuth, a well-known player and author of a dozen gambling books, estimates that there are only about 200 people in the US who earn $100,000 or more per year gambling. That's not a very big number when you think about the millions of people who gamble every year in casinos, in card rooms, and at racetracks across the country.*

## Winning games for players

Even with new games appearing regularly at casinos, there is a very limited number of games that can be consistently won by a serious player. If you want to be a professional or a semi-pro, or if you want to make gambling your number-one hobby, these are the games to play: blackjack, poker, video poker, casino tournaments, horse racing, and sports betting. In each case, skill – not luck – will be the deciding factor. You shouldn't go out and start to play, thinking you can beat the house or other players because of your experience at Friday night games in your hometown. To become even a moderately skilled gambler requires a lot of research, a great deal of studying, and loads of practice. Now let's look at each game.

## Blackjack

You have to know basic strategy for single-, double-, and multideck games. Card counting is a must. You should also pay attention to the little extra things, such as knowing about deck penetration and side counts. You'll want to use good money management skills, and, most of all, you'll have to develop an act to prevent yourself from being barred.

## Horse racing

To make money at horse racing, you must have lots of experience in handicapping races. You need to know which items are dominant, which must be weighted, and what must be considered when reviewing an upcoming race. You also need to learn to pass up races that you feel might be too close to call. Furthermore, you'll always have to overcome the house edge of 17 to 20 percent, which can be a very difficult task.

■ **You really need to know your stuff** *if you want to make money "betting the ponies."*

## Poker

In poker, you are always playing against your fellow players. It's often been said that poker is 50 percent skill and 50 percent luck, and it's difficult to tell which is which when you are playing. You can play poker almost anywhere: in casinos, in card rooms, even at home. When you first begin to play, I recommend that you specialize in one game, such as Texas hold 'em, five- or seven-card stud, or draw poker. Learning odds is very important in poker, as is learning to read other players. Remember, when it comes to bluffing, you have to know when, who, how, and a lot more.

## Video poker

When playing video machines, you're going one-on-one against the house. Unlike with "live" poker, you don't have to worry about other players. In video poker, you only have one draw. Thus, the strategy is a little different from that of live poker; but it can be easily learned. Knowing the right machines to play is the most important factor. The machines can be beaten, meaning that the return can be 100 percent or better. The real problem with this game is that over the long run, the return is limited to just a few dollars per hour.

■ **A lot of money is wagered on big-time boxing matches.** *It is unlikely, however, that many people would have tipped a third-round disqualification for Mike Tyson (right) in this famous bout with Evander Holyfield at the MGM Grand Casino in 1997, after he twice bit Holyfield's ear.*

## Sports betting

At present, Nevada is the only US state that legally accepts sports wagers. Of course, there is a lot of illegal betting that takes place with bookies, friends, coworkers, and on the Internet. How long it will last on the Internet remains to be seen, however, because of pending federal legislation. For now, though, if you want to make a formal bet on baseball, basketball, boxing, football, or hockey, your choices are the Internet or in Nevada only. As with horse racing, in sports betting you need to know a lot about teams, specific players, home field advantage, and much more. Note that most professional gamblers make their living by betting on sports.

## Casino tournaments

Many blackjack card counters have moved into tournaments because they have been banned by casinos. In addition to blackjack and craps competitions, there are slot, poker, and horse racing tournaments all around the country. These tournaments usually have hundreds and sometimes thousands of dollars as prize money, even for short one-day events (other events might be a weekend long). Entry fees can be small compared to the winning prizes. Many gambling magazines list tournament schedules, including entry fees and prize monies.

# Having fun

**WHAT IS YOUR IDEA OF FUN?** *Is it playing blackjack, roulette, craps, slots, or keno in one of the new mega-casino resorts? Or is it cruising on a luxurious ship in the Caribbean? Or how about Europe, in the casino at Baden-Baden, with its glamorous and intriguing decor? Whatever your idea of fun, you do not need to be a very experienced gambler or a high roller to enjoy the fun and excitement of gambling. You can play just enough to partake in every game offered in any casino or at any racetrack around the world. Just remember you don't have to win a fortune at gambling to have fun.*

■ **Become part of high society,** *if only for a day, at the lavishly appointed casino at Baden-Baden in south-west Germany.*

## Special playing

There are many ways in which you can spice up your casino visit, without spending or losing a lot of money. For instance, if you have the opportunity, you should play roulette at the few casinos that have those wonderful wooden masterpiece wheels with only a single zero. Or how about the very elite and formal surroundings of the baccarat area, where only a few brave players will venture? For fun, you might play blackjack at a reserve table and count how many floormen and pit bosses are mingling in the one small area that overlooks the game. Maybe you'll get invited to a special holiday event that is closed to the general public. You can always take some time between sessions to have a soothing massage in the casino spa. There are lots of different and exciting things a modern casino resort can provide to help bring fun and entertainment to your gaming experience. Try them all!

■ **Recharge your batteries** *in the hotel jacuzzi before another big night at a show or at the tables.*

## Hotel-casino amenities

Hotel-casinos offer much more than just gambling, though. First, there are pools in most hotel-casinos. Some of the largest and most interesting pools in the world can be found at the mega-resort hotel-casinos. Additionally, many of the large casinos offer live music throughout the complex, along with extensive bars to keep guests entertained. In fact, all the large hotel-casinos usually have big-name entertainment on their stages. Many have show lounges with up-and-coming comedy acts, music reviews, and magicians. And some of the world's finest restaurants now have outlets in the new mega-casinos. Are you the outdoors type? Well, resorts-casinos have golf and tennis to keep you alert during the daytime, and they usually offer exclusive spas and workout facilities. Some of the large casinos of Las Vegas also have water parks and fish aquariums. So don't spend all your time gambling; be sure to enjoy the amenities found in today's modern hotel-casinos.

■ **Modern hotel-casinos, like those on the Las Vegas Strip,** *aren't just about gambling. Music reviews, concerts, and magic acts are just some of the forms of entertainment on offer.*

# Your government wants to hear from you

*AS WITH YOUR EARNINGS from a job, you must declare all gambling winnings, regardless of the amount. You must have accurate records of your losses, too, or you could be dealing yourself a real problem. If you want to deduct your gambling losses, you can only claim them in the amount of your winnings. For example, if you win $5,000 gambling and you lose $10,000, you can only deduct $5,000.*

*Don't gamble with your tax return. Gambling winnings are considered income in the US by both state and federal governments.*

## Internal Revenue Service information

US Federal law requires that all casinos issue a W-2G form for slot machine winnings of $1,200 or more, and for keno winnings of $1,400 or more. However, you are required to report all winnings when filing your annual income-tax report. In fact, if you hit that jackpot of $1,200 or more on a slot machine, the casino will ask for your name, address, social security number, and positive identification, and then they will issue you a W2-G. Normally no tax is taken out at the time of the winning; however, before the casino will dole your winnings out to you, you will be asked to sign a statement that says that you will pay all the required taxes.

If you are not a resident of the US, the tax laws that relate to gambling will be different for you. Be sure to check with your local authority as to what your responsibilities are.

**INTERNET**

### www.rbstaxes.com

*This is an excellent site by the authors of The Tax Guide for Gamblers. It offers a very good article library, with lots of tax info for Americans and Canadians, as well as some good links to sites that deal with gambling and taxes.*

### Trivia...

*Every year, 3,000 players put up $10,000 to enter the World Series of Poker at Binion's Horseshoe in Las Vegas. They all have to pay taxes on their winnings . . . or do they? The 1990 champion, Mansour Matloubi of London, was able to avoid taxes on his winnings. How? Because there is no tax on gambling wins in the UK, and the US treaty with the UK exempts taxation of money won by British citizens in the US, Matloubi walked away not only as the champion, but with a tax-free $1,022,400.*

## Taxes for gambling

Only within the last few years did it become legal for a US citizen to claim him- or herself as a professional gambler. It happened when a laid-off auto worker began playing at the racetrack to supplement his income. It soon grew into a full-time job for him. When the IRS refused to recognize his new occupation, he took them to court, and he won! To do this, though, you must keep very good records: W2-Gs; wagering tickets; receipts with dates, times, and specific bets listed; cancelled checks; credit records; bank withdrawal slips; and any receipts provided by gambling establishments. You'll need all of the above if you want to claim yourself as a professional gambler come tax time.

# A simple summary

✓ Casinos, racetracks, and lotteries are all designed to win money from players. By playing carefully, though, you can collect from them instead of the other way around.

✓ There are some rare cases of cheating in casinos, but if you walk away when you think some cheating has taken place, you don't have to worry about it.

✓ Casinos love to give away comps. It doesn't matter what your bankroll size is, comps are there for you. Learn how to get them and enjoy them.

✓ It's very difficult to make a living at gambling, but it can be done.

You need to know which games will allow you to do it successfully. You must also know what is required, and you must have a complete understanding of the game itself before you even think about giving up your day job.

✓ Today's casinos and racetracks can offer a lot of fun and entertainment. There is more to it than spending all your time at the tables or machines. Learn to get the most out of every casino visit.

✓ Pay your taxes and keep good records, and you will keep the tax collector off your back.

# Chapter 3

# *Becoming a Better Player*

THE REAL OBJECT OF GAMBLING is to win. That sounds simple enough . . . . Well, it is and it isn't. Some players think winning is to get a 7 on the come-out roll at craps, or to get closer to 21 than the dealer at blackjack, or to pick a straight-up number at roulette. But this isn't necessarily true. To win, what you really want to do is beat the dealer. This concept applies to craps, blackjack, roulette, and many other games. At craps you want numbers; at blackjack you can win on 13 if the dealer busts; and you can win on a red or black in roulette. In other words, you don't have to hit a "jackpot" every time to be a winner. Look at it this way: Casinos win a little all the time, and those wins add up to a lot. If you win a little all the time, at the end of your visit or session, you could also end up with a lot.

## In this chapter...

✓ Player faults

✓ Player options

✓ Practicing your craft

49

# Player faults

CASINOS ARE WELL AWARE *of players' greed, selfishness, and lack of knowledge, and they take advantage of those human weaknesses. They provide glitter, free drinks, and friendly dealers to get you to play. They know the house advantage works best over the long run, so they want you to play and play for a long time. So, you should gamble with that in mind: Your gambling should be about self-control, pacing, and betting discipline. The facts are that winning is easy, walking out as a winner is hard, and walking on a losing night is harder still.*

## How do you look?

Casinos look at players in many ways. Casinos see "whales," who are maybe the top 200 biggest high rollers in the world; "high rollers" are those who bet $100 to $250 a hand; "median rollers" bet about $25 a round; and "low rollers" bet $3 to $10 a hand. Casinos also rate players as *easy* and *tough*. Players, on the other hand, tend to think that there are only two types of gamblers: winners and losers. Reading this book might not elevate you to the whale level, but it should at least put you in the winner's category.

> **DEFINITION**
>
> *An **easy** player, as rated by the casino, is one who doesn't know how to play or bet very well (for example, a player who bets on long shots at craps or takes insurance at blackjack). A **tough** player, however, only plays the games and bets that give the house the minimum advantage.*

## Things that prevent successful gambling

There are a number of factors that can work against your gambling success. The most common ones are:

● **Trying to prove that you're somebody you're not.** You're not James Bond, you don't have the wealth of Bill Gates, and you don't have to prove to your better half that you're always a winner.

■ Debonair, smooth, and in control – *we'd all like to be James Bond when we visit the casino, but the reality is likely to be otherwise. Don't impose unattainable expectations on yourself.*

● **Not knowing the house edge.** Every game in the casino has a built-in advantage over the player. Sometimes the house edge is very small, as with craps and blackjack. Other times it can be very large, as is the case with the wheel of fortune.

*You should know what the house edge or odds are for each and every game, and for each different bet you make.*

● **Not being mentally and physically alert.** You need to rest a little after a long drive or flight to your favorite gaming destination. To gamble, you need to be alert and in good shape mentally as well as physically. Not being 100-percent fit can affect your thinking and playing abilities. Lastly, if you are so tired you don't really know what is going on, you won't have much fun anyway.

● **Playing games you don't know much about.** Baccarat is a fun and easy game to play. There are no actions you need to consider because the dealer makes all the decisions. However, you need to read, study, and understand the game before you attempt to play. This principle is true no matter which game or machine you play. Knowing and understanding the games will set you on the road to winning.

> ## Trivia...
> *Louis Pasteur, the 19th-century French chemist, is quoted as saying, "Chance favors only the mind that is prepared."*

## Things that promote successful gambling

There are lots of things you can do to learn more about your favorite game and how to become a better player. It's really quite simple. To become a good player, you must practice three basic concepts: gambling know-how, self-control, and lots of common sense. Following are some of the specific things you can do to put these ideas into practice.

● **Take the free gaming lessons that are offered by most casinos.** You'll find lessons on craps, blackjack, roulette, Let It Ride, Caribbean stud, and more. Normally these free instructions are given in the mornings and afternoons. They can last anywhere from 30 to 60 minutes, and can be very helpful to a new player. They are honest and very instructive. Take them.

*Study the game you play. Today there is more information about gambling than ever before. No matter what your game might be, you will find new books coming out almost every month, and new Internet sites seem to pop up each week.*

● **Read magazines and newsletters.** There are many articles by experts that explain the newest table games and the most elaborate machines. The only real problem you're likely to have as far as information goes is finding the time to read it all.

● **Get some strategy cards.** Computers have helped make these cards readily available in simple and easy-to-learn formats. They're available for blackjack, craps, roulette, slots, and even video poker. With these cards you don't have to wade through all the mathematics – you just play the way the card tells you. Most cards are inexpensive, ranging from $3 to $7.

| | | | 2 | 3 | 4 | 5 | 6 | 7 | 8 | 9 | 10 | Ace |
|---|---|---|---|---|---|---|---|---|---|---|---|---|
| | | | | | | DEALER'S UP-CARD | | | | | | |
| PLAYER'S HAND | HARD HANDS | 8 or less | H | H | H | H | H | H | H | H | H | H |
| | | 9 | H | D | D | D | D | H | H | H | H | H |
| | | 10 | D | D | D | D | D | D | D | D | H | H |
| | | 11 | D | D | D | D | D | D | D | D | D | H |
| | | 12 | H | H | S | S | S | H | H | H | H | H |
| | | 13 | S | S | S | S | S | H | H | H | H | H |
| | | 14 | S | S | S | S | S | H | H | H | H | H |
| | | 15 | S | S | S | S | S | H | H | H | H | H |
| | | 16 | S | S | S | S | S | H | H | H | H | H |
| | | 17 or More | S | S | S | S | S | S | S | S | S | S |
| | PAIRS | 2-2 | H | H | SP | SP | SP | SP | H | H | H | H |
| | | 3-3 | H | H | SP | SP | SP | SP | H | H | H | H |
| | | 4-4 | H | H | H | H | H | H | H | H | H | H |
| | | 5-5 | D | D | D | D | D | D | D | D | H | H |
| | | 6-6 | H | SP | SP | SP | SP | H | H | H | H | H |
| | | 7-7 | SP | SP | SP | SP | SP | SP | H | H | H | H |
| | | 8-8 | SP | SP | SP | SP | SP | SP | SP | SP | SP | SP |
| | | 9-9 | SP | SP | SP | SP | SP | S | SP | SP | S | S |
| | | 10-10 | S | S | S | S | S | S | S | S | S | S |
| | | A-A | SP | SP | SP | SP | SP | SP | SP | SP | SP | SP |
| | SOFT HANDS | A-2 | H | H | H | D | D | H | H | H | H | H |
| | | A-3 | H | H | H | D | D | H | H | H | H | H |
| | | A-4 | H | H | D | D | D | H | H | H | H | H |
| | | A-5 | H | H | D | D | D | H | H | H | H | H |
| | | A-6 | H | D | D | D | D | H | H | H | H | H |
| | | A-7 | S | D | D | D | D | S | S | H | H | S |
| | | A-8 | S | S | S | S | D | S | S | S | S | S |
| | | A-9 | S | S | S | S | S | S | S | S | S | S |

| H = Hit | SP = Split | D = Double | S = Stand |
|---|---|---|---|

■ **A strategy card** *makes playing easy. Study the card and put your new-found knowledge to good use when you play.*

● **Download games from the Internet.** Craps, blackjack, roulette, and slots are all available online. Or, you can go to your favorite computer store and purchase casino game programs that will help you with your game. In addition to finding games on the Internet, you can stop by a game or novelty store and pick up a small game felt on craps, blackjack, or roulette, which will give you a more realistic feel for the game while you practice.

● **Watch before you play.** When you get to the casino, go to a craps, blackjack, roulette, or baccarat table and watch the game without making any bets. Stop by a table where a high roller is playing. Note that there is normally a security guard nearby to ensure that the crowd doesn't distract the player, but you can see it all by just standing a few feet away. Watch the betting as well as the strategy being used by the player.

*Be wary of trying to play the way a high roller might play; remember, the fact that someone has a large bankroll does not automatically make them an expert.*

**INTERNET**

**www.gamblersbook.com**

*The Gamblers Book Club has the largest selection of gambling books and videotapes in the world. No matter what game or sporting event you want to know about, they have information on it. You can order books and magazines directly online from this site.*

● **Play in tournaments.** Tournaments are an excellent way to get a lot of experience at little cost. Almost all casinos offer some type of tournament, usually slots, blackjack, poker, or even horse racing. Look in the tourist magazines and newspapers located throughout the casino. These publications usually contain listings of casinos with tournaments. Most tournaments have small entry fees, and they offer a lot of gaming and possibly even some extra amenities for entering. Remember, you will be playing against other players – not the house – when you're in a tournament.

**INTERNET**

www.casinogaming.com/
news/tournaments.html

*This site lists all the upcoming tournaments in Nevada, including types, dates, times, entry fees, prize monies, and telephone numbers. Many of the tournaments listed on this site are free.*

● **Look for the best games.** Find the casino, pit, and table that have the best blackjack rules; play at craps that offer at least double odds or better; play on single-zero-wheel roulette tables; and only play video poker on 9/6 or better machines. Once you have obtained some knowledge of the game and have learned which games are the best ones to play, use that knowledge to your advantage. Be selective and only play where you have a better than reasonable chance to walk away a winner.

● **Manage your bankroll carefully.** You know the house has an advantage over the long run, but you can win in the short run by starting with small wagers and progressing to larger ones only when you are on a winning streak. You don't want to be out of funds when the dealer finally gets cold. Properly managing your funds will help you to minimize your losses and maximize your wins. There's nothing fun about losing. It's important that you have the discipline to limit your losses.

■ **You don't exactly** *need the skills of an accountant, but you'll play better and have more fun if you put some thought into properly managing your bankroll.*

# Player options

THERE ARE MANY ADDITIONAL things you can do to improve as a player. In fact, as a player, you have more options than the casino has. Study the following options and try to practice them. They will help you become a better player and end up a winner.

## Select the best casino

You can pick and choose which casino to play in. Remember, not all casinos are created equal. Consider the following factors when choosing a casino.

**a** **Best rules**: Look for the best rules at the blackjack, craps, and roulette tables and on video poker machines, and watch for the best payout on slots.

**b** **Best prices**: Keep an eye on the minimum betting requirements at tables, and make sure a casino offers lots of quarter slot machines.

**c** **Atmosphere**: Look for a friendly, helpful, and enjoyable staff.

## Select the best games

As I mentioned in previous chapters, there are good games and not-so-good games. Again, you'll want to pick the ones with a house advantage of less than 2 percent.

**a** **Best odds**: You'll find the best odds with double or better craps odds, single-wheel roulette, Las Vegas blackjack rules, 98-percent slot payback, and 9/6 video poker machines.

**b** **Lowest house advantage**: Know your game, and know what are the good odds or rules when you play.

**INTERNET**

**www.casinocenter.com**

*Casino Center is the web site of gaming enthusiasts. It features extracts from six leading gambling magazines, current news articles about the gaming industry, a gaming catalog, listings of upcoming gaming conferences and tradeshows, and a free monthly news service that can be sent directly to you via email.*

# Select the best table or machine

Take the time to check out which tables and machines are best.

*(a)* **Winning signs:** Look for players with lots of chips, dealers with lots of tips, and a low chip tray. Listen for sounds of happy players; noisy equals happy when it comes to craps, roulette, or slot players.

*(b)* **Casino staff recommendations:** Find out where the casino staff and locals play.

# Walk and not play

Recognize when it's better to walk than to play. You'll thank yourself in the morning.

*(a)* **Not in the mood:** Don't play if you don't feel comfortable or can't keep your mind on the game.

*(b)* **Don't like conditions:** Avoid a game/casino that is crowded, has rude dealers, offers few choices, or has poor rules.

*(c)* **Poor bankroll:** Manage the size of your bets based on your total bankroll; save it for another day if you don't have a reasonable bankroll.

# Quit after winning

The old adage "Quit while you're ahead" is still the best advice you can take. The longer you play, the better chance the house will win: The game odds are set up at a fixed rate to give the house an advantage over the long run. Win and walk in a short period if you want to end up a real winner.

■ **Now might be a good time to quit.** *You've got another blackjack, you've won a lot of money, so why give the house an opportunity to win it all back?*

# Practicing your craft

*IF YOU ARE A GOLFER, you might want to play a round at St. Andrews. If you play tennis, maybe you wish you could play a few matches at Hilton Head. If you bowl, you might want to check out the Reno National Bowling Center. Likewise, if you want to gamble, you might want to go to Las Vegas, Atlantic City, or Monte Carlo. But before you play in these places, you need to practice and become good at your game.*

## Practice, practice, practice

In real estate it's location, location, location. When it comes to playing casino games, it's practice, practice, practice. Get yourself a deck of cards, a set of dice, or even one of those small plastic roulette wheels you find in game stores. You know what to do when you get an ace–10 in blackjack. You should have the same mental reflex when you get a 14 against a dealer's 5 up-card. Practicing beforehand will pay off substantially when you get to the casino.

*You need to practice your game so you know what your next action will be or how much your next bet will be without even thinking about it. Practice enough that your actions become habits.*

■ **Even if you just keep track** *of the numbers as they come up on a toy roulette wheel, it will help you formulate a strategy for the real thing.*

## Using the computer

There are lots of inexpensive and very good computer games on the market today that provide excellent programs to play and practice on. There are even some that offer a variety of games, including some that you might not have played yet (such as three-card poker and Let It Ride). Use these programs to help familiarize yourself with these new games or to practice your favorite game. This type of computer training is so good because it provides a "hands-on" learning experience, which is one of the best learning techniques you can use.

## Casino time

You don't have to play every minute you are in a casino. Take your time and look around. There is a saying that can be applied to gambling: "Stop, look, and listen." Remember this: It's important that you see and understand what is going on around you. Make a note of where your favorite tables or machines are located. Watch other players, particularly if you play poker. Find the high-roller areas and see what is going on there. If you want to become a good player, or even make gambling your hobby, you need to know all about the gaming place you're visiting. You should know what is going on in front of you as well as all around you.

## A simple summary

✔ Casinos cater to players' weaknesses, but you can use self-control, patience, and discipline to overcome your disadvantages. You need to become a "tough" player, one who knows what he or she is doing at all times while at the tables or machines.

✔ Gambling sometimes turns people into someone they are not. You don't have to show off in a casino; don't play the role of a high roller if you don't have the bankroll for it. You should try to become more knowledgeable than the person sitting next to you, and possibly even smarter about the game than the dealer.

✔ Use all the tools available to you, such as the Internet, magazines, newsletters, and books about your favorite game. Try to become an expert.

✔ You have lots of options available to you; use them all. You can play in any casino, at any game, at any level. You can also choose not to play. It is all up to you.

✔ Use your time in a casino to your advantage. Stop, look, and listen to everything that is going on around you. It will help make you a better player.

# Chapter 4

# Managing Your Funds

MANAGING YOUR BANKROLL is as important as knowing the correct game strategy. Don't underestimate the importance of a sound money-management program. As you know, you cannot win all the time, so you have to develop a program or plan that will leave you with some funds to help play your way back to a win. Poor money management will leave you without the ability to remain in the game. Have the courage to bet more when you're winning, and have the self-discipline to bet less when you're losing. There is an old gamblers' saying: "It's not difficult to win; what is difficult is to walk out with it."

## In this chapter...

✓ Money management

✓ Betting systems

✓ Tipping

✓ Gamblers Anonymous

✓ Record keeping

IT TAKES MORE THAN A FISTFUL OF DOLLARS TO BE A GOOD GAMBLER

# Money management

WHEN IT COMES TO MANAGING *your bankroll for gambling, you must have a basic plan; however, it's also important for you to remember that a* **money-management** *plan will not help you win at the tables or machines. Rather, a good financial plan will help you reduce your losses and give you a better chance to come out ahead in the long run. To be successful, you need to win more frequently than you lose, and you need to restrict your losses to a minimum when you do lose. Your plan should consist of the following steps.*

## Set aside gambling funds

Start with establishing a set amount for your entire trip. Next, set an amount for gambling for each day of your trip. Finally, establish an amount to play with during each session. For instance, you might want to play three sessions per day: one in the morning, one in the afternoon, and one in the evening. It's important that you do not intermix session monies. That is, don't use your afternoon funds to help a losing morning session. Each session's funds must be separate from the others.

## Establish goals

Setting goals is very important in gambling. Having a goal enables you to reach for a specific and reasonably attainable objective. It teaches you self-control, and – most of all – it forces you to gamble responsibly. Consider this technique for leaving a winner: Set a firm goal of doubling your buy-in amount; for example, if you buy in for $100, you should stop playing when you reach $200. You'll find that you can usually reach your goal at some point during a session. Most players don't stop when they hit a set level. Remember, though, that the longer you stay at a game, the more chance the house will have to beat you down to zero. The object of playing is not to keep playing until you run out of funds. Instead, think about it this way: A 30-percent return on your investment is very good; a 50-percent return is excellent; and a 100-percent return is out of this world. So, doubling your buy-in (your investment) is a very nice, reasonable goal to set when gambling.

■ **Keep track of your winnings**
*versus your buy-in amount: Doubling your buy-in is a reasonable goal to aim for in any game.*

## Establish a "stop-loss" limit

This technique is very similar to working with a stockbroker. When the price of a stock you bought for $30 goes up to $40, you tell your broker to sell only if the stock drops back down to $35. The broker will do this automatically so that you still come out with a profit. You should follow the same principle when gambling. Keep this in mind: If you win early and significantly, leave. Don't give the casino an opportunity to get its money back. Again, it's not that difficult to win in a casino; what's difficult is to walk out with your winnings.

*Set a loss limit of 50 percent of your session funds. This will help to stop you from experiencing a big loss during a losing streak (which you will run into every so often).*

## Keep trip expenses separate

The last part of your plan involves your trip expenses. Set aside the money you need for transportation, lodging, eating, sightseeing, and shows; this money should always be kept separate from your gambling funds. Don't mix them together; otherwise, you will not know how you did gambling versus total expenses.

## Establish the size of your bankroll

The size of your bankroll will have a large effect on what you do and how you do it. Set aside a given amount as your bankroll. Once you have settled on an amount, resist the temptation to supplement your bankroll with any other monies.

*Your bankroll determines what games you should play, what bets you should make, how big your bets should be, and the amount of time you can play.*

■ **It helps to have a big bankroll,** *but even that won't guarantee success if you disregard sound money-management strategies.*

## The ten positive rules for gambling

Following are some rules for managing your bankroll:

1. Budget your gambling funds for the entire trip, for each day, and for each session.

2. Gamble only with money you can afford to lose.

3. Decide beforehand how much you want to spend during your gambling session. Don't exceed your spending limit if you lose. Remember, there is always another day, and another trip.

4. Preset a goal for your winnings, for example, 50 percent or double your buy-in money.

5. When you're winning, increase your bets; when you're losing, decrease your bets.

6. Never play when you're tired or have had too much to drink.

7. Play only at tables you can afford. Your session bankroll should be sufficient to cover at least 20 bets.

8. Keep your gambling expectations reasonable. Don't expect to make $1,000 if you start with $100.

9. After analyzing five consecutive actions of play, decide to continue or leave the table or machine.

10. Have fun, and always quit while you're ahead.

# Betting systems

THERE ARE MANY DIFFERENT *betting systems out there, most of which claim you can be a winner all the time if you just follow that system. Some of these systems seem very good when you first look at them, but over the years they have all been proven not to work. The following sections examine a few of them.*

# The Martingale system

This system can dig you into a deep hole very quickly. It is an easy system to understand. Say your first bet is $1. If you win the bet, you start again at $1. If you lose the bet, you double the next bet. Winning the next bet gives you a win of $1 ($1 lost, followed by $2 won). If you lose again, though, you double your bet again, this time to $4. And again, a win at this stage results in $1 ($1 lost, $2 lost, and $4 won). So it continues until you win. Given a "normal" sequence, it should not be too long before you register a win that covers your losses and provides a profit of $1. Using blackjack as an example, in only eight hands, you would have to bet $128 to win back $1. So, this is not a good system to use.

*Casinos will establish table limits to prevent a player from using the Martingale system. For example, at a $5 table, after seven losses you would have to bet $640; but say the table limit is $500. You are now behind by $140 because you cannot bet the required $640 using this system.*

# D'Alembert system

With this system you increase your wager by one *unit* after each loss. You decrease by one unit after each win. For example, say you begin at $5. If you lose, you bet $10, or two units. If you lose again, you bet $15, or three units. If you win the third bet, you drop back to $10. Another immediate win will cause you to drop to one unit, or $5. In other words, you change your unit after every win or loss. The problem with this system is that you will most likely experience a big loss after working up your wins to a very high level.

# Other systems

There are many more systems, which you will find advertised in popular magazines and newsletters. Take them all with a grain of salt. They don't work. The cards, the dice, and the wheel do not know what system you are using; therefore, you cannot expect them to respond in the positive. Ask yourself this question: If this system is so good, why is the person who is advertising it willing to part with their winning strategy, selling it to you and other gamblers? The reason is simple: They are trying to make money by selling the system, not by using it.

## Author's system

When I'm winning two out of three hands, I'll begin to bet $10 or $15 instead of $5. If I'm losing two out of three hands, I'll reduce my bets or stay at the $5 level. You should analyze every three to five hands. If you're on a winning steak, continue to raise your bets. If you are losing more hands than you are winning, reduce your bets to one unit, or move to another table, pit, or casino.

*What system do I recommend? It's simple: Start to increase your bets when you are winning, and decrease them when you start to lose.*

# Tipping

**THE AVERAGE PLAYER** *is not sure how or when to tip. Tipping is very important in the gambling world, especially in the US. Most employees in casinos and racetracks make only minimum wage. So, to make a decent living, those employees depend greatly on tips to supplement their take-home pay. Tipping a slot attendant, blackjack dealer, or cocktail waitress also shows good form on your part.*

■ **It never hurts** *to give your cocktail waitress a decent tip: then even if you lose, at least you won't go thirsty.*

## When to tip

When to tip is a more difficult question. Although drinks are free in almost every casino, it is recommended that you tip the cocktail waitress when you receive a drink. The amount of the tip depends on the denomination you are playing. When you are playing at the quarter machines, two or three quarters is a fair tip for a drink. If you are playing dollars, you probably want to tip a dollar for a drink. If you are playing at the $25 table, tipping a little extra is appropriate. How much you tip is always up to you. Big winners give bigger tips, but it's always your call. I find that my tipping habits have become more generous over the years. Here's why: I'm going to drop that money into the machine anyway, so a good tip may mean a few less spins, but a lot more ginger ale will come my way.

*In the UK, dealers in casinos are forbidden by law to accept tips from players.*

# WHAT TO TIP: SOME GUIDELINES

1. If you're lucky while playing the slots or video poker, you should give a couple of bucks to the change person (especially if they pointed you to a winning machine).

2. At craps, it is always a good idea to make a wager for the dealer(s). A dollar or two on a hardway bet is an acceptable tip. Another way to tip is to throw a $5 chip (or more, depending on your level of play) on the table "for the boys" when leaving.

3. At blackjack, you can tip by making a bet for the dealer; simply place a chip in front of your bet. If you're betting $5 to $10 a hand, a $1 or $2 dealer bet is fine. If you are playing at a higher level, a higher bet is appropriate. I usually make a dealer bet after I get a blackjack, on the very next hand.

4. When I win at roulette, I will ask the dealer for his or her favorite number and put a dollar or two on that number for them. If it hits, he or she wins $35. Alternatively, I might toss a few bucks toward the dealer and say, "This is for you," as I leave the table.

5. In keno, it's customary to tip a few bucks when you are finished playing.

6. Bellmen and doormen customarily receive $1 or $2 for each bag they handle for you. Hotel maids and housekeepers traditionally get $1 or $2 per day. Ordering room service is just like having a waitress serve you – 15 percent is the standard. (Be sure to review the bill first, as some hotels add the tip automatically.)

7. If you attend a showroom with open seating, giving a $5 to $20 tip to the maître d' will improve your seating.

8. At restaurants, waiters expect the standard 15-percent tip for good service. At buffets, servers usually receive $1 per person.

9. Taxi drivers are given $1 to $2 for fares below $10, and more if they help you with your bags. Limousine drivers are normally tipped 15 percent for their services. It's also nice to tip tour guides and bus drivers $1 to $2 per person at the end of a trip.

10. Valet parking attendants normally get $2 for quick service.

Of course, all tipping is based on good, prompt, and friendly service. If the service doesn't meet those standards, adjust your tip accordingly. The reverse is also true: If you receive extra service, be sure to increase the tip accordingly.

# Gamblers Anonymous

JUST AS WITH ALCOHOL *or drugs, people can get in over their heads with gambling. Having a cocktail or a beer at the end of the day is one thing; having a half-dozen is something else. Having a losing streak and dropping $200 will not change your lifestyle; but losing $2,000 in one session could cause some problems. Take a look at the following questions put together by Gamblers Anonymous and see if they apply to you or someone you know.*

**INTERNET**

**www.gamblersanonymous .org**

*This excellent site explains the organization's overall program, offers a very good question-and-answer page, and lays out the recovery program. Use this site to get both state and international help.*

## GAMBLERS ANONYMOUS 20 QUESTIONS

1. Did you ever lose time from work due to gambling?

2. Has gambling ever made your home life unhappy?

3. Did gambling affect your reputation?

4. Have you ever felt remorse after gambling?

5. Did you ever gamble to get money with which to pay debts or otherwise solve financial difficulties?

6. Did gambling cause a decrease in your ambition or efficiency?

7. After losing, did you feel you must return as soon as possible and win back your losses?

8. After a win, did you have a strong urge to return and win more?

9. Did you often gamble until your last dollar was gone?

10. Did you ever borrow to finance your gambling?

If you, or someone you know, has a gambling problem and wants or needs help, write to the Gamblers Anonymous international service office, PO Box 17173, Los Angeles, CA, 90017, or contact them at www.gamblersanonymous.org, or by phone (in the US) at (800) GAMBLER. They know all about problem gambling and are experts at helping people.

■ **If you think you might be getting in** *over your head, it's important that you seek help. Gamblers Anonymous is a good place to start.*

11 Have you ever sold anything to finance gambling?

12 Were you reluctant to use gambling money for normal expenditures?

13 Did gambling make you careless of yourself or your family?

14 Do you ever gamble longer than you had planned?

15 Do you ever gamble to escape worry and trouble?

16 Have you ever committed or considered committing an illegal act to finance gambling?

17 Does gambling cause you to have difficulty in sleeping?

18 Do arguments, disappointments, or frustrations cause you to gamble?

19 Do you have an urge to celebrate any good fortune by a few hours of gambling?

20 Have you ever considered self-destruction or suicide as a result of your gambling?

# Record keeping

KEEPING GOOD RECORDS is also an important part of a good money-management program. How well you're doing at a specific casino or game will become clear if you keep accurate records. Adding comments about particular rules at a blackjack table in a certain casino, for example, can be helpful to you when planning a future trip. Don't overlook the value of record-keeping as part of managing your funds.

## Gambling log

You should keep a log to record detailed information about all your visits, where you played, and how much you won or lost. Also record how much time you spend at each game. Over time, this data will aid you in future gambling endeavors. See the Appendices at the back of the book for sample records for each specific game you might play.

## Analyze your log

Be sure to review and analyze your history of playing. This will help you see your progress as you continue to play and learn. For example, you might feel that you have been doing well in a specific casino. However, your records might tell a different story. Use record-keeping as a tool in your arsenal of knowledge. Review your logs before each visit to a gambling destination.

### Record Keeping: Blackjack

Shift: D=Day S=Swing G=Grave

| Date | Casino | Shift | Number decks/ number players | Playing time | Win/Loss | Remarks |
|------|--------|-------|------------------------------|--------------|----------|---------|
| 3 Feb | Harrahs | D | 6 / 3 | :30 | +55 | |
| 3 Feb | Caesars | D | 1 / 2 | :40 | +110 | Slow dealer |
| 3 Feb | NY NY | S | 6 / 4 | :55 | +180 | Good rules |
| 4 Feb | Tropicana | S | 2 / 3 | :20 | -40 | All neg. shoes |
| 4 Feb | Treasure Is. | D | 6 / 2 | :20 | -60 | Rude dealer |
| 4 Feb | Paris | D | 2 / 2 | :40 | +80 | |
| 4 Feb | Venetian | S | 6 / 4 | :45 | +205 | Fun place to play |

■ **A gambling log** *gives you incontrovertible data on which to base your future gambling strategy. Don't rely on remembrances that may be blurred by the many distractions to be found at the casino.*

## Use of your log

In addition to helping you see your progress at gambling, you can use your log to help you with taxes. In the US, the IRS will want to see lots of documentation if you decide to list gambling as a deduction. Thus, a log can be a very important item in helping to substantiate figures that might be reviewed during a tax audit.

# A simple summary

✔ Money management is an important tool when it comes to any type of gambling. Learn the techniques and tools of a sound money-management plan. It will help you to play more successfully.

✔ Establish specific funds for your entire gambling trip, for each day, and for each session. Don't mix the funds together, and be sure to keep travel expenses separate from gambling funds. This is an important foundation for a money-management program.

✔ Through the years, a lot has been written about betting systems. Betting systems just do not work. Sometimes they look good on paper, but they don't hold up when you are playing for real.

If you need a system, consider simply increasing your bets when you are winning and reducing them when you're on a losing streak.

✔ Tipping is important in the world of gaming. Knowing who, where, when, and how to tip can make a visit to a resort-casino more satisfying.

✔ If you or someone you know has a gambling problem, seek out Gamblers Anonymous for help. They have been helping players for many years, and know how to help fix problems.

✔ Keep good records of your visits to casinos and racetracks. This can be helpful in many ways. Record all the information you can.

# PART TWO

IT'S THE SMART BET THAT MAKES YOU A WINNER

# TABLE GAMES

THERE ARE A VAST NUMBER OF TABLE GAMES available in today's *modern casinos*. In the United States you'll find baccarat, blackjack, Caribbean stud poker, craps, Let It Ride, poker, roulette, Spanish 21, three-card poker, and the Wheel of Fortune. In other  areas of the world, such as Europe, Canada, Asia, and Latin America, in addition to the games found in the US, there are other table games like chemin de fer (similar to baccarat), boule (similar to roulette), monte bank, Pai Gow, and Sic Bo.

All of these are considered table banking games in which the house is the banker and the player tries to *win against the house*. I'll try to cover the most popular games available in today's casinos. And most of all I'll try and keep it simple.

# Chapter 5

# Basic Blackjack

BLACKJACK, VINGT-ET-UN, PONTOON, and Van-John are the variants of, or alternative names for, the game twenty-one. The game derives from a family of card games designed by the French in the late 18th century. During World War I, the game became very popular with Allied troops. Gradually, any two-card count of 21 became known as a blackjack, and the game acquired a new name. During World War II, blackjack was the most popular banking game of soldiers in the barracks. After the war, blackjack replaced faro as the predominant card game in the casinos of Las Vegas and Reno.

*In this chapter...*

✓ *A simple card game*

✓ *Playing the game*

✓ *Options*

✓ *Basic playing strategy*

# A simple card game

TODAY, BLACKJACK, OR TWENTY-ONE, *is one of the most popular of all casino table games. It is played from Arizona to Wisconsin in the United States and throughout the world from Antigua to Zanzibar. The reasons for its popularity are obvious. First, it is a simple game to understand and play. Also, many people believe that it is one of the few casino games at which a skilled player can beat the house most of the time.*

## How the game is played

Blackjack is played on a special half-round table with six to seven spots that serve as the designated betting areas for each player. The game uses a standard deck of 52 cards. All numbered cards, 2 through 10, are counted at face value. The court, or picture, cards are all counted as 10s, with kings, queens, and jacks having no special value. The same is true of the different suits: the spades, clubs, hearts, and diamonds are not relative to any of the game results. Aces are different from all other cards because they can be

■ **Blackjack is one of the few casino games** *that relies as much on chance as skill. However, by learning the basic strategy, players can place their bets knowing they have some control over the outcome.*

counted as either a 1 or an 11. This choice – which way to count the ace – is up to the player, not the dealer. You will also find many casinos that use two decks for blackjack, and others that use a box-like device called a "shoe" to deal multiple decks of 4, 6, and 8.

# CARD VALUES

In blackjack only the number value of the cards has any importance in the game, the four suits are of no significance. Cards ranked 2 through 10 are scored according to their face value, all picture cards are worth 10 points, and the aces are semi-wild and can be worth either 1 or 11.

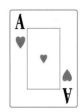

1 OR 11

ALL ARE 10 POINTS

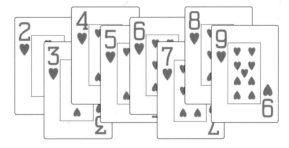

ALL ARE FACE VALUE

## The objective is to win

Some people think the objective of blackjack is to try to get 21, or to get closer to 21 than the dealer without "busting" (going over 21). That's wrong! The real objective of the game is to beat the dealer. There are three ways a player can beat the dealer at blackjack:

1. The player receives an ace and a 10-value card for a blackjack.

2. The player gets closer to 21 than the dealer.

3. The dealer goes over 21 and the player, regardless of the total of his hand, does not.

> **Trivia...**
> It is well documented that Napoleon Bonaparte played and loved the game of twenty-one above all other card games.

# Playing the game

THE GAME CAN BE PLAYED *one-on-one with the dealer or with a full table of seven players. You select which casino and table you want to play and how much you want to wager, and you can quit any time you want. These are very good options for you, the player, to start with.*

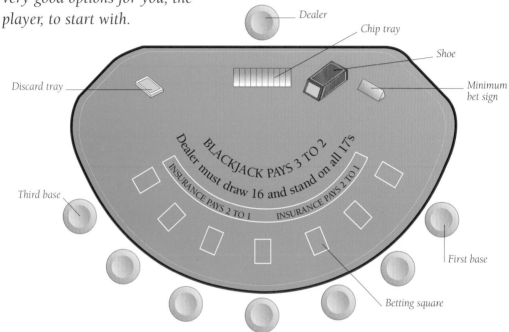

Dealer

Chip tray

Shoe

Minimum bet sign

Discard tray

BLACKJACK PAYS 3 TO 2
Dealer must draw 16 and stand on all 17s
INSURANCE PAYS 2 TO 1          INSURANCE PAYS 2 TO 1

Third base

First base

Betting square

■ **Most casinos have blackjack tables** *that accommodate six or, more often, seven seated players and a standing dealer. The position you choose to sit at the table should have no effect on the cards you're dealt, but may influence the way you play, so choose a position that suits your game.*

## Selecting a seat

Normally, any seat is as good as any other. However, there are some small differences that can help your game. When first learning the game you might want to avoid the first-base seat, as this position will be under the gun to play first. You might find yourself feeling rushed, thereby opening yourself to the possibility of making a mistake. The last seat, or third base, allows you plenty of time to play your hand. If you're new at the game, though, sitting in the third-base seat might bring you some undue pressure from other players to play correctly. This is because your play is immediately before the dealer's, and any table losses might be blamed on you. Always remember this rule: Play your hand correctly, regardless of anyone else's comments.

It doesn't matter if the dealer sees a player's hand because the dealer is required to play his or her hand in a set manner regardless of any other hands. In fact, if you have trouble determining your hand total, particularly when you have an ace or a couple of aces, ask the dealer what you have. He or she will tell you if you disclose your hand to them.

## The game begins

You must wager before any cards are dealt out by the dealer. Each player does this by placing his or her bet in the center of the designated spot in front of his or her position. The placard on the side of the table will alert you to the minimum and maximum bets for that specific table. The dealer begins by shuffling the cards. One player cuts the deck. The dealer then begins to deal cards from left to right, one card to each player, and then one for the dealer. The dealer then deals a second card in turn to each player. Cards can be dealt either face down or face up. In single- and double-deck games they will normally be face down; four, six, and eight decks will be dealt face up.

It is important to note that one of the dealer's cards will be turned face up, and the other face down. This is important to you when it comes to make decisions about what action needs to be taken with your hand. After the cards are dealt, each player is given the opportunity to play his hand in turn, starting at the dealer's left and going around the table from left to right. After all players have acted on their hands, the dealer will play his hand.

*A basic rule for you, the player, should be to always look at three cards before making a decision. Look at the two cards that are dealt to you, and then look at the dealer's up-card.*

All casinos in the United States and around the world use the same house rule: The dealer must hit any hand with 16 and below, and stand on 17 and above. Therefore, it's important to know what the dealer is most likely to do before you have to act on your hand. The player, however, can stand on any card and is not restricted by the same rules as the dealer.

■ **Check out the dealer's up-card** *before deciding the best course of action to take with your own hand.*

# Options

THERE ARE A VARIETY OF OPTIONS *for how each hand can be played. How liberal these options are depends on the "house" rules established by each individual casino. For example, one casino might use a single deck, whereas the casino next door might use the shoe exclusively. One casino's rule might allow doubling down on any two cards, while another casino might allow doubling on 10 and 11 only.*

The point is that each casino has its own specific rules, and it's important for you to know what they are when playing. Many casinos have placards with the minimum and maximum bets listed; these placards might also list some of the house rules for that table. If you're not sure of the rules, just ask the dealer.

BLACKJACK SHOE

## Player options

When the cards are dealt, each player has the following options available to them as they play their hand in turn.

● **Hit** If you want an additional card, you indicate this to the dealer by lightly scraping your cards toward you. If you need another card, repeat the motion. This is the standard procedure when the cards are dealt face down. In a face-up game you indicate a hit by scratching or tapping the table with your fingers or pointing at your cards. Telling the dealer verbally that you want a hit will not work. You must give a hand signal to make the dealer respond. You can continue to receive cards as long as their total doesn't exceed 21.

■ **Tapping or scratching the table** *with the tip of your finger will signify to the dealer that you wish to hit, or be dealt another card, in a face-up game.*

● **Stand** If the first two cards in a face-down game have a satisfactory total, you should slip the cards under the chips in the betting spot. It's important that you don't touch the bet directly. If you are playing in a face-up game and you want to stand, hold your hand, palm down, over your cards and move it sharply left to right in a "no"-type of motion.

● **Pair splitting** When you are dealt two cards of the same point value, you are allowed to "split," or divide, them. The dealer will give you additional cards on each of the split pairs. In effect, you now have two separate hands. You must put up an equal bet on the new split hand. You stand or hit each new hand as needed. If you should receive another card of the same point value, most casinos will allow resplitting up to a total of four hands. Note that there is a special rule for splitting aces: most casinos will only give one card to each ace and move on regardless of its point value. If a 10-value card is received you will have 21, which is very nice. However, if it's a 4, resulting in a total of 15, you will not be allowed to hit again.

● **Double down** After receiving the first two cards you can "double down." You must make an additional wager, no higher than the original bet, and you will receive only one additional card. All casinos allow doubling down on a two-card total of 11; most casinos include 10, though, and many will let you double-down on a total of 9. Some permit doubling down on any two-card hand. This is an excellent option for you – it means you can double on a soft hand (one that contains an ace, such as ace–5). Again, it's important to see what the dealer is showing. If the dealer has a busting hand (2 through 6 up-card), doubling on your ace–5 is a great play because you cannot bust with this hand, but the dealer can. When playing a face-down game you must turn over your hand and add an additional bet. In a face-up game, just add the additional bet next to your original wager.

*A few casinos will allow doubling down after a split, which is an excellent option for you, the player. For example, if you split 8s and receive a 3 as the next card, you'll want to double down on the new hand, which totals 11.*

● **Insurance** When the dealer's up-card is an ace, the dealer will stop the game and offer an optional side bet, called "insurance." To play this side bet, you place a new wager equal to half of your original bet in the insurance box. The dealer looks at the down-card, and if the card is a 10, the dealer will turn it over for a blackjack. You lose your original bet, but win the insurance bet and are paid at 2 to 1. If the dealer does not have a 10-value card, you lose the insurance bet, and the hands are played out normally.

*Trivia...*

*Is it chips or checks? What's the official name for the disc or token that is imprinted with a cash value and used in place of money in all casinos? Casino management uses the word check, whereas the general public uses chip. You can consider the two words interchangeable.*

The insurance bet has almost a 6-percent house advantage and is considered a poor bet for the player. Another technique employed by the casino is to offer "even money" for your blackjack in lieu of the bonus of 3 for 2 payout.

*Don't take either insurance or even money.*

● **Surrender** This option is not offered in many casinos. However, this is a good option for you, the player. There are two kinds of surrender: early and late. Early surrender allows you to throw in your hand, or "surrender," before the face-down card of the dealer is looked at. Late surrender allows you to throw in your hand after the down-card is seen by the dealer. You must state "surrender" to the dealer while discarding your hand. (There is no hand signal for this action, so you must speak to the dealer directly.) The cost of surrender is one-half of the original wager, and you are out of that specific round. Your surrender options are:

*a)* Surrender 9–7 or 10–6 against dealer's 9, 10, or ace

*b)* Surrender 10–5 against dealer's 10

If you have a 16 or a 15 hand, you have the worst and second-worst hand in blackjack, respectively. With the dealer showing a 10 or an ace, you have a greater than 75-percent chance of losing that round. Surrender is an excellent option in this case, as it allows you to save some of your wager for the next round .

SOFT 17

● **Soft hand** This is not really an option for the player but should be discussed in detail. Any hand containing an ace is said to be a "soft hand." An ace–7 can be counted as an 8 or an 18 (it's the player's choice). If two aces are received along with, say, a 5, the player will have 5–ace–ace, which can be counted as a 7 or a 17. Soft hands can be confusing to a player. When you are not sure what your hand totals, ask the dealer what you have. He will tell you.

The ace can be confusing in the heat of the game. Try using this technique: always count the ace as a 1, and then total all the cards in your hand, including the aces, and then add 10. For example: ace + 2 + ace + 7 = 11 + 10 = 21. If you go over 21, discard the 10. Counting this way will help prevent you from hitting a soft 19, 20, or even 21 by mistake.

HARD 17

## Dealer options

The dealer does not really have any options open to him in the game. However, knowing what the dealer is required to do will greatly affect your decisions about your hand.

- **Dealer hits on 16, stands on 17** The dealer must hit on 16 (or any hand totaling less than 16), and stand on 17 (or any hand higher than 17). This is a standard rule in any blackjack game worldwide. Some casinos also require the dealer to hit on a soft 17 (ace–6), which is a disadvantage for the player. If possible, avoid those casinos that do hit on a soft 17. This is the only option that the dealer has.

- **Push** A push is not really an option, but it is an important action in the game. If you and the dealer end up with the same total value hand – for example you both have 18 – it is considered a tie, or "push," and no chips change hands. Also, if you and the dealer both get a blackjack, again it is a tie or push, and no one wins or loses. The game continues.

### Trivia...

*When dealers gets a 10 or an ace as their up-card, they will check their down-card to see if they have a blackjack. To prevent dealers from unintentionally (or intentionally) letting the player know what the down-card is, casinos have installed little mirrors in the center of the tables and marked the 10s and aces on the corners of the cards. If dealers have a blackjack, they will turn over the card; if not, they can't tell what value the card is.*

## HOUSE RULES

One big variation in the game lies in the casino options, or house rules. These will vary from casino to casino, from pit to pit, and even from table to table. For instance, one set of house rules will be based on using a single deck, whereas others are based on a six-deck shoe. Most rules around the country, and even around the world, are based on what is commonly called "Las Vegas Strip rules." These so-called standard rules are as follows:

- Single deck
- Dealer stands on all 17s
- Double on any first two cards
- No doubling after split
- Split up to four hands
- Split aces, one card only
- No surrender

In many European casinos the dealer will not take the down-card (also known as the hole card) until all players have played their hands. The main problem with this is that if you double down or split and the dealer gets a blackjack, you lose your total bet – your original and your additional bet. In the United States, on the other hand, they will only take your original wager and return your double or split wager.

## HOUSE RULE VARIATIONS

Some variations on these house rules can be helpful, while other rule changes will reduce your advantage. Knowing what the house rules are will allow you to pick and chose which casino is the best to play in. The following table shows what the effect of variations will be against Las Vegas Strip rules.

| Rule | Effect on player | Rule | Effect on player |
|---|---|---|---|
| Two decks | -0.31% | Double on 10, 11 only | -0.26% |
| Four decks | -0.48% | Dealer wins ties | -9.00% |
| Six decks | -0.52% | Double after split | +0.14% |
| Eight decks | -0.55% | Double on more then two cards | +0.24% |
| Dealer hits soft 17 | -0.20% | Resplit aces | +0.32% |
| No dealer hole card | -0.11% | Early surrender | +0.62% |
| No resplitting of pairs | -0.03% | Late surrender | +0.02% |

Using standard Las Vegas rules the house advantage is almost zero. You can calculate to determine if you are playing at a good or poor game.

| Example 1 | | Example 2 | |
|---|---|---|---|
| Eight deck game | -0.55% | Basic single deck game | 0.00% |
| Dealer hits soft 17 | -0.20% | Dealer hits a soft 17 | -0.20% |
| Dealer wins ties | -9.00% | No resplitting pairs | -0.03% |
| Total | -9.75% | Double 10, 11 only | -0.26% |
| | | Late surrender | +0.02% |
| | | Total | -0.47% |

This is a poor game and should be avoided.

This is less than ½-percent house advantage and a game you should play.

# Basic playing strategy

*WHEN IT COMES TO DECIDING what course of action to take for a given hand, you need to know how to do it the right way – using what is commonly called basic strategy. This is the correct mathematical way to play each and every hand of casino blackjack. You do not want to play hunches, use intuition, or guess – if you want to win, you must play what the basic strategy chart tells you to do. Even after you have played for some time it is always a good idea to review the chart before each casino visit.*

# BASIC STRATEGY CHART

In the chart below, the player's two-card hand is listed down the left side and the dealer's up-card is shown across the top. If the dealer is showing an 8 and the player has a total of 14, follow across and down to where those columns intersect: that is the correct strategy. In this example, the player would hit.

| | | | 2 | 3 | 4 | 5 | 6 | 7 | 8 | 9 | 10 | Ace |
|---|---|---|---|---|---|---|---|---|---|---|---|---|
| | | | | | | DEALER'S UP-CARD | | | | | | |
| PLAYER'S HAND | HARD HANDS | 8 or less | H | H | H | H | H | H | H | H | H | H |
| | | 9 | H | D | D | D | D | H | H | H | H | H |
| | | 10 | D | D | D | D | D | D | D | D | H | H |
| | | 11 | D | D | D | D | D | D | D | D | D | H |
| | | 12 | H | H | S | S | S | H | H | H | H | H |
| | | 13 | S | S | S | S | S | H | H | H | H | H |
| | | 14 | S | S | S | S | S | H | H | H | H | H |
| | | 15 | S | S | S | S | S | H | H | H | H | H |
| | | 16 | S | S | S | S | S | H | H | H | H | H |
| | | 17 or More | S | S | S | S | S | S | S | S | S | S |
| | PAIRS | 2–2 | H | H | SP | SP | SP | SP | H | H | H | H |
| | | 3–3 | H | H | SP | SP | SP | SP | H | H | H | H |
| | | 4–4 | H | H | H | H | H | H | H | H | H | H |
| | | 5–5 | D | D | D | D | D | D | D | D | H | H |
| | | 6–6 | H | SP | SP | SP | SP | H | H | H | H | H |
| | | 7–7 | SP | SP | SP | SP | SP | SP | H | H | H | H |
| | | 8–8 | SP | SP | SP | SP | SP | SP | SP | SP | SP | SP |
| | | 9–9 | SP | SP | SP | SP | SP | S | SP | SP | S | S |
| | | 10–10 | S | S | S | S | S | S | S | S | S | S |
| | | A–A | SP | SP | SP | SP | SP | SP | SP | SP | SP | SP |
| | SOFT HANDS | A–2 | H | H | H | D | D | H | H | H | H | H |
| | | A–3 | H | H | H | D | D | H | H | H | H | H |
| | | A–4 | H | H | D | D | D | H | H | H | H | H |
| | | A–5 | H | H | D | D | D | H | H | H | H | H |
| | | A–6 | H | D | D | D | D | H | H | H | H | H |
| | | A–7 | S | D | D | D | D | S | S | H | H | H |
| | | A–8 | S | S | S | S | S | S | S | S | S | S |
| | | A–9 | S | S | S | S | S | S | S | S | S | S |

H = Hit    SP = Split    D = Double    S = Stand

The basic strategy chart is considered a universal chart that can be used in any casino worldwide. In those casinos where house rules will not allow doubling on any two-card total, you'll want to hit those soft hands instead of doubling.

## Basic strategy summary

This is a summary of the basic strategy chart. This summary will help you by lessening the time of the learning process (learning the entire chart normally takes 8 to 12 hours to memorize).

- Little to little = stand (12–16) vs. (2–6) or (your little hand vs. dealers little hand)
- Little to big = hit (12–16) vs. (7–ace) or (your little hand vs. dealers big hand)
- Always split = aces & 8s
- Don't split = 4s, 5s, or 10s
- Always hit or double down a soft 17 (ace–6)
- Don't take insurance
- Double down 11 verses dealer's 2–10
- Double down 10 verses dealer's 2–9
- Surrender 15 & 16 verses dealer's 10

*Never guess when practicing your blackjack game. If you are not certain of an action to a specific play, stop and review the basic strategy chart.*

Using the basic strategy chart as you play will help you reduce the house odds to less than 1 percent. Of course, this doesn't mean you will come out even during every visit to the blackjack table. There could still be a lot of volatility (or streaks) before the odds are finally balanced out. You will experience both winning streaks and losing streaks. We don't always know why streaks happen, but you should watch for them and pay close attention to them while playing. The house advantage is based on thousands of hands over a long period of time. You don't play that many hands. Instead, you might play a few hundred hands over a short period of time. That's why streaks are important to you.

*When you find yourself on a losing streak move to another table, pit, or even another casino and make smaller bets. Stay and bet more when you find a winning table.*

**INTERNET**

### www.bjmath.com

*This excellent site has all the mathematics (maybe more than you want) involving probability, averages, formulas, house rules, betting strategies, counting, and much more – all about the game of blackjack.*

## European rules

In European casinos you will generally find a minimum of four decks, although six is becoming more popular. The croupier will be cutting a substantial amount of cards out of the shoe to prevent card counters from having any real advantage (see Chapter 6). Also, you will find certain rules, such as not being allowed to split 4s, 5s, or 10s (which is good for the player), and no insurance (which is not good for the card counter). Dealers will not take their second card until all the players have played out their hand. If you end up with a multicard hand of 21 and the dealer turns up a natural 21, it's considered a push.

### Trivia...

*In some European casinos, additional players are allowed to make bets on the seated player's box. These additional players will place their wager on the corner of the players box. Up to four additional player bets are allowed.*

## Asian rules

The surrender option, which is a good rule for the player, came out of East Asian casinos. Some of these casinos also offer a five-card option. If you get five cards without busting, you can turn in your hand for half your original bet. It seems like a different version of surrender, and is a good option for the player.

**INTERNET**

**www.blackjackinfo.com**

*This great site allows you to input specific blackjack rules and receive custom basic strategy charts for any specific casino.*

## A simple summary

✔ Blackjack, has been played in one form or another for nearly 200 years. It's played in almost every casino in the world, making it the most popular casino table game.

✔ Blackjack is a simple game to understand and play. Knowing the real objective – beating the dealer – gives you a good basis for playing the game successfully.

✔ You have lots of options, whereas the dealer can only hit on 16 and under and stand on 17 and above. Knowing all the options and table rules available can really help you at the game.

✔ Learning, practicing, and using blackjack basic strategy at the table will reduce the house odds to less than 1 percent. Use basic strategy if you want to win.

# Chapter 6

# Advanced Blackjack

ＷITH 28 STATES, MORE THAN 100 COUNTRIES, and 130-plus cruise ships with casinos on them, you can play blackjack almost anywhere. You've already learned that knowing basic strategy will reduce the house odds to less than 1 percent. Knowing a few other things, such as card counting, will enable you to move those odds to your favor. Keeping track of what cards have been played will enable you to figure out what cards are left in the deck, in turn allowing you to adjust your wagering and playing strategy to make the game one that favors you most of the time. It might sound easy, but it requires lots of practice and work on your part.

## In this chapter...

✓ Card counting

✓ What card counting does for you

✓ Other skills

# Card counting

BLACKJACK, OR TWENTY-ONE, *is different from most other games the casino offers because it is a game of dependent events. The cards that remain in a deck are dependent on which ones have been played or removed from that deck previously. Blackjack is a game that involves a great deal of skill; in fact, the skill factor is so great that if you use the correct strategies in addition to card counting, you can beat the casino most of the time.*

This is the reason casinos will ask you to leave if they think you are a card counter. It's important to understand that card counting is not illegal in any casino, but casinos abide by the old English law that says, "Management has the right to refuse service"; therefore, you can be denied the privilege of playing blackjack in their casino.

## A little history

In the mid-1950s a group of young army engineers stationed in Maryland – Roger Baldwin, Wilbert Cantey, Herbert Maisel, and James McDermott, known today as the Baldwin group – discovered the correct mathematical way to play blackjack. They used desktop calculators to establish the correct ways to hit, stand, split, and double down. In other words, they discovered what is commonly known today as basic strategy. Upon their discovery, they published an article in a trade journal, but did not really enlighten the casino world. However, the article was noticed by a Dr. Edward Thorp, who used high-speed computers to confirm the Baldwin group's data and improve the numbers. In

1962 Dr. Thorp published a best-selling book entitled *Beat the Dealer*, showing how blackjack could be beaten in the casino. His book changed the way casinos dealt and played blackjack.

■ **By the 1960s,** *the Baldwin group's complicated mathematical theories had been refined and popularized to provide players with the basic winning strategies for casino blackjack.*

Dr. Thorp's system, the 10 count, proved quite complicated for card counters. Later, though, simpler counting systems were developed. One of the early counts was the ace–5 count. It turns out that keeping track of these two cards has a very big impact on the deck. Other counts were developed after the ace–5 count, some for certain areas such as Atlantic City and Las Vegas, and others for general use in any casino. Almost all the new counts were simpler and easier to play than the original 10 count.

*It's important to remember that to be a consistent winner at blackjack, the game must be played mathematically correctly (basic strategy), and card counting must be added to the skill of the player. With this combination, a player can move the odds to his favor.*

## System selection

The easiest card-counting systems are those called "level one." These counts only assign values of +1 and –1. Multilevel systems, on the other hand, may assign values of plus or minus 2, 3, or 4 for various cards. Some systems even use "side counts," for example, keeping a side count of aces along with the plus and minus count. The main point to remember is that there is no memorization required: just add or subtract each card value when you see it.

There are some important considerations involved in selecting a counting system. For one thing, the count should be simple, practical, and powerful, and one that you can use easily and effectively in the casino. But though some experts believe the simple counts will result in fewer mistakes and more reliability, others advocate more complex counts that will help improve the odds.

Another consideration to weigh when choosing your system is speed. You must keep the count, even against a very fast dealer. This can create problems. You might find yourself mentally fatigued after only a few hours at the table. You might start to make mistakes or lose your count frequently. Also, the concentration necessary for counting cards probably will not allow you to make small talk with the dealer or other players, which could in turn raise casino suspicions that you are a card counter. All these things must be taken into consideration when choosing a counting system.

The multilevel systems with additional multiparameters – such as side counts of aces, deuces, 8s, and so on – can lead to a very powerful and winning system. In computer simulations it has been found that these counts will outperform all simple systems, thus allowing you to greatly improve your win-rate.

## Trivia...

*The blackjack shoe was first introduced in Cuba in the early 1950s. Young Cuban dealers who dealt cards all day long got to be pretty skilled at handling them. When management started to suspect dealers were being too helpful to their friends at the table, they introduced a dealing box known today as the shoe. Later, when casinos got worried about card counters, the shoe was called on again to help prevent a house loss.*

# LEARNING AND PRACTICING THE COUNT

One of the most popular counts is the hi-opt 1 count, in which you count each card at the value listed here:

2, 7, 8, 9, A = 0 POINTS

3, 4, 5, 6 = +1 POINT

10, J, Q, K = –1 POINT

Now, here are some techniques to help you to learn a counting system. Start with a standard deck of cards; simply turn over the top card and announce the value. (For example, if it is a 4, you say, "plus 1.") Continue with the next card, determining its value and announcing it. Continue through the deck until you have seen all 52 cards. The objective is to recognize each specific card's point value relative to your counting system. Speed is not important at this stage.

Next, start counting a deck by reciting the cumulative value of the deck. For instance, let's say the first card is a 10; you'll say "minus 1"; if the next card is a jack, you'll say "minus 2." Then, say a 5 comes up; you'll say "minus 1," which is the cumulative total of the three cards. If the next cards are a 6 and a 4, you'll end at "plus 1." Start the deck at zero and continue to add or subtract only one, up and down the scale, as you see each card. After 52 cards you should end at 0. If not, you made a mistake.

## Trivia...

*Some cruise ships and individual casinos have been known to use three or five decks. The only reason for this unusual number of decks is to help make the counting process more difficult for card counters.*

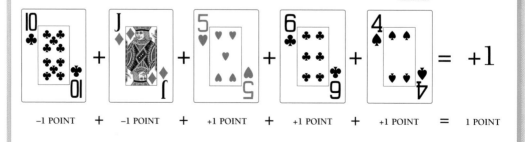

−1 POINT  +  −1 POINT  +  +1 POINT  +  +1 POINT  +  +1 POINT  =  1 POINT

# COUNT DOWN DRILLS

To play at the professional, or even the semi-professional, level, you must be able to keep up with the fastest dealer you might face. To do that you need to count through a deck at the following speeds:

- One deck – 30 seconds
- Two decks – 60 seconds
- Four decks – 2 minutes, 30 seconds
- Six decks – 3 minutes, 30 seconds
- Eight decks – 4 minutes, 30 seconds

## Running count versus true count

Keeping track of the big cards versus the little cards is called keeping the running count. This count doesn't differentiate between a +6 count with a half deck remaining to be dealt in a single deck game, or with a +6 count with 2 decks left in a 6-deck shoe game. But one is four times stronger than the other. You must use the true count to determine the real value of the count. In order to find the true count, you have to use a conversion.

*The true count is determined by dividing the running count by the amount of the deck(s) that is remaining.*

In a single deck, you divide by a fraction of the deck (such as ¼, ½, or ¾):

$$\frac{+6}{\frac{1}{2}\ (\text{deck remaining})} = +12 \text{ (true count)}$$

In multideck games you divide the running count by the number of half decks remaining.

$$\frac{+6}{2\ (\text{decks remaining})} = +3 \text{ (true count)}$$

### Trivia...

*Mathematically, in 100 hands the dealer will win 48 hands, the player will win 44 hands, and the dealer and player will tie eight hands. However, the player can win more money in the 44 hands through a type of "bonus" system such as the following: 3 to 2 for blackjack, splitting, doubling down, and surrendering.*

# What card counting does for you

CARD COUNTING *does two big things for you. First, it tells you when to increase your bet. For example, if you know the next round of a deck will produce a lot of big cards (such as 10s), you'll want to make a larger bet than normal, with the expectation of getting a 20. Second, when you count cards you can adjust your basic strategy to compensate for what cards you expect to receive as the hand is played. These two things – adjusting your bet and adjusting how you play your hand – are what make card counting such a powerful tool in blackjack.*

■ **You'll know when the odds** *are in your favor and when to increase your bet accordingly once you've mastered the skill of card counting.*

*Card counting can be very strenuous, both mentally and physically. Limit your playing to 45 minutes to 1 hour, and then take a 30-minute break. This will prevent you from becoming too tired and possibly making mistakes with the count.*

## Betting the true count

I suggest you use the true count as your betting guide. If the true count is +3, bet three units, or three times your basic bet. (For example, if $5 is your basic bet, three units would be $15.) If the count is –2 (or any negative number), bet one unit or the minimum allowed.

*It's important that you do not jump your bets.*

For example, if your last bet was two units and you immediately go to eight units because the true count went to +8, you will attract the attention of the pit boss. I suggest you *let your winning bet ride*, thereby doubling your bet to 4 units. This will look more natural to the casino staff. If you win and the count is still +8, let it ride again. In other words, don't jump your bet so high in one step that you get noticed.

## Playing the true count

Now that you know how to find the true count for betting, you should also use the count to adjust your basic strategy. You do this to compensate for how you expect the remaining cards in the deck to play. You will find it is not as difficult as it might first appear. For example, in basic strategy you normally hit a 12 against a dealer's up-card of 2 or 3. However, if you know there are a lot of big cards remaining in the deck (10s), you shouldn't hit. A +2 or more true count indicates that there are more big cards than little cards left in the deck. So, in this case it boils down to the following question: Do you want the 10 or do you want the dealer to get it? Let the dealer hit. Remember, the dealer always hits on 16 and stands on 17; you can stand on 12 and win!

## GENERAL CARD COUNTING RULES

Here are some rules to obey when counting. But remember: The situations and conditions you'll encounter at any particular casino will vary, and that these rules form only part of the basic blackjack-playing strategy. When you're ready for more advanced card-counting techniques, take a look at one of the blackjack books listed in the Appendices.

### True count of +2 or more

- Take insurance
- Stand on 12 versus dealer's 2 or 3
- Double 10 versus dealer's ace
- Surrender 14 versus dealer's 10
- Surrender 8s versus dealer's 9, 10, and ace

### True count of −2 or more

- Hit 10 versus dealer's 10
- Hit 9 versus dealer's 2
- Hit 12 versus dealer's 4
- Hit 13 versus dealer's 2 or 3
- Hit more and double less
- Hit more instead of standing
- Hit more instead of splitting

You might be wondering about all the specific variations to basic strategy; there are many. First, you have to know how many decks are in play: one, two, four, or six. How about rules? Does the dealer stand or hit on a soft 17? What about double on any two cards and double after split? There are so many variations that they cannot all be listed here.

*To be a successful card counter you must practice. Use a deck of cards, use a computer or flash cards – but practice, and practice regularly, especially in the beginning.*

# Other skills

BESIDES CARD COUNTING, *there are many other techniques to use to help make you a winning blackjack player. Each of these techniques will help reduce the house odds and increase your chance of winning.*

## Deck penetration

How far down into the deck does the dealer go before reaching the cut card and shuffling? Knowing this is important to you, the card counter, because with this knowledge your advantage can get very high, particularly toward the end of the deck. If most of the little cards are gone, the odds, with the big cards left, increase substantially in your favor. If the dealer never gets to these favorable situations, your win rate can suffer. Years ago, dealers would go to the end of the deck, which was very good for the card counter, but this isn't the case today. You should look for a 65 to 70 percent or better deck penetration in any game you play. If you don't see good penetration, move to another table, pit, or casino.

By being the last to play, the dealer or house will always have the advantage over all the players at the blackjack table. Consider this: if all the players bust, the house still wins, regardless of the dealer's total hand. Playing last is really the only advantage the house has over you, the player. Note that because many European dealers do not take their second card until all the players finish their hands, you want to double down and split less when the dealer is showing an ace or 10. This is because the dealer will take both bets if he turns up a blackjack. Conversely, in the United States, the dealer returns your double or split wager and only takes the original bet if he gets a blackjack.

# GAME EVALUATION

There are numerous factors to consider in evaluating any blackjack game. You want to play under the best conditions and have the best possible advantage over the house. You should consider the following factors before you play:

- Number of decks – one is best, eight is worst
- Rule variations – Las Vegas Strip rules are best
- Level of deck penetration – 65 to 70 percent is minimum; the deeper the better
- Number of other players – one-on-one is best, three becomes marginal, four or more is bad
- Management "heat" – continue to observe pit boss and floor man actions

## Developing an act

Card counting is not illegal. However, many casinos have the right to refuse service and can ask you to leave and bar you from playing. In the US, if you fail to leave when you are asked to, you are subject to arrest under the trespassing law – but not for being a skilled card counter. Therefore, knowing how to prevent casino management from identifying you as a skilled card counter and barring you from playing is very important.

There are literally dozens of techniques you can use to camouflage your play so as not to get barred. Maintaining anonymity and a low profile is your objective. So try to fit in, and try to look and act like a typical casino-resort tourist. Remember, you can be the best blackjack player around, but you must be able to play in a casino, or else all that expertise is wasted.

■ **Attracting unwanted** *attention, like the player on the left, arouses suspicions and may result in you being forced out of the casino.*

*Sitting in third base, the last seat, will allow you to obtain the best up-to-date information before you and the dealer play. But remember, the house reads the same books you do, so be sure to develop an act.*

## Counter measures against barring

The practice of barring skilled players from casinos has been tested in US state courts, and the courts have ruled that casinos have the right to refuse service to anyone. They can ask you to leave the blackjack table, and they can enforce that action by having you arrested for trespassing. As you become more skilled, you must work harder to prevent getting barred. Here are some suggestions:

- Don't play for more than an hour in any one casino.
- Don't jump your bets; instead, wait until your bet wins and then let it ride if the count is plus.
- Don't move your lips while you count.
- Don't move your head while following the cards as they are being dealt. Be sure to sit in a seat that gives you a direct visual perspective of the entire tabletop.
- Never leave the betting square in front of you empty. Always have a bet in the square.
- At the start of a new shoe, don't always bet your minimum amount.
- Don't hold up the game in any way.
- Dress and act like the other players.
- Try not to be the biggest bettor at the table.
- Don't attract attention in any way.
- Tip the dealer by placing a wager for him.
- Don't vary the size of your wager when a pit boss is watching.
- Be alert when the pit bosses are nowhere in sight. Remember, the eye in the sky is always watching.
- Don't talk at the table unless necessary; when you speak, be brief and polite.
- Smile! Don't look glum or serious while playing, or else you may alert management.
- Don't drink alcohol while you play, but do have some kind of drink in front of you.
- Play with a companion of the opposite sex (it looks natural), but teach him or her basic strategy first.

■ **Scotch on the rocks** *may be your favorite tipple at the bar, but if you want to keep your head clear stick to a nonalcoholic drink when you're at the blackjack table.*

# SIDE BETS

To help increase the house's take at blackjack, a lot of side bets have been introduced over the last few years, and new ones are always popping up. Side bets are not good for you. The house advantage is so high on these bets that they just don't pay. I've listed the most common side bets in blackjack; if you see one that's not listed, don't play it, either.

| Game | House advantage |
|---|---|
| Over/under 13 | 10 percent + |
| Pair square | 10 percent + |
| Streak | 8 percent + |
| Royal match | 6 percent + |
| Super 7's | 11 percent + |

## A simple summary

✓ Card counting has been around for some time now. Some of the counts are easy, whereas others can be quite complicated. Pick one that you can learn and use easily in the casino.

✓ Card counting can move the house odds to your favor. By adjusting your wager based on card counting, you'll have a very big advantage over the house.

✓ Knowing what the best blackjack rules and conditions are will enable you to start all your sessions in a positive way.

✓ As you get better at blackjack, you must also develop an act, or a set of personal rules to prevent you from being identified and barred from a casino as a skilled player.

✓ Stay away from side bets at blackjack. The house advantage is just too high.

# Chapter 7

# Craps Part 1

THE OLDEST CONFIRMED RECORD of a game of chance in which dice were used was in 1573 BC by the Egyptians. These Theban dice, as they are known today, are resting for all to see (but not to play with) in the Egyptian Museum in Berlin, Germany. But the legacy of this game lives on. The modern game of craps is an American game that was developed on the Mississippi and other inland waterways during the great steamboat era of the 1800s. Today's modern craps game is considered the fastest, noisiest, and most exciting game in the casino. It also has the best odds for the player of any casino game.

## In this chapter...
✓ Playing the game
✓ Some technical stuff
✓ Game bets

WHO'D HAVE THOUGHT THAT TWO LITTLE DICE COULD LEAD TO SO MUCH COMMOTION?

# Playing the game

WHEN YOU FIRST *see a craps table in action, with a dozen or more players all yelling, your first impression might be that it's a wild and confusing game. That's partially because this game seems to bring out players' emotions more than any other. Also, as you look at the layout of the table, you might think you will never learn this complex game. Craps can be wild and noisy, but it really is a simple game to play.*

At first you might not agree, but after I show you the correct and simple ways to bet and play craps, you'll wonder why other players make so many bad and foolish bets. To help convince you, I'll give you a brief description of a craps betting and playing scenario that you can use in any casino, at any time.

■ **Craps tables** *are often the noisiest and most action-intensive places in the casino, but don't be intimidated: Craps is an easy and fun game to play if you take the time to learn the right bets to make.*

# The making of a craps player

When a new player is given the dice for the first time, I suggest that you put a $5 bet on the pass line (the ribbon-like area that runs around the table layout), directly in front of you. This is known as a come-bet. (This first *throw* of the dice is called the "come-out *roll*.") When you do this, both you and the shooter will be hoping for a 7 or 11 to roll; if it happens, you win! On the other hand, if a 2, 3, or 12, also known as "craps," comes out, you lose. If any other number, such as 4, 5, 6, 8, 9, or 10, comes out, a "pass-line point" is established and the shooter hopes (as do you) that that number will be thrown again before the 7 comes up. If it does, you win; but if the 7 comes first, you lose, and the *hand* is over and the dice move to the next player.

If the shooter does throw a point number, you should put $10 directly behind your original $5 bet. This additional wager is called a *free-odds* bet or an "odds bet." The casino will pay you the *true-odds* money for that number bet when it wins, as opposed to the *even-money odds* they pay for your original pass line bet. So, even though you have to put up additional funds to make this bet, it is an excellent wager because the house edge is zero on this specific bet. The layout doesn't show this bet because it is so good for the player and so bad for the house. Review the chart below to see what the different numbers will pay out for the free-odds bet.

You can play this way all day long in any casino with great success. You can also be the shooter and throw the dice yourself. Whether you throw the dice or not, you should still bet the pass line and add odds bets the same way. So, now you're a craps player! Simple, wasn't it?

# $10 FREE-ODDS BET

The payout for a $10 free-odds bet will differ according to the point number thrown. Remember, this is a very good bet for you because the house advantage is zero.

| Pass-line point | House odds | Payout |
| --- | --- | --- |
| 4 or 10 | 2 to 1 | $20 |
| 5 or 9 | 3 to 2 | $15 |
| 6 or 8 | 6 to 5 | $12 |

# Some technical stuff

OF COURSE, *there are some "rules" that need to be followed at the craps table. Some of these are for the casino's benefit, and others are for your benefit. Take note because you will find these rules in almost all casinos around the world, and all dealers will insist that you abide by them at all times.*

## Buying chips

When you walk up to a craps table, the first thing you should do is look for the placard that shows the table limit. When you are first learning to play, you should start with a limited bankroll and always play within your means. You'll want to start at a $2 to $5 table. To exchange money for chips, you just place the funds on the table in front of a dealer and say, "Change." It's important to note that dealers are forbidden to take money from customers' hands. The dealer will take the money from the table and hand it to the boxman, who will count it and tell the dealer the amount. The dealer will then place the correct amount of chips on the table directly in front of you. You should take the chips from the table and place them in the groove provided on the table railing. At any time during a round you can ask for additional chips by simply calling, "Change."

## Making bets

You can place all the pass-line, don't-pass, come-line, field, and Big-6 or Big-8 bets yourself. Just put your chips on the designated area on the table and then watch the dice roll. Note that you can't make a bet directly on a numbered spot or in the proposition areas. If you want to bet in one of these areas, toss your chips in and call out your bet, and the stickman or dealer will place the bet for you in the appropriate area.

*Any time a die flies or bounces off the table or lands on the chip railing, in the dice bowl, or on top of the chips in front of the boxman, the stickman will call a "no roll" and that throw will not be counted. In that case, no bets are exchanged, and the shooter will be offered new dice to throw.*

## Right or wrong player

A player who bets with the dice, (one who wants the shooter to win), is known as a "right" bettor. This title has nothing to do with morality; it is the term used for a player who is betting with the dice. Players who bet against the dice, hoping the shooter will lose are known as "wrong" bettors. The game is dominated by "right" bettors.

## Who's who

The craps table usually operates with a team of five employees: the boxman, two dealers, a stickman, and one relief dealer. The boxman, who is a casino executive, sits opposite the players at the center of the table. He or she oversees the entire game, watches everything, and resolves any disputes. The boxman is also responsible for all currency that is accepted at the table, which is counted before being dropped into the money box. During games that have lots of action or when a high roller is playing, a second boxman will join the game.

The two dealers stand on either side of the boxman. They pay off the winning wagers, collect the chips on all losses at their end of the table, and make change for players. The stickman stands in the center of the players' side of the table. He or she is responsible for the handling of the dice and all the proposition bets in the center of the table. The stickman will call the game by announcing each roll of the dice, advertise betting options that are available to players, and generally set the pace of the game itself. The relief dealer is brought in to rotate the entire crew, except for the boxman.

Finally, there is the shooter, who is the player who rolls the dice during that specific round.

> ### Trivia...
> *Paul-Son Gaming Supplies, Inc., located in Las Vegas, manufactures 25,000 pairs of dice every month. Their dice are produced to a tolerance of 0.0003 inches (0.01 mm). Casinos normally change all the dice at the beginning of every shift.*

Stickman
Shooter
Dealer
Pit boss
Boxman

■ **It takes a good-size crew to run a craps table.** *The stickman and dealers rotate positions normally every 20 minutes, and additional supervisors will appear when a high roller is playing.*

# Game bets

THERE ARE MORE THAN *120 different bets that can be made at a craps table. There are bets that the dice will roll a natural, and there are bets that the dice will "crap out." In fact, it seems that for every bet you can make, there is an opposite bet. Additionally, there are hardways, buy bets, lay bets, one-roll bets, all-day bets, hopping bets, and many, many more.*

I'll discuss the majority of these plays in this chapter. For your part, as you progress as a crap shooter, you may want to review the appendices for some advanced books on playing. Keep in mind that some of those exotic bets give the house a very large advantage; therefore, many of them are not recommended.

## A new shooter

When a new shooter is ready to throw the dice, the stickman will push five dice toward him. The shooter selects any two, and the stickman retrieves the remainder.

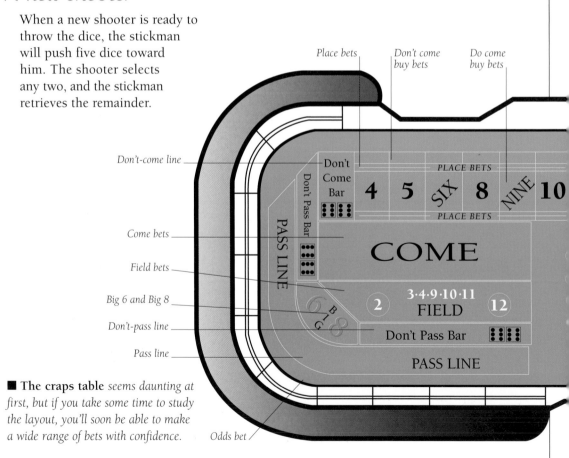

*Place bets*

*Don't come buy bets*

*Do come buy bets*

*Don't-come line*

*Come bets*

*Field bets*

*Big 6 and Big 8*

*Don't-pass line*

*Pass line*

■ **The craps table** *seems daunting at first, but if you take some time to study the layout, you'll soon be able to make a wide range of bets with confidence.*

*Odds bet*

You do not have to throw the dice to bet craps. You can pass and let the next person (moving clockwise) shoot. The only rule is that you must have a pass-line or don't-pass wager to throw the dice yourself.

## The come-out roll

The first throw is called the come-out roll. On this roll, you win if a 7 or 11 appears; you lose if a 2, 3, or 12 comes up (this is known as a craps). If a 4, 5, 6, 8, 9, or 10 comes up, that number becomes the pass-line point. To win now, the pass-line point number must repeat before the 7 appears; otherwise, the hand is over.

## Pass line

When you bet on the pass line as a right bettor, you are betting that the shooter will win by rolling a 7 or an 11 on the first throw of the dice, or that he will roll a number and repeat that number before a 7 is rolled. To make this bet, you put your bet on the pass line, (also known as the front line, because it appears at the front of the table). The pass-line bet is paid at even money. This is a **contract bet**.

> **DEFINITION**
>
> A **contract bet** is a wager that cannot be removed, reduced, or "taken down" once it is made. It must remain until it is won or lost by the player. Note that this applies for the original bets made on the pass line and come-point numbers.

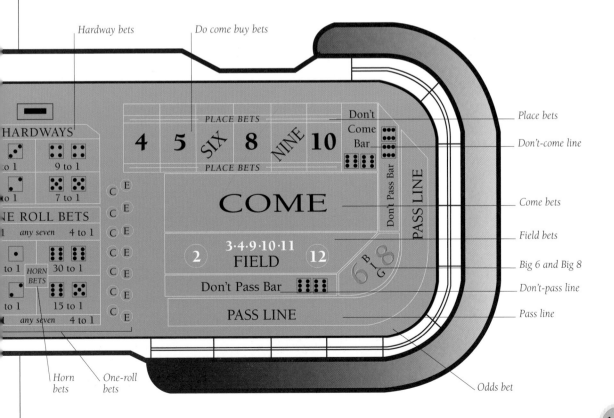

Hardway bets

Do come buy bets

Place bets

Don't-come line

Come bets

Field bets

Big 6 and Big 8

Don't-pass line

Pass line

Odds bet

Horn bets

One-roll bets

Pass-line and come bettors actually have an advantage over the house on the come-out roll. Because there are eight ways to win and only four ways to lose, you have a 2-to-1 odds favor. However, the advantage clearly shifts to the house whenever a point is established. That is why the pass-line and come bets (contract bets) cannot be picked up or changed after a point is established. This is the price the house exacts for being generous during the come-out roll.

PASS-LINE BET AREA

## Don't pass

Don't pass is the opposite of a pass-line bet. On the come-out roll you win on a 2, 3, or 12 (12 is a tie, or push, in some casinos; others use 2 as a tie). You lose if a 7 or an 11 appears on the first throw. You win if the shooter throws a 7 before making the pass-line point. The don't-pass area is known as the "back line." When the back line wins the dealer will say, "Pay the back line." This bet is paid at even-money.

DON'T-PASS BET AREA

## Come

When you place your wager in the "come" spot, which you can do yourself, you are betting on the very next throw of the dice. You win even money if 7 or 11 comes up, and you lose on 2, 3, or 12. If none of these numbers are thrown, your bet will go on the number that did appear, and you'll win when that number is thrown again. You'll lose if a 7 appears first.

COME BET AREA

DON'T-COME BET AREA

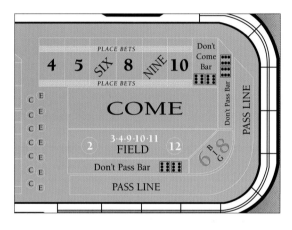

PLACE BET AREA

FIELD BET AREA

# Don't come

This bet is the opposite of the come bet. You win if the next throw is a 12 or a 3 (2 is a usually a tie; some casinos use 12 as a tie), and you lose if a 7 or an 11 comes up. Otherwise, your wager goes against the number thrown, and you win if the shooter throws a 7 before the come number appears.

# Place

Another way you can bet is to "place" a number. When you place a number, you select the point yourself instead of making a come bet and waiting for a point to be established by a throw of the dice. This bet can be made at any time. To wager on a number, after the come-out roll, you simply tell the dealer at your end of the table that you want to place the 4, 5, 6, 8, 9, or 10. Do not reach across the come line; just toss your chips toward the dealer so he can reach them. The dealer will take your chips and place the bet in a specific spot on the edge of the number so that he can identify whose bet it is.

# Field

This is a one-roll bet that you can make at any time. You are betting that 2, 3, 4, 9, 10, 11, or 12 will appear on the next throw of the dice. You win even money on 3, 4, 9, 10, or 11. Many casinos will pay double on 2 or 12, and some casinos will pay triple on 12. You will lose the field bet if 5, 6, 7, or 8 appears.

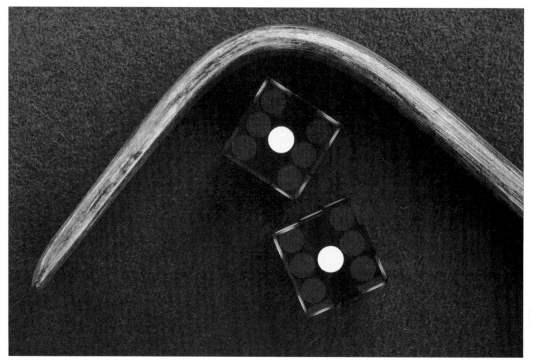

■ **The dreaded "snake eyes."** *But don't be too concerned – what happened on the last throw theoretically has no bearing on the next one. That said, they do often seem to run in streaks, both hot and cold.*

## Big 6 and Big 8

This is a bet you can place yourself on the spot marked Big 6 or Big 8. It pays even money when a 6 or 8 is rolled. You lose if 7 comes up, and nothing happens as long as other numbers continue to appear. It is an all-day bet, and you can remove the bet at any time. The house edge is 9.09 percent.

*Betting on the Big 6 or Big 8 is a poor bet for you. In fact, the New Jersey Gaming Commission thinks this is such a bad bet that they have prohibited Atlantic City casinos from offering it. You will not see the Big 6 or Big 8 on their craps table layouts (it's the same in some European casinos).*

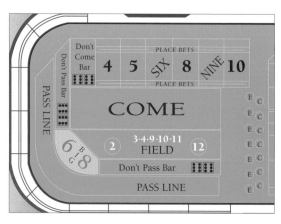

BIG 6 AND BIG 8 BET AREA

# Proposition

Proposition bets are in the center of the table, directly in front of the stickman, who is responsible for placing them. These bets are used for a wide variety of both one-time roll and all-day wagers, with large payoffs that you can make at any time. To wager on a specific proposition bet you toss your chips toward the stickman (not one of the dealers) and announce what bet you would like to make (for example, "$5 on a hard 4"). The stickman will place the bet for you. When you win one of these bets, the stickman will instruct the dealer at your end of the table about the correct payout, and that dealer will pay your winnings.

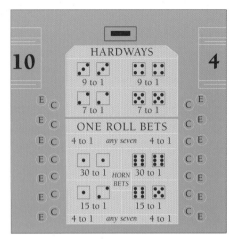

PROPOSITION BET AREA

*Avoid proposition wagers. They have the highest house advantages, ranging from 9.09 percent to a high of 16.67 percent, which makes them "long shot" bets.*

www.conjelco.com/faq/
craps.html

*This site has answers to those frequently asked questions (FAQs) about casino craps, including how the game is played. It also has a large listing of terminology and definitions.*

■ **There are over 120 types** *of bets available to the craps player. It makes sense to know about as many of them as possible, to sort the good bets from the bad.*

# TYPES OF PROPOSITION BETS

The following are the various proposition bets that are available in most casinos.

*a* **Two or twelve** This one-roll bet is a straight-up throw of a 1–1 or 6–6 combination. The payout is 30 to 1 on each number. The correct odds are 35 to 1. The house edge is 13.89 percent. In some casinos in the UK, the payout on this bet is 33 to 1.

*b* **Three or eleven** This one-roll bet is a straight-up throw of a 1–2 or 5–6 combination, with a payoff of 15 to 1 on each number. The correct odds are 17 to 1, with a house advantage of 11.1 percent. Again, in British casinos, you will find payouts on the 11 at 16 to 1 instead of the 15 to 1, which is good for you.

*c* **Horn** The horn bet is a popular one-roll bet that can be made on any throw of the dice. The horn bet is a combination bet defined as the two lowest and two highest numbers on a pair of dice. Consequently, any wager made on the horn is a bet that 2, 3, 11, or 12 will come up on the very next throw. Instead of placing a dollar on each number, the entire bet is placed on the horn space in the center of these numbers. Depending on which number rolls (2, 3, 11, or 12), one number will win, and three will lose.

It's important to note that the payoff varies depending on the specific number that is thrown. A $4 horn bet has $1 on each of the four numbers. The 2 and 12 each pay 30 to 1, and the 3 and 11 each pay 15 to 1 odds. For example, if either the 2 or 12 rolls, the bet will pay $30; but you must subtract the three losing $1 bets, leaving a $27 win. So, the $1 bet pays $27. If either the 3 or 11 rolls, the bet pays $15; but again, you must subtract the three losing $3 bets, which leaves you with a $12 win. Remember, if any other number is thrown you will lose this one-roll bet.

*d* **Any seven** This one-roll wager bets that the shooter will roll 7 on the very next throw. You will get a payoff of 4 to 1. The true odds are 5 to 1, which translates to a high house advantage of 16.67 percent. This is not a very good bet for you.

*e* **Any craps** This one-roll bet on the 2, 3, or 12 has a 7-to-1 payoff. That might sound good, but if you do the math, you'll find that it's not. There is one way to roll 2, two ways for 3, and one way for 12; the result of this is that you can roll four ways out of 36, which results in 8-to-1 true odds, giving the house an 11.1 percent advantage. Again, this is how the casino pays the rent.

In blackjack, a popular bet is insurance. Well, there is a type of insurance in craps, also. Many shooters will place an any-craps bet of $5 on the come-out roll only as a type of insurance bet to cover a large pass-line wager. If you lose the pass-line bet because of a craps, you win $35 on the craps wager. Remember, any craps pays 7 to 1, or $35 to $5.

*f* **Craps–eleven (C & E)** This is also a one-roll bet that the shooter will throw 2, 3, 11, or 12 on the next throw of the dice. To place this bet, toss your chips toward the stickman and call the bet "$2 C & E." The payout is three times the amount of your bet if the 2, 3, or 12 comes up, and seven times the amount of your bet if an 11 comes up.

*g* **Hardways** In the proposition area there is also a group of bets called hardways. These are all-day bets (rather than the one-roll type). They are the 2–2, 3–3, 4–4, and 5–5 combinations. (The 1–1 and 6–6 are not considered hardway bets because 2 and 12 can only be rolled one way, with no "easy way.") You can make these hardway bets any time, regardless of whether it is a come-out roll or the point has already been established by the shooter. With hardways, you are betting the shooter will roll a pair before the 7 and before the point number rolls in another form, which is called the easy way. For example, if you bet on the hardway 8, you want the two 4s to show up before the 2 and 6 or 3 and 5 do, and before any type of 7 appears. You win this hardway bet if the 4–4 rolls, but lose if the easy way comes up (2–6 or 3–5) and if any 7 rolls. The same is true when you wager on other spots that can be matched or paired.

## Hardways payoffs and odds

| Hardway number | Payoff | True odds | House advantage |
|---|---|---|---|
| Hard 4 | 7 to 1 | 8 to 1 | 11.1 percent |
| Hard 6 | 9 to 1 | 10 to 1 | 9.09 percent |
| Hard 8 | 9 to 1 | 10 to 1 | 9.09 percent |
| Hard 10 | 7 to 1 | 8 to 1 | 11.1 percent |

*Most British casinos pay out 9½ to 1 (19 to 2) on hard 6 and 8, and 7½ to 1 (15 to 2) on hard 4 and 10, making the UK a good place to play craps.*

## Buy

Another way to get true odds on a place bet is to "buy" a number. A buy bet is a special type of place bet that is normally made only on 4 or 10. It generally requires a $20 minimum wager. The house will charge an additional 5-percent commission. This commission, called the vigorish, or vig, will result in the house paying true odds of 2 to 1 instead of 9 to 5 for that bet. For example, a $20 wager on 10 will normally pay $36, but a buy wager of $21 ($20 plus $1 commission) will pay $40. If you want to buy 4 or 10, inform the dealer which one you want, and then toss your wager toward the dealer, who will mark the bet for you.

*When the bet is for more than $20, 4 and 10 are the only numbers you should buy. All the other numbers (5 and 9, 6 and 8) should remain as place bets.*

To distinguish a buy bet from a come-point bet, a special "buy" button is placed on top of the chips or wager.

## Lay

Lay bets are the opposite of buy bets because you win on 7 and lose when the point comes up. These bets are normally made by "wrong" bettors. The lay bet is similar to "giving" odds on any of the don't come bets. In theory, giving means you must lay down, or bet $2 to win $1. The casino also takes a 5-percent commission of the lay bets, just as it does with buy bets. For example, if you bet against the 4, you have to lay $41 to get $20. (The extra $1 represents the 5-percent commission.) Review the following lay bet payout chart to see the house advantage; then you'll understand why this is not a good bet.

## LAY BET PAYOUTS

Your best lay bet is against the 4 or 10; bet against the 6 or 8 and the house advantage becomes prohibitively high.

| Point | Odds | House advantage | Payout |
|---|---|---|---|
| 4 or 10 | 1 to 2 | 2.44 percent | $40 to win $20 |
| 5 or 9 | 2 to 3 | 3.23 percent | $30 to win $20 |
| 6 or 8 | 5 to 6 | 4.0 percent | $24 to win $20 |

■ **Once you understand** *the game, and know the best bets to make, playing craps should provide you with many memorable and fun times at the casino.*

# A simple summary

✔ Craps can be a simple game with simple bets. In fact, the simple bets offer some of the best odds in the casino. The more complex bets, on the other hand, give the house a larger advantage.

✔ There are some specific procedures to follow in craps. You can place some of the bets yourself, whereas others must be placed by the dealer or stickman.

✔ The table staff of boxman, dealers, and stickman are assigned very specific tasks. They can help you. Play with them, not against them.

✔ The come-out roll is the first important roll for all the players. The player has an advantage during this roll, but subsequently the advantage switches back to the house.

✔ There are more than 120 types of bets. Some are one-roll bets and others are all-day bets, and all have different odds. Smart players know which bets to take and which to avoid.

✔ Knowing which bets have less house edge will enable you to play long and effectively without risking a lot of funds.

# Chapter 8

# Craps Part 2

N O ONE CAN REALLY EXPLAIN IT, but casino revenue figures show that craps is attracting more new players than any other table game. Players are learning that craps is not difficult to understand, and the odds of less than 1 percent make it an excellent game to play in the casino. As you saw in Chapter 7, there are lots of different bets you can make, some of which are good for the player. In this chapter you will see the specific numeric odds for all the bets, and then you'll know precisely which ones you should make and which ones to avoid.

## In this chapter...

✓ Odds are everything

✓ The house edge

✓ What to learn and know

✓ The best and worst bets

# Odds are everything

**THESE DAYS YOU'LL FIND** *fierce competition for the player's dollar, particularly at craps. Many casinos will allow you to make odds bets of double, triple, 5, 10, and even 100 times the amount of your pass-line bet. They generously offer this betting to get your business. So what does this mean to you?*

If you bet $5 on the pass line with 100-times odds, you can wager $500 behind it. As the amount of allowed odds increases, the house advantage decreases considerably. The following chart shows what the house advantage is with the amount of odds offered.

## HOUSE ADVANTAGE

Note how the house advantage diminishes as the odds increase. If you're prepared to play at 100-times odds, the house advantage reduces to practically nothing.

| | | |
|---|---|---|
| ● | Single odds | 0.8 percent |
| ● | Double odds | 0.6 percent |
| ● | Triple odds | 0.5 percent |
| ● | 5-times odds | 0.3 percent |
| ● | 10-times odds | 0.2 percent |
| ● | 20-times odds | 0.1 percent |
| ● | 100-times odds | 0.02 percent |

## 100-to-1 odds?

Odds of 10 times or 100 times sound really good for the player; however, think about what kind of bankroll you need to play at that level. A $10 pass-line bet with 10-times odds would require you to bet $100. A $25 bet requires $250 on the odds. Imagine what happens when you are allowed 100-times odds on those types of wagers!

Finding a casino with 100-times odds is very rare; however, Binion's Horseshoe casino in downtown Las Vegas has such high odds available.

BINION'S HORSESHOE CASINO

*In general, the odds bet is a very good optional bet. The stickman will never solicit this bet because it aids the player and reduces the house advantage so much.*

# COUNT THE WAYS

Each die has six sides, so there are 36 possible numerical combinations when you throw a pair of dice (6 x 6 = 36). While there is only one combination that results in 2 (1 and 1) and one that results in 12 (6 and 6), the number of possible combinations increases as you move forward from 2 or backward from 12 until you reach 7, which has six possible combinations (1 and 6; 2 and 5; 3 and 4; and so on).

Your odds of rolling a particular number in craps is based entirely on the number of possible ways you can roll that number. For example, to determine your chances of rolling a 4, divide 36 by 3. (You use 3 because there are only 3 ways to throw a 4.) The result is 12, which means you have a 1 in 12 chance of rolling a 3. In other words, the odds are 11 to 1 against you for rolling a 4. If you compare the following chart with the one on page 118, you will see how the house makes its edge. As I said earlier, the true odds of rolling a 4 are 12 to 1, but the house pays only 11 to 1, which gives the house an 11.11-percent advantage. This is how the casino wins even when you win.

> ## Trivia...
> When you look at a die, notice that every number when added to the number opposite it on the die will always total 7. For instance, the 5 is opposite the 2; the 1 is opposite the 6; and so on. Crooked dice do not match. This is the first thing a boxman or player will look for if he doubts the dice are on the up and up.

| Dice total | Possible combinations | Number of ways | Odds |
|---|---|---|---|
| 2 | | 1 | 1 in 36 |
| 3 | | 2 | 2 in 36 |
| 4 | | 3 | 3 in 36 |
| 5 | | 4 | 4 in 36 |
| 6 | | 5 | 5 in 36 |
| 7 | | 6 | 6 in 36 |
| 8 | | 5 | 5 in 36 |
| 9 | | 4 | 4 in 36 |
| 10 | | 3 | 3 in 36 |
| 11 | | 2 | 2 in 36 |
| 12 | | 1 | 1 in 36 |

## Odds bets

Taking odds on pass-line and come bets is the best bet anywhere in the entire casino. Why? Because the casino has zero advantage, or edge, over the player when adding odds to these original bets. The casino will pay you the true odds when you win an odds-type bet at craps. Remember that you can make an odds wager on the pass line and on the don't-pass line after a point has been established. Also, you'll want to take odds on a lay bet and on a don't-come bet after the bet has been moved to a number.

*The odds bets, also known as free odds, can be removed or reduced at any time. But because they work to the player's advantage, you shouldn't take them down or reduce them.*

# CRAPS PAYOUT ODDS

By looking at the payout odds versus the house edge for the various bets in craps, the wise player should be able to ascertain which bets to make regularly, and which to avoid.

| Bet | Payout odds | House edge |
|---|---|---|
| Pass-line bet | 1 to 1 | 1.4% |
|     Single odds | 1 to 1 | 0.8% |
|     Double odds | 1 to 1 | 0.6% |
| Don't pass-line bet | 1 to 1 | 1.4% |
|     Single odds | 1 to 1 | 0.8% |
|     Double odds | 1 to 1 | 0.6% |
| Come bet | 1 to 1 | 1.4% |
| Pass-line point 4 or 10 w/odds | 2 to 1 | 0% |
| Pass-line point 5 or 9 w/odds | 7 to 5 | 0% |
| Pass-line point 6 or 8 w/odds | 7 to 6 | 0% |
| Field Bet 3, 4, 8, 10 or 11 | 1 to 1 | 5.5% |
| Field bet 2 or 12 (double) | 2 to 1 | 5.5% |
| Field bet 2 or 12 (triple) | 3 to 1 | 2.8% |
| One-roll bet any 7 | 4 to 1 | 16.67% |
| One-roll bet any craps (2, 3, or12) | 7 to 1 | 11.11% |
| One-roll bet any 2 or 12 | 30 to 1 | 13.89% |
| One-roll 3 or 11 | 15 to 1 | 11.11% |
| Don't pass-line point 4 or 10 | 1 to 2 – 5% vig | 2.44% |
| Don't pass-line point 5 or 9 | 2 to 3 – 5% vig | 3.23% |
| Don't pass-line point 6 or 8 | 5 to 6 – 5% vig | 4.00% |
| Big 6 or Big 8 | 1 to 1 | 9.09% |
| Hardways 6 or 8 | 9 to 1 | 9.09% |
| Hardways 4 or 10 | 7 to 1 | 11.11% |
| Place 4 or 10 | 9 to 5 | 6.67% |
| Place 5 or 9 | 7 to 5 | 4.00% |
| Place 6 or 8 | 7 to 6 | 1.52% |

If you look at the "Craps payout odds" chart, you will see that you have to wager more to get less on the don't-pass bets. For example, you must bet $2 to win $1 on the don't-pass 4 or 10; $3 to win $2 on don't-pass 5 or 9; and $6 to get $5 on 6 and 8 numbers.

*It's always a good idea to keep your original line bet small and your free-odds bet large. That way, if you win on the come-out roll, you can save your winnings so that you can increase your odds bet later. You'll then have a better advantage over the house.*

## Are the odds "on" or "off"?

Come-bet odds are always temporarily off during the come-out roll, and are automatically put back on once a point is established because players hate to lose the entire bet when a winning 7 is thrown. Remember, the dice don't know you have a bet working, so they're just going to follow the laws of probability. You can tell the dealer, "Odds work on the come-out," and the dealer will place a special "on" button on your bets. That way, if the shooter does throw a point number, you'll be paid even money for your come bet and true odds on your odds bet. Most players accept the common procedure of odds being "off" on the come-out roll.

The main marker that is used to tell everyone whether the odds are on or off is called the puck. The puck is white on one side, with ON printed in bold letters; the other side is black and is painted with the word OFF. The puck is handled by the dealers at each end of the table. After a point is established, the dealers will first turn the puck to the white side, and then place it on the point the shooter established.

■ **The puck denotes** *here that the odds are ON, and that the point number is 5. All "right" bettors hope that another 5 is thrown before a 7.*

# The house edge

THE HOUSE EARNS A PERCENTAGE *on every bet that is made at the craps table. This is how they pay for the overheads of running a casino. However, the choice of how much you want to pay for the privilege of playing is entirely up to you. At craps you can almost play for "free" when you make the proper odds bet, or you can pay a large vig when you bet on one of the proposition bets (such as a one-roll any 7). I suggest that you consider your options any time you're at the craps table.*

In craps there is a big difference between 10 to 1 and 10 for 1. For example, when you are paid at 5 to 1, you'll be paid $5 and the $1 original wager. In the case of $5 for $1, you get paid $5 only, which includes your original dollar bet. This really reduces the true payout to 4 to 1.

*You should avoid any "for" bets you see at the craps table — all they do is give the house an extra percentage toward their edge.*

## Player advantage

You do have some advantages over the house. For one thing, you can always quit when you want to. Also, you decide how much to bet, and when, and where. You can skip bets, and you can bet big or little, and the house must cover you every time. Don't be intimidated by all the action and noise – you now know the good bets to make, and which ones to stay away from. The key to playing craps is to play smart. Obtaining knowledge will give you that ability.

## Hot tables

When first picking a table to play, be alert to the pit supervisor's attitude as you approach the craps area. Pit bosses and floor men normally will give their full attention to the "hot tables" – tables where there is a lot of action and the players are winning. For that reason, you should look for the table that is getting all the attention. Conversely, if the staff appears to be chatting, joking, and generally relaxed rather than tense, it's a sure sign that none of the tables are "hot." You are better off moving to another pit, or even another casino, when you encounter this "cold tables" type of situation.

### Trivia...
*Even though a knowledgeable player can reduce the house edge to less than 1 percent, the Nevada Gaming Commission reports that casinos are earning approximately a 16-percent return at craps.*

# What to learn and know

*MANY PEOPLE WILL NOT JOIN a craps game because it appears wild and confusing; as you have already learned, though, it really isn't. But it is true that in addition to all the different ways to bet, there are some important procedures you'll need to understand before joining a game.*

## Throwing the dice

The house wants a true and clean throw of the dice. Using only one hand to hold and throw the dice is the accepted (and acceptable) method at any craps table. Be careful – rubbing the dice together with two hands will draw a sharp remark from a stickman. Instead, shake them using one hand, as this is the standard way to do it. The dice should be thrown hard enough so that they both hit and bounce off the opposite end of the table from the shooter. Any time a die bounces off the table it will be inspected by the boxman before it can be reintroduced to the game.

■ **Don't be shy, let 'em fly!** *When it's your turn to shoot, give the dice a shake and send them on their (hopefully lucky) way.*

## Establishing a point

When the come-out roll is thrown and any number other than a craps, 7, or 11 is made, this new number becomes the "point" for the shooter. Each dealer will move the puck onto that number, thus allowing everyone to see what number needs to roll before the shooter craps out. Once this point has been established, no numbers other than the point and 7 will affect the outcome of the roll.

## Pressing your bet

When you start to win you will want to increase the size of your bets. One way to do so is to "press" your bets. When you press, you are doubling your bet by the amount you originally wagered. For example, a $6 bet, when pressed, will go to $12 on the next roll; $12, when pressed, goes to $24; and so on. Most players will press their place bets. To press or double your wager, just tell the dealer to "press the 5" or "press the 8." Do this when the dealer starts to make your particular bet payoffs.

# ETIQUETTE

There's an etiquette to playing craps. Many actions are purely social or superstitious in nature, but some others help ensure that the game runs smoothly and efficiently. You should try to practice all of the following etiquette rules when playing craps:

**a** If you want to be part of the "team," be a "right" bettor: Always bet with the shooter.

**b** Never let your hands interfere with the roll of the dice; this is a big no-no in craps.

**c** Don't hold a drink over the lip of the table, where it could possibly spill onto the table.

**d** Collect your winnings and make your bets quickly so as not to delay the shooter.

**e** Never, never use the word "seven" at the craps table – it's bad luck. Of course, this is only superstition, but you don't want the table angry at you for using that word. Instead, use the nickname "big red" or "six–ace" when referring to a seven.

**f** It's popular to call 3 as "ace–deuce" or "craps," 11 as "yo," and 12 as "boxcars."

**g** Use only one hand when throwing and handling the dice.

**h** A good way to tip the dealers is to place a bet next to yours on the pass line. The dealers will know it's for them.

## Free lessons

Take advantage of the free craps classes offered by the major casinos. They are normally given in the morning and afternoon. A knowledgeable and outgoing dealer will conduct short, 1-hour introductory classes right in the main casino using a real table. The information is basic and factual, and allows for questions by the participants. These classes can be helpful to the new player, and I recommend that you take them.

**INTERNET**

**gambleup.com/free games/craps.html**

*This interesting site allows you to play craps for free. The graphics are lifelike, and it's a fun place to practice playing casino craps.*

*i*    Another way to tip is to throw a $1 (or more) on a hardway and announce "a hard 8 for the boys." If it rolls, the "boys" will get a $9 tip. (See the section "Tipping dealers" at the end of this chapter for more information.)

*j*    After the dealer pays you, he or she will put your chips down on the layout. It is your responsibility to pick them up before the next throw of the dice, or they may be declared a bet. The expression for this is "They lay . . . they play." Act promptly.

*k*    First-time female shooters always seem to be lucky. This might just be another superstition, but you should always ride with them.

■ **Take a ride with Lady Luck.** *Female shooters, like Sharon Stone in* Casino, *often seem to be lucky, especially if it's their first time at the tables. Why not bet accordingly?*

## Coloring up

When you are ready to cash in your winnings, the dealer will ask you to "color up," or exchange small denominational chips for larger ones (which are easier for you to carry). This also allows the small denomination chips to remain at the table so they don't run out and require constant refills. In addition, it lets management know how much you are leaving the table with so they can keep track and rate you as a player. If for any reason you don't want to color up, you don't have to.

# The best and worst bets

*IF YOU EXPECT TO BEAT the house at casino craps, you need to know which are the best bets you can make and which ones to avoid. You can beat the house in the short run by making the bets discussed in the following list and then taking your winnings and leaving. Keep in mind that the longer you stay, the more the house edge will get to your bankroll.*

(a) Adding odds to the pass line or the come, don't-pass, and don't-come spots are considered the best bets in the entire house. Always make those bets.

(b) Always place the 6 and 8 instead of betting on the Big 6 and Big 8. The house will pay you even money on the Big 6 and 8, but they will pay you $7 for $6 when you place these same numbers. Placing the 6 and 8 is one of the best bets in craps.

■ **Don't do it!** *Betting on the Big 6 and Big 8 is never a good idea; you can get better odds by placing the 6 and 8.*

(c) Stay away from field bets. These one-time bets have a high house edge of 11.1 percent.

(d) Only play craps in casinos that offer double odds or better. With single odds, the house will have a 0.8 percent edge over you. With double odds, the house edge will be further reduced to 0.6 percent. This means, technically or in theory, that over the long haul you can expect to lose only 60¢ for every $100 wagered.

(e) Remember, every hand will end in a 7-out. If you insist on leaving your bets on the table until the 7-out and relying on the length of the hand to make you a winner, you'll lose. The only way to be a long-term winner is to make smart bets, win, and move on.

(f) Like most other games, streaks in craps will happen. Shooters will start to make numbers and hold the dice for lots of rolls. You need to take advantage when that starts to happen.

## Tipping dealers

When playing craps, one way to tip the dealers is to make a hardway bet for them. If you are the shooter and your point is one of the numbers in the hardway box (such as 4, 6, 8, and 10), make a small wager bet for the dealers. If you hit your number, you will have made a nice tip for "the boys," and if you don't, they will still appreciate the effort. Another way to tip the dealers is to place a bet next to your bet on the pass line. Dealers will recognize that the bet is made for them. The main idea behind tipping dealers is to get them on your side, working against the house.

■ **Tipping the dealers,** *especially when you're enjoying a winning session, is recommended: It's nice to have allies when playing against the casino.*

# A simple summary

✔ The house advantage varies a great deal in craps and you, the knowledgeable player, can place bets with a house advantage of only 2 percent or less.

✔ Looking for "hot" tables and learning to "press" your bets can lead to a higher return, but it should always be managed in a sensible way. Learn to "win and walk."

✔ There are some very good bets in craps, and by learning the odds you can have fun playing – and be very successful.

✔ Etiquette is very important at the craps table. Use the terms, become a "right" player, make bets for the dealers, and be part of the team. You will have more fun if you follow these simple rules.

## Chapter 9

# Baccarat

THE GAME OF BACCARAT can be traced back to the latter part of the 1400s, during the reign of Charles VIII, King of France. The game became very popular in French casinos in the 1830s, and is still extremely popular in European and South American casinos today. It is the simplest table game in the casino to learn and play. Its simplicity lies in the fact that the player has only three choices, and all three deal with the betting; no other playing skill is required. There are two versions of the game: the American version and the European version.

## In this chapter...

✓ Traditional and mini-baccarat

✓ How the game is played

✓ The game objective

✓ Playing strategy

DON'T WORRY, HE WON'T HURT YOU – THE BACCARAT PADDLE IS PART OF THE GAME'S ALLURE

# Traditional and mini-baccarat

YOU WILL FIND *two different environments that accommodate* **baccarat** *players. The size of your bankroll normally determines which area you play in. One baccarat area is the formal, traditional, special, roped-off area of the casino, with a full staff of three dealers on a large table that will allow as many as 14 players. Many casinos will even have a strict dress code for the customers who play in these special areas.*

## DEFINITION

*We aren't sure where the word* **baccarat** *(pronounced bah-cah-rah) comes from. Most agree that it derives from the French "baccara," but that word's origin is unknown, and does not translate to English.*

## Trivia...

*In most casinos around the world, the number 13 position will not be found at a baccarat table. The number is eliminated to accommodate any superstitious beliefs on the part of any players who consider number 13 to be unlucky.*

■ **Traditional baccarat,** *with its formal atmosphere and tuxedo-clad dealers, is often the game of choice for the high-rolling gambler.*

The second environment in which you can play is the little-brother table, called mini-baccarat. This area has only one dealer and a much smaller table that allows only seven players. In mini-baccarat the dealer deals all the cards, and the players are not allowed to touch them. In addition, mini-baccarat is a much faster game than traditional baccarat. No matter which version you play, though, the objective is always the same: to arrive at a total of 9, or as close to 9 as you can get. Unlike in blackjack, where you are out of the round if you exceed 21, in baccarat you are still in the game even if you exceed 9.

# How the game is played

THE AMERICAN GAME *is dealt from an eight-deck shoe, although from time to time you will encounter casinos with six-deck shoes. All the numbered cards, 2 through 9, are counted at face value, with the suits having no relative value. The ace is counted as 1. Tens and all face cards are counted as zero. Any hand that adds up to more than 9 is counted by the second digit only. For example, if your hand totals 14, the hand is counted as 4; likewise, 11 becomes 1. Using this system, the highest possible score is 9.*

## EXAMPLES OF CARD TOTALS

| Cards | Total baccarat hand |
|---|---|
| 5 and 6 | 1 |
| 2 and queen | 2 |
| 4 and 9 | 3 |
| 8 and 8 | 6 |
| 9 and ace | 0 |
| 10 and jack | 0 |
| 4 and 6 and 9 | 9 |
| 3 and 8 and jack | 1 |
| 10 and king and 2 | 2 |

You can sit in any open seat: The seating position does not affect the play in any way. Each seat corresponds to a number on the layout. There are three dealers at the traditional table. The one standing in the middle, known as the caller, runs the game. The caller places the cards in the appropriate boxes, sometimes using an elongated paddle or palette to move the cards around. He calls for additional cards and declares winners, all according to the rigid rules of the game. Across from him will be two additional dealers, who pay off the winning bets, collect from losers, and, if the banker's hand was the winner, post the commission in the appropriate player box on either end of the table.

# TRADITIONAL BACCARAT

Traditional baccarat is played in an area that is normally reserved for high rollers, where minimum bets can range from $100 to $500 and player bets can be as high as $50,000 per hand. Dealers wear tuxedos, and you might find male and female *shills* in formal dress who are there to help keep a solo player company or to keep a game moving. Normally, you will encounter about 50 to 70 hands or rounds per hour, which makes the game slow and relaxed.

### DEFINITION

*People who are hired and financed by the gambling establishment to act as players are called **shills**. They make minimal bets and do not affect the outcome of the game in any way. Their role is only to attract other players to the game. You will not see them in Atlantic City, however, because the New Jersey Gaming Commission does not permit the use of shills.*

■ **At the traditional baccarat** *table the caller may use an elongated paddle or pallette to move the cards around and collect the chips.*

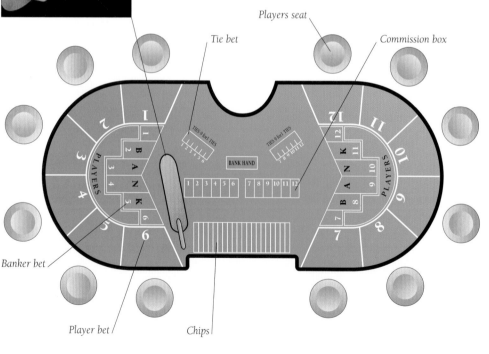

Players seat

Tie bet

Commission box

Banker bet

Player bet

Chips

Trivia...

*In 1959 baccarat was introduced to the American gambler for the first time at the Sands Hotel-Casino in Las Vegas. During the first 24 hours, two high rollers from Texas won almost a quarter of a million dollars. During the next 24 hours, the rules of the game were changed, reducing the player's advantage. These revised rules formed the basis for the American version of baccarat.*

# MINI-BACCARAT

You won't find James Bond in a tux at the mini-baccarat table on the main floor of the casino, among the blackjack and craps tables. However, you will find all the same rules and procedures at mini-baccarat as at the traditional table. Here, minimum table limits might range from a low of $5 to only $10. With fewer players and less formality, you can experience 100 to 150 hands per hour – almost twice as many as at the traditional table. This accelerated rate is something to consider when you figure what your bankroll needs to be to play.

■ **In mini-baccarat** *cards are dealt from a 6- or 8-deck shoe by a single dealer; the players do not handle the shoe or the cards.*

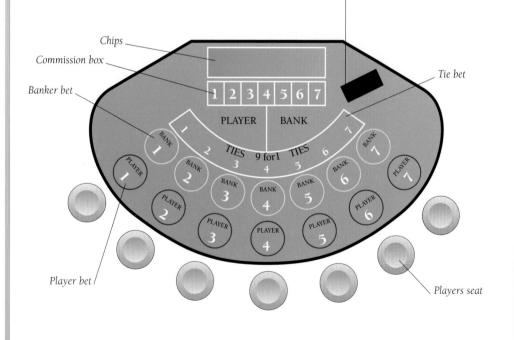

Chips

Commission box

Banker bet

Tie bet

Player bet

Players seat

## A good game

Baccarat is a very good game for you, the player, primarily because it has a relatively low house advantage. Additionally, it's important for you to know that there is a very strict set of playing rules that have been established and that cannot be changed by the player or by any actions of the house. In other words, in baccarat there are no decisions or options, and no degree of skill is required to play as either the player or the banker.

*When you first sit down, you will be given a pencil and a tracking card or chart. The card can help you to keep track of which hands are winning (banker, player, or tie), and can also reflect short-term streaks. You should use the card to help you tailor your betting strategy.*

■ **Using tracking cards** *helps you monitor winning hands and allows you to see streaks as they develop. Use them to help determine your betting strategy.*

## Shuffling the cards

The elaborate shuffling procedure used in baccarat seems to add to the aura of importance that the game exudes. First the eight decks are laid out on the table, and then scrambled about by all the dealers in a large, ever-moving "muck." The decks are then shuffled into various stacks and, finally, into one row. One player cuts the deck, which is then placed into a card-dealing box called a sabot, or shoe. The dealer exposes the first card, which indicates how many cards will be removed or "buried" before play begins. For example, if a 7 is exposed, the dealer buries the first seven cards before starting to deal the regular game.

## Dealing the cards

Two sets of cards are dealt out of the shoe, regardless of the number of players. One set, consisting of two cards, is for the player position; the other set of two is the banker's hand. Any hand with two original cards totaling 9 is known as a natural or, more formally, le grande natural. A hand of 8 is also considered a natural, or le petit natural. A natural hand is an automatic winner unless there is a tie. According to the strict set of game rules, if additional cards are required, the player hand always draws first.

*A tie can be expected in one out of ten hands. The bet, however, is only paid out at 8 to 1, resulting in a 14.4-percent return for the house and a poor bet for the player.*

## Additional cards

If neither hand is a natural (8 or 9), each hand is required to receive an additional card. It is important to remember that the banker hand is completely dependent on the player hand total when it comes to taking additional cards (because the banker's next action – drawing or standing – depends on the player hand total). This is the one small advantage the banker hand has over the player hand. The banker doesn't have to guess, the percent is in the banker favor. If he takes an additional card on his own the odds would be against him. Because it is the caller–dealer's job to enforce the draw rules, you, as a player, really have no need to know all the rules because you cannot play a different way than what has already been established.

## BACCARAT RULES FOR DRAWING

**Player hand**

| Player having | Action |
|---|---|
| 0–1–2–3–4–5 | draws |
| 6–7 | stands |
| 8–9 | natural (banker cannot draw) |

*Note: Natural = automatic winner (9 beats an 8) – no cards are drawn*

**Banker hand**

| Banker having | Draws when giving | Does not draw when giving |
|---|---|---|
| 0–1–2 | draws | |
| 3 | 1–2–3–4–5–6–7–9–0 | 8 |
| 4 | 2–3–4–5–6–7 | 1–8–9–0 |
| 5 | 4–5–6–7 | 1–2–3–8–9–0 |
| 6 | 6–7 | 1–2–3–4–5–8–9–0 |
| 7 | stands | |
| 8–9 | natural (player cannot draw) | |

The rules make the game interesting. For example, if the player receives an ace and a 2 (for a total of 3), the player must draw according to the set rules. Now suppose the player draws an ace, making the total hand equal 4. And say the banker gets a 5 and queen, for a total of 5. Even though the banker has a winning hand if he is allowed to stand pat, he must abide by the rules and draw another card. What if the card drawn is an 8? The banker hand is now 5–queen–8, for a total of 3, which loses to the player hand of 4. This makes for an interesting situation, particularly if a large bet is involved.

*In the European version of the game, the player and banker make their own decisions about whether to draw or stand on individual hands.*

# The game objective

THE REAL OBJECTIVE *of both baccarat and mini-baccarat is to correctly guess which of the three possible outcomes will come up on the next round. If you bet the player, the house edge is 1.36 percent; if you bet the banker, the house advantage is only 1.17 percent; and if you bet a tie, the house advantage is 14.4 percent. If the player and dealer hands end in a tie, and if you did not bet a tie, it's a push (with no win or loss), and no chips change hands.*

There are only three actions that can be played in baccarat:

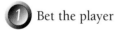 Bet the player

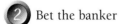 Bet the banker

 Bet a tie

*Don't bet on a tie hand: it is considered the worst bet in baccarat. It might seem like a good bet because it pays 8 to 1. However, because the house has a 14.4-percent advantage, this is rarely a good bet for the player.*

With only these three choices and the dealer making all the required plays, it is important for you to concentrate on how much to wager on each hand. That's really all there is to this game.

## The commission

It's important to note that in the American version of baccarat, a 5-percent commission is exacted on a winning banker bet, but not on any losses. For example, if you win $10, you owe 50¢ in commission; if you win a $100 banker bet, you owe the house $5. Note that after the adjustment for the 5-percent commission, all the banker bets result in a 1.17-percent casino advantage.

Some casinos will offer a lower commission on banker hands in an effort to attract more players. Most will lower the commission to 4 percent, and occasionally drop it to a low of 3 percent, which is a very good arrangement for the player.

The banker bet has an actual player advantage of winning 50.68 percent of the time, and losing only 49.32 percent of the time. If the setup were allowed to stay this way, all players would bet the banker spot and the casino would go bankrupt very quickly. However, the 5-percent commission returns the house advantage to a minus 1.17 percent for the bettor. Thus, when you lose a bet you lose $49.32 for every $100, but when you win you win $50.58 – except when you multiply by 0.95 percent, to accommodate the 5-percent commission rate), in which case the return is only $48.15. That is a loss of $1.17, which, you'll notice, is also the percentage of the house edge.

When you look at the player hand, you'll find that the opposite is true: The bettor wins only 49.32 percent of the time, and loses 50.68 percent of the time, which is okay with the casino. Looking at it from a dollar point of view, you find that for every $100 wagered on the player bet over the long run, you will lose $1.36 ($50.68 minus $49.32). Thus, the casino has a 1.36-percent edge on the player hand.

*Rather than collecting a 5-percent banker commission after each round, a record of what is owed by each player is kept on the table in a numbered box corresponding to each player seat. Normally, players pay this accumulated amount after the finish of each shoe and before leaving the table.*

## The European advantage

In the European variant of baccarat, chemin de fer, the banker hand is given a slight edge over the player hand. The reason for this seeming generosity on the part of the casino is that the individual banker hand is required to finance the entire round. The banker will be paid even money when he wins, while the player will only get less than even money because of the 5-percent commission. Confused? Well, it's even more complicated than it first seems. For example, if the banker funds total, say, $1,500, and the player in the first seat to the right bets $1,000, there will only be $500 left for the remaining players to wager. This poses a problem because when all the banker's funds are covered, no further bets are allowed. The banker can only cover the bets his total bankroll has. (It should be noted, by the way, that the casino risks no money in this situation, but charges a fee to the player–banker. When the American casino finances the game, it is awarded the 5-percent commission on the banker hands for doing so.)

In the European game, if one player wants to cover the entire banker's bet, he calls out "banco." No other player is allowed to bet during that specific round. You might recall that this was the type of game James Bond played in the movies.

**INTERNET**

www.thehouseofcards.com/baccarat.html

*This central resource of information related to baccarat includes rules and some great links to other sites (such as Sancho's Free Baccarat web site).*

# Playing strategy

*STRICTLY SPEAKING, there is no playing strategy that will affect the outcome of any hand or round. There are, however, some betting strategies that can result in a winning session for an alert player. So, when you play baccarat, consider these strategies:*

1. Because the banker hand has a slight edge over the player hand, consider betting the banker hand most of the time.

2. Streaks can be important in any card game, but especially in baccarat. Good tracking can help identify short-term streaks, so pay attention and be alert when they appear.

3. The tie bet has the highest house edge; therefore, you should normally avoid it. However, occasionally a run of ties will appear, and when it does, you should consider the high 8-to-1 payout that this bet awards.

4. You should start your game by making bets at the table minimum. This will give you some time to track results, so that you are better able to judge the flow of the game before making any large bets.

**5** You can count cards in baccarat, just as you can in blackjack. However, because there are eight decks in play and any real advantage will be near the end of the shoe, many experts believe that card counting will not help very much in baccarat.

**6** Consider the game to be one of chance, even though it is officially a game of skill. A little bit of luck, along with some streaks, can result in a winning session over a short period of time. The "win and walk" strategy can bring you good fortune in this game.

# A simple summary

✓ Baccarat is generally considered to be a high-roller's game, and is played in an elegant and special area of the casino. However, you can also play mini-baccarat for much lower stakes, and with all the same rules and procedures, but at a much faster rate.

✓ You, the player, make no decisions, except for betting. When you bet, you can choose a banker, player, or tie bet. Remember that with a house edge of more than 14 percent, a tie bet has the worst odds for the player.

✓ The game has a strict set of rules that are enforced by the dealer. All rules for standing, hitting, and drawing are already established and are carried out by the caller–dealer. You don't even have to know the specific rules to play and win at baccarat.

✓ The banker bet has a slight edge over the player hand, but requires that a commission of 5 percent be paid to the house on every winning banker hand (but not on any losses). Still, the banker hand is the best bet in the game. In addition, you can bet the tie hand, which pays 8 to 1.

✓ In some parts of the world you will find variations to the game rules, such as the player–dealer financing the game or options for drawing cards. However, despite these differences, trying to draw to an 8 or 9 remains the main objective of the game.

# Chapter 10

# Roulette

FOR MANY YEARS, ROULETTE was known as the glamour game of European aristocrats. In fact, it is still the most popular table game in European casinos. Roulette is a French word meaning "small wheel," and the game evolved from a number of pocketed wheel games that originated in England and continental Europe in the 18th century. The layout we see today was designed in the early 1800s by brothers François and Louis Blanc, early concessionaires of the world-renowned Monte Carlo Casino. Today, almost every casino in the world has a roulette wheel and it is still played in what is essentially its original form. Roulette is simple, easy to play, and exciting, with a wide variety of possible bets on each and every spin of the wheel.

## In this chapter...

✓ How the game is played

✓ Inside and outside bets

✓ The real odds

✓ A good way to play

THE ELEGANCE AND HISTORY OF ROULETTE IS STILL THERE FOR ALL TO SEE

# How the game is played

ASK ANYONE ABOUT THE CASINO *and there's a good chance that the first thing to spring to mind is the roulette table: the fantastic rotating wheel – a wood-and-chrome precision masterpiece – inset in a sea of multicolored felt. There are 38 blocks on the wheel, with numbers ranging from 1 through 36, colored red and black (alternating), plus a zero and a double zero that are colored green. The French wheel, however, which is used throughout the world and in a few casinos in Las Vegas and Atlantic City, has 36 numbers but only one zero. Shaped like a bowl, the wheel is spun in one direction by the dealer, who then spins a small ivory ball around the outer rim in the opposite direction. When the ball slows, it drops into one of the pockets of the wheel.*

## Trivia...

*Some history experts believe the original design of the roulette wheel was done by the French mathematics scholar Pascal, who was experimenting with perpetual motion machines. The basis for this conclusion is that Pascal gave the name "roulette" to the wheel he was experimenting with.*

It pays to look for the right table. In Reno, I found one casino that had a double-zero game on the first floor and a single-zero game on the second floor. On the Las Vegas Strip are two casinos that have both a single- and double-zero wheel within the same gambling area. As you will see later, your odds are better at the single-zero wheel than at the double-zero wheel.

■ **Though most casinos in the US** *play American roulette with the double-zero wheel (right), if you find a casino that has the French wheel (left), the one less pocket will increase your chances of winning.*

## Betting the wheel

Normally, between one and eight players can play the game at one time. However, some casinos have two layouts, with one wheel that allows additional players to participate. There are a large number of bets allowed in casino roulette. They range from single-number selection to numerous numerical variations up to 18, in addition to a large number of combinations. You are allowed to make as many bets as you want, and you may continue making them until the dealer or *croupier* calls "no more bets" or, in French, "rien ne va plus."

## Roulette chips

In American casinos you will be given special colored roulette chips when you first buy in to the game. You declare their value to the dealer (this can be any amount between the minimum and maximum table limits). The dealer places a value button (marker) on your colored chip, and then places both on the rim of the wheel to remind himself and to alert the next dealer of the value of your chips. Every player at the table will use different-colored chips to prevent confusion and to help the dealer determine which wager belongs to whom.

In many casinos around the world, all the players use the same "house" chips, which can lead to lots of confusion. When playing under such conditions, it's important that you keep track of your own chips.

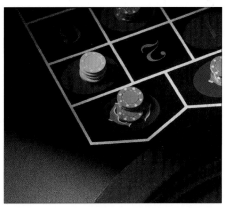

■ **American roulette** *is the only casino game where every player has their own colored chips with which to make their bets.*

*Be careful that each chip fits clearly on the spot you want because every wager wins or loses on every spin of the wheel.*

If you cannot reach a betting spot, slide the chip toward the dealer and ask him or her to place it for you. The placard on the table will inform you of the minimum and maximum bets. If a specific bet you would like to make is already covered by someone else's wager, simply stack your bet on top of theirs. In American roulette you can do this because each player uses a different colored chip. In other countries, however, its gets confusing, so be careful. Remember to cash in your roulette chips for regular chips before you leave the table – roulette chips cannot be used anywhere else in the casino.

# Inside and outside bets

THE TABLE IS DIVIDED *into two sections, called the inside and outside bets. On the inside of the layout you can wager between one and six numbers. Payouts vary depending on what spots or combinations you bet on. The outside bets include red or black, even or odd numbers, low numbers 1 to 18 and high numbers 19 to 36, column bets (which represent the 12 numbers in each of the three columns), and, finally, the dozen bet (which consists of the first, second, and third 12-number sections). Each wager will pay out differently, depending on which bet you select.*

## PLACING YOUR BETS

Study the tables below to get a feel for some of the different types of inside and outside bets you can make on the American and European roulette tables.

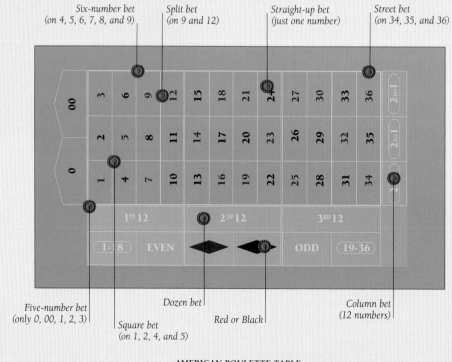

Six-number bet
(on 4, 5, 6, 7, 8, and 9)

Split bet
(on 9 and 12)

Straight-up bet
(just one number)

Street bet
(on 34, 35, and 36)

Five-number bet
(only 0, 00, 1, 2, 3)

Dozen bet

Column bet
(12 numbers)

Square bet
(on 1, 2, 4, and 5)

Red or Black

**AMERICAN ROULETTE TABLE**

# Inside bets

All bets on any of the numbers are known as inside bets. You are allowed to make inside bets on as many combinations of numbers as you want. It's important to note that most casinos will also have a minimum "inside" wager requirement. Even though the table minimum might be $1, there usually is a minimum "spread" requirement of $5 on all inside bets. This means that you need to bet a total of $5 when betting on inside numbers. You can do this as a single $5 number bet, or as five $1 number bets.

 **Straight-up, or single, bet** You can wager on a single number by placing it, centered, on any specific number from 1 to 36, or on 0 or 00. The payout will be 35 to 1 on both the American and French wheels. (Remember, the French wheel lacks the 00.) This is the highest payout on the table, and also the highest odds to win against.

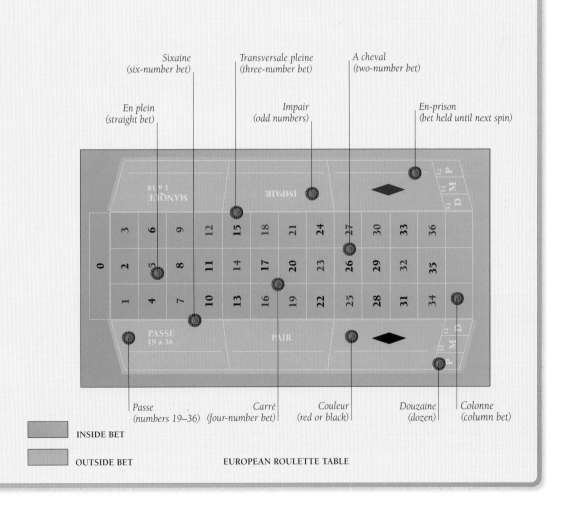

Sixaine
(six-number bet)

Transversale pleine
(three-number bet)

A cheval
(two-number bet)

En plein
(straight bet)

Impair
(odd numbers)

En-prison
(bet held until next spin)

Passe
(numbers 19–36)

Carré
(four-number bet)

Couleur
(red or black)

Douzaine
(dozen)

Colonne
(column bet)

INSIDE BET

OUTSIDE BET

EUROPEAN ROULETTE TABLE

143

**b** **Two-number, or split, bet** You can make the two-number, or split, bet by placing a chip across any line that separates any two numbers on the board. The payout for this bet is 17 to 1.

**c** **Three-number, trio, or street bet** To make a three-number bet, place your chip on the line at either end of a row, making sure it doesn't touch any other line. You can also bet the 0, 00, and 1 by placing your chip on the intersecting line where these numbers come together. The three-number, or street bet, pays 11 to 1.

**d** **Four-number, four-spot, or square bet** Placing the four-spot bet is easy. Put your chip over the spot where any four numbers come together. The four spot pays 8 to 1.

**e** **Five-number, or five-spot, bet** The five spot is only found on the American wheel. It is the intersection of the 0, 00, 1, 2, and 3 spots. This bet is placed at the end of the row, on the line where the 0 and 1 come together. When you place this bet, you want any of those five numbers to come up. The five spot pays 6 to 1. This bet gives the house the highest advantage for the entire game – a whopping 7.29 percent.

*Don't make a five-spot bet. It's the worst bet you can make in roulette on the American wheel.*

**f** **Six-number bet** Make a six-number bet by placing your chip on either end of a row, like you do for a three-number bet, except this time you'll cover the line where two rows come together. You want any number in those two rows to come up. The six-number bet pays 5 to 1.

> ## Trivia...
> In January 1963, Sean Connery, also known in the movies as James Bond, was playing at Casino de la Vallee in Saint-Vincent, Italy. His game was roulette. He played the number 17 three times in a row and won! The true odds of hitting the same number three times in a row are 50,653 to 1. After his third win, he left the casino with $30,000 in winnings.

■ **For a six-number bet** *place a chip in between two rows on the outside line. If the ball lands on any number in the two rows, you win your bet with a payout of 5 to 1.*

# Outside bets

Outside bets are those that are placed on spots other than the numbers 0, 00, and 1 through 36. On the table layout you will find the outside bets in the sections closest to the players. They are the even-money, column, and dozen bets.

*(a)* **Red** When you bet red, you are betting that the next spin of the wheel will result in any red number coming up. This will result in an even-money, or 1-to-1, payout. For example, if red comes up and you had a $5 wager, you will win another $5.

*(b)* **Black** When you go with black, you want any black number to come up on the next spin. This is also an even-money, or 1-to-1, payout wager. The only ways you can lose on this bet are if a red or a green number comes up.

*(c)* **Even** When you bet even, you are wagering that the next spin will result in an even number coming up (not including 0 and 00). This is an even-money (1-to-1) payout bet.

*(d)* **Odd** With odd, you are wagering that the next spin will result in any odd number coming up (again, not including 0 and 00). This is also an even-money (1-to-1) payout.

*(e)* **Column** With a column bet, you are wagering that on the next spin a number from one of the three columns of 12 numbers will come up. This bet is placed at the end of the layout, in the box marked 2 to 1, which signifies that it is a 2-to-1 payout wager.

*(f)* **Dozen** With a dozen bet, you are wagering that on the next spin a number from a particular group of 12 numbers will come up. You have three wager choices: 1 to 12, 13 to 24, or 25 to 36. Each dozen has its own specific wagering box (labeled 1st 12, 2nd 12, and 3rd 12, respectively). The payout is 2 to 1.

*(g)* **Low number 1 to 18** With this bet, you are wagering that on the next spin a number between 1 and 18 will come up. The payout is even-money, or 1-to-1 odds.

*(h)* **High number 19 to 36** With this one you are wagering that on the next spin a number between 19 and 36 will come up. This is also an even money, or 1-to-1, payout.

■ **The red chips above** *have been stacked on the third 12 bet (numbers 25 to 36); this outside bet pays 2 to 1.*

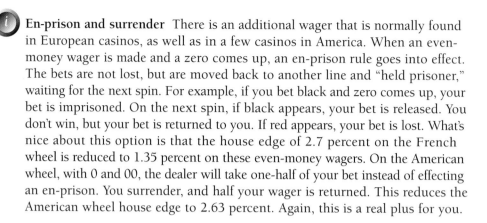

**En-prison and surrender** There is an additional wager that is normally found in European casinos, as well as in a few casinos in America. When an even-money wager is made and a zero comes up, an en-prison rule goes into effect. The bets are not lost, but are moved back to another line and "held prisoner," waiting for the next spin. For example, if you bet black and zero comes up, your bet is imprisoned. On the next spin, if black appears, your bet is released. You don't win, but your bet is returned to you. If red appears, your bet is lost. What's nice about this option is that the house edge of 2.7 percent on the French wheel is reduced to 1.35 percent on these even-money wagers. On the American wheel, with 0 and 00, the dealer will take one-half of your bet instead of effecting an en-prison. You surrender, and half your wager is returned. This reduces the American wheel house edge to 2.63 percent. Again, this is a real plus for you.

## Payouts

When the ball stops, the dealer or croupier will announce the number and color, and whether it is odd or even, high or low. He'll also place a marker on the winning spot. The dealer will remove all losing wagers, and then begin to make all the required payouts. This ensures that a new bet is not removed as a losing one by mistake, and it prevents cheaters from trying to place a bet after the fact. Dealers are very fussy about this and will tell you bluntly if you violate the rule. Betting can resume once the marker is removed.

*Make sure you don't touch your winnings or make any new bets while the dealer's marker is on the table.*

■ **If you strike it lucky** *and the ball lands on your number, the croupier will place a marker on the winning spot and gather up all the losing bets before paying off your bet in wheel chips.*

# The real odds

**THE HOUSE HAS A GUARANTEED** built-in win rate for roulette, no matter what bet is made. Using the American wheel, with 38 numbers, the payout is 35 to 1 for a straight-up win; however, the true odds are 37 to 1. This means that the casino will win an average of 2 chips for every 38 played.

*If you wager one chip on number 17 for every spin, in a cycle of 38 spins you will lose on 37 numbers (37 chips) and win once for 35 chips, and the casino will be ahead 2 chips. This results in a 5.26-percent house advantage on the American wheel and a 2.70-percent advantage on the French wheel (which uses only 37 numbers).*

## Payouts versus true odds

The following table lists the payouts and the true odds for all roulette bets. Remember, the house has to pay for the mortgage, salaries, free drinks, air conditioning, lights, and all the other things it takes to run a large casino. The difference between the payout and true odds is what pays for all those overhead expenses.

## ROULETTE PAYOUTS AND TRUE ODDS

| American bet | European bet | Payout | True odds (US) | True odds (European) |
|---|---|---|---|---|
| Single/one number | En plein | 35 to 1 | 37 to 1 | 36 to 1 |
| Split/two number | A Cheval | 17 to 1 | 18 to 1 | 17.5 to 1 |
| Street/three number | Transversale pleine | 11 to 1 | 11.67 to 1 | 11.33 to 1 |
| Square/four number | En carré | 8 to 1 | 8.5 to 1 | 8.25 to 1 |
| Five number | – | 6 to 1 | 6.6 to 1 | – |
| Line/six number | Sixaine | 5 to 1 | 5.33 to 1 | 5.17 to 1 |
| Column | Colonne | 2 to 1 | 2.17 to 1 | 2.08 to 1 |
| Dozen | Douzaine | 2 to 1 | 2.17 to 1 | 2.08 to 1 |
| Even | Pair | 1 to 1 | 1.05 to 1 | 1.01 to 1 |
| Odd | Impair | 1 to 1 | 1.05 to 1 | 1.01 to 1 |
| High/19–36 | Passe | 1 to 1 | 1.05 to 1 | 1.01 to 1 |
| Low/1–18 | Manque | 1 to 1 | 1.05 to 1 | 1.01 to 1 |
| Red | Rouge | 1 to 1 | 1.05 to 1 | 1.01 to 1 |
| Black | Noir | 1 to 1 | 1.05 to 1 | 1.01 to 1 |

## The odds are everything

The fixed odds in roulette are how the house makes its money. There can be some very big odds to overcome, but at the same time, there are some odds that are very small. A bet with big odds, such as a straight-up bet, is often called a long shot. For example, compare the odds of hitting any red number versus the odds that one specific number out of 38 will come up. As you can see, the odds against you vary a great deal, depending on which bet you make. You can play any way you want at the roulette table. You make the choices, you select the odds, and you make the bets. When it comes to roulette, play smart – play the odds. The main thing to remember is that the game is based on independent events or trials.

*In roulette, each and every spin is a new spin, and the outcome is never determined by a prior spin. What happened before makes no difference to what will happen next.*

■ **The spinning wheel** *is what makes roulette such a game of chance: Each spin is new so that no matter how many times a number has recently come up, there's simply no way of predicting where the ball will fall. As a novice player, the skill lies in being aware of the odds and placing your bets accordingly.*

# A good way to play

THERE HAS BEEN A SUBSTANTIAL *number of books written about roulette systems. Among the most popular systems is the Martingale system, in which you double your bet after each loss; and then there is the reverse Martingale system, in which you cut your bet in half after a win. With the cluster system, if you think number 11 will come up, you bet on the cluster numbers on the table layout next to the 11 (7, 9, 13, and 15). Another system (similar to the cluster system) involves betting the neighbor numbers on the wheel itself. Again, if you were to wager on 11, you would also make additional bets on the 7 and 30 because they are neighbors on the wheel.*

My advice to you is to not put too much stock in any particular roulette system. There is no mathematical certainty that one system or another will provide any extra chance of winning, and some systems can actually be downright costly to your bankroll.

## Some simple tips

Now that you know how the game is played, and you know how to play it (which is considerably different), you want to have the best possible chance of winning. Following are some tips that should help you along that winning road.

*a* Don't bother to look for a biased wheel. Today's casinos examine and measure the ivory ball; the wheel is inspected and balanced frequently; and the dealers are scrutinized closely. It would be unusual for you to find a biased game.

*b* Since the house odds are cut in half when you play the French wheel versus the American one, you might want to look for a single-zero wheel to play. It shouldn't be difficult; many American casinos are starting to use the French wheel.

*c* Only wager on even-money and low-odds choices at roulette. They offer the lowest house advantages of any bets available to you.

*d* Never play the five-spot (0, 00, 1, 2, 3) on the American wheel.

*e* Because roulette is a game of chance, you should just play the game for fun, excitement, and entertainment value.

*f* Manage your session money carefully. Set aside a given amount to play with; if you lose 50 percent of it, it's time to quit. Set a win target, and when you reach it, quit.

## Some simple strategies

There are lots of books that advertise successful winning and betting strategies for roulette. However, when they are analyzed in detail, most of these strategies don't work. But a smart, knowledgeable, and observant player such as yourself can get in, make some bets, win some wagers, and leave. To help accomplish this, review these following tips:

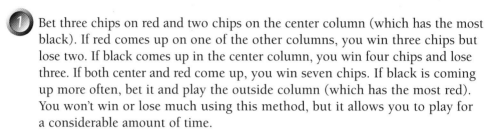 Bet three chips on red and two chips on the center column (which has the most black). If red comes up on one of the other columns, you win three chips but lose two. If black comes up in the center column, you win four chips and lose three. If both center and red come up, you win seven chips. If black is coming up more often, bet it and play the outside column (which has the most red). You won't win or lose much using this method, but it allows you to play for a considerable amount of time.

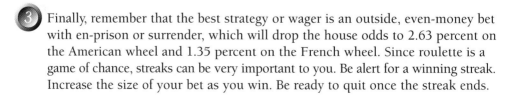 Look for someone who's winning at the table. Start making the same bets they're making. Maybe they know something or are on a lucky streak.

■ **Though roulette, with its high odds,** *should be played for fun and not profit, by incorporating a little strategy into your game you may be pleasantly surprised when you find yourself on a winning streak.*

Finally, remember that the best strategy or wager is an outside, even-money bet with en-prison or surrender, which will drop the house odds to 2.63 percent on the American wheel and 1.35 percent on the French wheel. Since roulette is a game of chance, streaks can be very important to you. Be alert for a winning streak. Increase the size of your bet as you win. Be ready to quit once the streak ends.

In the United States, many casinos have an electronic display, or scoreboard, that shows the results of the last 20 spins. In other countries, the croupier will supply a tracking card, allowing you to "manually" record the result of each spin of the wheel. Tracking will help you to recognize short trends that develop and can be helpful in making decisions about what to play next.

# A simple summary

✓ Roulette is the oldest known casino game, and is played in almost every casino in the world.

✓ The game is played using a simple bowl-like wheel and a colorful table layout with 36 numbers and one or two zeros. As many as eight players can wager all at the same time, and even on the same numbers.

✓ Roulette has a large variety of bets that can be made all at the same time, but that result in different payouts, ranging from very high odds for long shots, down to 1-to-1 (even-money) payouts.

✓ American roulette is different in many respects from the French game. Some of these differences are the amount of numbers available, what type of chips are used, and even the name of the person managing the game. The French wheel, with its single zero, gives a much better return on your money and should be played instead of the American wheel if possible.

✓ There is no foolproof strategy that will stand up mathematically, so play smart and choose the bets with the best odds.

✓ Always aim for a fun and entertaining experience, and remember that if you manage your session bankroll properly, you will almost certainly have a good time playing roulette.

# Chapter 11

# Poker

POKER, POKER EVERYWHERE . . . just how many games are there? I've been able to identify at least 120 different games that claim to be poker, in one form or another: Chicago, five-card draw, five-card stud, Texas hold 'em, Omaha, low ball, seven-card, whiskey poker, and (of course) strip poker. The game we know today was developed in the US in the early 1800s. Some scholars believe that brag, a type of mini-poker game popular in the UK, is the true ancestor of poker. Others believe the game comes from New Orleans, from the French game poque. But regardless of where it originated, poker has become a billion-dollar-a-year industry.

## In this chapter...
✓ Types of games
✓ General game rules
✓ Choosing your game
✓ The art of poker
✓ Where to play

WITH A GOOD HAND AND GOOD LUCK YOU'RE A WINNER

# Types of games

ALMOST ALL POKER GAMES *can be divided into two major types: stud and draw. In stud, cards are distributed to each player, and no changing of cards is allowed. In draw poker, cards can be exchanged for new ones. There are really only two ways to win at poker: one way is to have the highest-ranking hand (see the "Ranking order of hands" chart opposite), and the other way is to bluff other players into thinking you have the highest hand, thereby encouraging them to drop out of the round.*

In both types of games, you can play in one of three ways: high, low, or high-low. When a poker game is played high, the highest hand wins the pot. When a game is played low, the lowest hand wins. When playing high-low, the pot is split between the person with the highest hand and the person with the lowest hand.

## Poker games

Even though there are more than 120 different poker games, only a few are normally found in card rooms and casinos around the world. These are:

a Five-card stud

b Seven-card stud

c Five-card draw

d Texas hold 'em

e Omaha

■ **In card rooms** *around the world, at all hours of the day and night, you will be able to find – and join – some poker variant being played. Thankfully, card-room etiquette has improved since the days of the Wild West!*

# RANKING ORDER OF HANDS

There are 2,598,960 five-card combinations in a standard 52-card deck with no wild cards. The value of each possible poker hand is based on the likelihood of it being dealt. For example, there are only four royal flushes among the available combinations, making it the rarest – and most valuable – hand.

| Hand | No. of possibilities | Probability |
|------|:---:|:---:|
| Royal flush (A, K, Q, J, 10 of same suit) | 4 | 1 in 649,740 |
| Straight flush (e.g., 6, 5, 4, 3, 2 of same suit) | 36 | 1 in 72,193 |
| Four of a kind (e.g., four 7s) | 624 | 1 in 4,165 |
| Full house (three of a kind plus a pair) | 3,744 | 1 in 694 |
| Flush (any five cards of same suit) | 5,108 | 1 in 509 |
| Straight (e.g., 6, 5, 4, 3, 2 of mixed suits) | 10,200 | 1 in 255 |
| Three of a kind | 54,912 | 1 in 47 |
| Two pair | 123,552 | 1 in 21 |
| One pair | 1,098,240 | 1 in 2 |
| No pair | 1,302,540 | 1 in 2 |

Note: In games in which a joker is used, five aces is the highest-ranking hand.

■ **The holy grail?** *Your chances of being dealt a royal flush are unbelievably slim – but anything's possible.*

# General game rules

PLAYING IN A CARD ROOM or casino is considerably different than playing at home. First, the dealer will be a professional who will deal all the rounds. Everyone gets to be the nominal dealer, though, thanks to the "dealer button," which moves from one player to the next after each hand, establishing who is dealt the first cards in each round and is first to bet (the person to the "dealer's" immediate left).

Another important difference in a casino is that table stakes are used. This means that you can bet only with the funds you have on the table during a particular hand or round.

*When table stakes are used, you can't go into your wallet for new money during a hand.*

Furthermore, you won't find yourself pushed out of a hand because you run out of funds. Instead, you can go *all-in*. A *side pot* will then be set up for the other players. Remember, though, that you can only win the pots you have paid into.

## How the house makes money

Normally, you play poker against other players, and whoever wins the pot "takes all." So how does the house make money? Poker games in card rooms and casinos operate differently than your kitchen poker games. There are two ways in which the house makes money. First, the casino or card room charges a fee by the hour, a sort of "seat fee" to pay for the staff and facility. Every hour, management collects a set amount from every player, depending on the table limits. Second, the house will charge a fee, or "rake," on every pot that is played. Casinos really don't make a lot from poker; it's more of a "convenience" game for the patrons.

## Entering a poker room/casino

Casino and card-room poker is played around an oval table that seats between seven and ten players, depending on the specific game. Unlike other casino table games, you can't just walk into a poker room, pick any seat, sit down, and start to play. Instead, you must first contact a floorman or supervisor who will inform you what games are being played, what limits they have, and whether there's an available seat.

> ### DEFINITION
>
> A poker player who goes **all-in** gambles all of his or her remaining chips or cash on the strength of a hand. The pot with all the wagers you had participated in will be set aside, and a new wagering pot, called a **side pot**, will be established with all subsequent wagers by other players. You will have no part in this side pot.

# Betting levels

You will find different betting levels or limits for each poker game. For example, you might play in a $1 to $4 Texas hold 'em game, which means a $1 minimum bet and a maximum bet of $4. Or you might find a higher stakes hold 'em game at the very next table, with limits of $5 to $20. Whenever you play poker, always make sure you know what the betting limits are for the table you are playing.

# The ante

As the dealer shuffles the deck, each player puts up an "ante," which is a small flat fee you pay to purchase the right to play in that round. If you don't pay the ante, you are "sitting out." Many games have what is called the "blind," which is the ante for a particular round. With blinds, only the first and second players (after the "official" dealer) put up an ante, called the small blind and big blind respectively. The small blind is normally half the minimum bet, and the big blind is the same as the minimum bet. This requires the third player to call the minimum bet, to fold, or to raise.

# Betting order

When you are betting, it's important that you bet in order, or in proper sequence. Betting normally starts from the left of the dealer and goes around the table clockwise from player to player. You must wait your turn before betting in any poker game. All raises and calls must be the correct amount for each player. It's the dealer's job to see that each player puts in the proper amount when it is his or her turn to bet. After all bets are made, the dealer sweeps all bets into the center of the table, making one big pot. In games in which cards are dealt face up, the highest hand starts the betting.

*Do not bet out of sequence — it will only slow the game down, so wait your turn. Also, you should never throw your chips into a pot. Whether it is a call or a raise, you should always place your bet directly in front of you.*

■ **In casino or tournament play,** *the dealer will ensure that everyone bets the required amount and will also announce who wins each hand.*

## The pot

The ante and all other wagering money in the round go into the center of the table, into a pile called the pot. Additional side pots are formed whenever one player runs out of table funds and goes all-in. These additional pots grow from the wagering that is still being done by other players as the round progresses.

## Player options

There are different numbers of betting rounds for different games. During each round, players can choose to "check," "call," "raise," or "fold." When you check, it means that you want to stay in the game, but don't want to bet. After someone makes the initial bet, all other players can call, raise, or fold, but not check. When you call, you wager the same amount of the original bet and remain in the game. When you raise, you match the

■ **The more chips** *that you personally invest in the pot, the less keen you will be to pull out. But you might want to consider cutting your losses . . . .*

original bet and increase the wager by a given amount. When you fold, you are declaring that you are out of the round, and you discard your hand.

*Normally, when you check you forfeit the right to raise in the current round unless a "check and raise allowed" rule was agreed before the game started.*

## Cards speak

The value of the hand is as it lays. This means that regardless of what a player might declare or claim, the cards that are exposed are taken at face value. In fact, a player does not have to verbally declare his hand at all. The dealer normally determines and declares the highest or lowest hand during a showdown.

# Choosing your game

*MOST POKER GAMES are not difficult to learn, as far as rules are concerned. The ranking of hands can be easily learned, as can rules about how many cards are dealt and how they are distributed for a specific game. On the other hand, it has been said that poker is 50 percent luck and 50 percent skill. In many poker games, bluffing can be a deciding factor; consequently, your skill at bluffing your opponents can make a big difference. It boils down to a simple concept: It's not what cards you are holding, but how you play them.*

In this chapter, the strategies listed for each game are intended mainly for beginners. I have omitted many advanced strategies and various other concepts that you will eventually need to learn if you want to play poker as a hobby, or even as a career.

## Five-card draw

**Number of Players**  2–8

**Initial deal**  Five face-down cards are dealt to each player.

**The play**  There is a betting round after the initial deal. The player to the immediate left of the dealer starts the betting. After the betting round, each player can exchange as many as three cards. (Sometimes a player can draw four cards if he shows that his remaining card is an ace. And some games even allow you to exchange all five cards! Check which rules you are playing before you start.) Another round of betting ensues, followed by the showdown.

**Strategy**  Stay in for additional cards if you have the following hands:

- A pair or better
- Four cards to a straight or flush
- A pair of kings, if someone else opened (i.e., was first to act)
- Any two pair, raise

*Who opens and bets first is important: that player must be the first to bet after the draw.*

**Showdown**  The player makes his best five-card hand using all the cards in his hand.

**Determining winner**  Highest hand

# Texas hold 'em

**Number of players** 2–12

**Initial deal** Two cards are dealt, face down, to each player. (Later, a total of five cards will be placed in the center of the table – these are called community cards.)

**The play** A round of betting is held after the deal, and then three of the community cards are dealt face up (this is called "the flop"). Another round of betting follows. One more community card (called "fourth street," or "the turn") is dealt face up, followed by another round of betting. The last card (called "the river") is dealt face up, and a final round of betting follows.

*Players can check, bet, call, raise, or fold during each round.*

**Strategy** Stay in the game if you hold the following cards:

- Any high pair (10s, jacks, queens, kings, or aces)
- Ace–court card of any suit
- King–queen (or, possibly, king–jack) of any suit
- Queen–jack of any suit (if you are raised, fold)
- Jack–10 of the same suit
- King–10 of the same suit
- Pair of 9s or less (use caution)
- High–low, same suit (for example, ace–3 of hearts)

**Showdown** The players make their best five-card hand using their two cards and the table's five cards.

**Determining winner** Highest hand

### Trivia...

*Texas hold 'em is the game of choice for the World Series of Poker, which is held annually at Binion's Horseshoe Casino in downtown Las Vegas. More than 500 players compete, and the entry fee is $10,000. The winner of the 2000 Series took home $1.5 million in prize money.*

■ **Texas hold 'em** *is the poker variant played in the 1998 movie* **Rounders,** *starring Matt Damon, Edward Norton, and John Malkovich (as Teddy KGB, left).*

# Five-card stud poker

**Number of players** 2–8

**Initial deal** One card down, one card up to each player.

**The play** Betting begins after the deal. The highest (showing) hand starts the betting. After the betting, each player is dealt one additional card face up. This is followed by more betting, and then more cards face up, for a total of four face-up cards and one face-down card, with a round of betting after each deal.

**Strategy** Stay in the round if you hold the following hands:

- Any pair *in the hole*
- Any three of a kind
- Any three to a straight flush
- Three high cards to a flush
- A pair of kings or aces in the hole
- A pair of aces or kings including one face up
- Queens or jacks in the hole
- A three-card flush
- Three high cards to a straight
- Jacks or queens including one showing

**Showdown** This occurs after the last round of betting.

**Determining winner** Highest hand

> **DEFINITION**
>
> *Cards that are dealt face down and remain unseen by the other players are said to be* **in the hole**.

■ **With an ace** *as the hole card and the face-up ace, this started as the top hand available. But when the 4, 3, and 2 came in the successive rounds, this player would have been wishing his hole card was an unassuming 5: As nice as a pair of aces is, it's not as nice as a straight.*

# Seven-card stud poker (America's favorite poker game)

**Number of players** 2–7

**Initial deal** Two cards face down and one card face up to each player.

**The play** After the hands are dealt, the highest (showing) hand bets first. After each round of betting, each player is dealt one additional card, face up. A total of four face-up cards are dealt to each player, and then the last (or seventh) card is dealt face down. Betting follows each deal. The highest visible hand in each round starts the betting for that round.

**Strategy** Your first three cards are the most important. Bear the following points in mind:

- A hand that is weak to start will end as a weak hand
- A hidden strong pair with a high card showing will be strong until the end
- After the fourth card, you need a high pair, a four-card straight or flush, or a three-card straight or flush to stay in
- After the fifth card, you need at least a pair of queens or a four-card straight or flush
- A four-card straight or flush is worth staying for the sixth and seventh cards
- Fold if one of your opponents holds a higher-ranking hand
- Fold if the odds of filling your hand are not worth what the pot contains

**Showdown** Each player makes his or her best five-card hand from the seven he or she holds.

**Determining winner** Highest five-card hand, or high-low hands split (this is decided before the start of the game).

■ **With the** *innocent-looking 7, 4, 9, and 2 face up, this doesn't look like much of a hand to the other players at the table. But it's the best five-card hand that counts, and this player can make two pairs.*

# Omaha

**Number of players** 2–10

**Initial deal** Four cards are dealt face down to each player. Community cards will be dealt face down in the middle of the table during each round, to a total of five.

**The play** Identical to Texas hold 'em, but the final hands must include two of the player's four cards and three of the table's five community cards. However, Omaha can be played two ways: high or high-low split. When played high-low, the low hand cannot be higher than an 8. When played this way the game is often called Omaha 8 high-low split.

**Strategy** Know the rules for splitting the pot, and bear the following points in mind:

- You need a strong high pair in the *pocket* to stay
- You need a pocket ace–2 to stay
- Fold if you don't have four cards that are 6 or lower
- Ace, 2, 3, 4, 5 is the perfect low hand, plus a high straight hand
- Three of a kind in your hand is not a good hand
- Evaluate your hand before the flop and decide whether it's worth calling or raising
- After the flop, consider the odds of seeing additional good cards
- After the fourth and fifth cards, basic poker skills come into play

**Showdown** Players make their best five-card hand using two cards in their hand and three from the table. When playing Omaha 8, players declare in betting order if they are playing "high," "low," or "both."

**Determining winner** Highest five-card hand. When playing Omaha 8, the high and low hands split the pot evenly, but the low hand must be no higher than 8, or else the high hand gets it all. When a player declares "both," he can use all four of his cards, splitting them into two groups to form a high hand and a low hand.

■ **Three of a kind** *may look nice in your hand, but in Omaha it's really no good. Omaha hands must be made up of two hole cards and three community cards. But this player need not despair: he's got a nice little straight!*

# The art of poker

AS I SAID EARLIER, *poker is 50 percent skill and 50 percent luck. The part about skill is a given – you need it to play successfully. The other 50 percent, luck, will come to you in various degrees. Sometimes you'll be dealt excellent cards round after round, and other times you will not get any decent cards during a whole session. The thing to remember is that winners make good hands out of bad ones; losers always get bad hands.*

Successful poker play could be said to derive from several different factors. The four main necessities are:

1. Strategy is the principal ingredient

2. Short-range knowledge of your opponents (a variable)

3. Immediate action awareness of the situation (a variable)

4. Long-range understanding of the game (a constant)

## How to become a good poker player

Because playing poker requires at least 50 percent skill, it only stands to reason that a player needs to do a lot of reading, studying, and practicing before any real success can be expected. You need to know and understand the rules, odds, and expectations of each poker game you want to play. There is a lot to know about calling, raising, and bluffing in poker. Indeed, there are whole books on facial and body expressions. It's important that you know how to read the other players at a table.

The other 50 percent of poker, on the other hand, deals with the luck of the draw. You can be a very skilled player and not draw decent cards for some time. I call this being in a "slump" – just like a professional baseball player. Just as the team MVP can get into a hitting slump, a skilled poker player can have a dry spell. Sometimes you just get lousy cards, round after round. My advice in this situation is the same for poker as it is for any other game: Reduce your bets or stop playing for a while when you consistently get poor hands.

**INTERNET**

**www.pokercentral.com**

*This site provides a place for people to come together and explore the world of casino poker. It contains a good listing of more than 450 US poker rooms, articles about poker, information on where and when poker tournaments are held (and their results), and a large selection of links.*

# Bluffing

Poker wouldn't be poker without the bluffing, body language, intimidation, and everything else that comes into play when you look at your opponents across a table. The phrase "poker face" has a very real meaning – your poker face can be a deciding factor in your game. Learn all you can about the technique called bluffing. Here are some quick tips:

*a*   Whenever you are not involved in a pot you should be observing other players to categorize their play as being loose, strong, tricky and so on.

*b*   When bluffing against a single player try to estimate how likely it is he or she will fold. Try to judge the size of the pot – the bigger the pot the more reluctant your opponent will be to fold.

*c*   You can bluff on a weak flop with a strong bet; in hold 'em, you should see most weak players fold.

*d*   A bluff that you start early should be continued as though you hold a strong hand.

*e*   Knowing how to bluff is only part of the skill, you need to know when your opponent is bluffing.

*f*   If you think your opponent is bluffing and you have a strong hand, call once, then review the pot to see if it is worth going in all the way for.

■ **W.C. Fields** *demonstrates his irrefutable poker-face skills. Would you fancy your chances against this man?!*

# Basic poker strategy

The players' face-down cards should never be revealed until the final showdown: Even when you fold a hand, you should never expose your cards to other players.

When it comes to strategy, there are a few general rules that you need to understand, regardless of which poker game you are playing. Aside from the draw, you will find that all decision-making is done during the betting rounds. Following are some more good poker strategies:

*a* The biggest mistake poker players make is playing too many hands

*b* Don't play cash poor: a good rule of thumb is that your bankroll should be 40–50 times the table limit

*c* There's an even chance that you won't better your opening hand

*d* If you've got nothing in your hand, fold

*e* If you've got a sure-bet hand, make the other players pay to see it

*f* If they've got you beat, don't fool around – fold

*g* The goal is to beat the other players, not have the highest hand. If everyone else folds, you win the pot

*h* The more players at the table, the greater the chance that one or more players has a pair; if you haven't got a high pair or better, or four cards to a flush or straight, fold

*i* The better your openers, the better your chances of improving your hand

*j* Make sure you know all the rules of the specific game you're playing

*k* When you get a weak hand in the initial deal, fold early instead of in the middle or at the end – and save money!

*l* Even a poor player can get lucky and get good cards once in a while

*m* Don't play unless you can give it all you've got

*n* If it isn't fun, don't play

**INTERNET**

**www.pokerdigest.com**

*Poker Digest magazine's home page has lots of poker articles by noted player/authors. There's an interesting readers' poll on specific poker questions, as well as a listing of upcoming poker cruises and a bunch of links to other poker-related sites.*

# Reading other players

Whenever you are not involved in a pot, you should always be observing all the other players. You want to categorize their play as being one of the following:

- Aggressive
- Conservative
- Loose, or wild

You want to look for signs of bluffing; you want to be able to identify any *tells* that will help you analyze another player's hand when you play against him or her.

# Tells

There are whole books written about tells and it would be hard to list them all in this chapter; however, here are a few to be on the lookout for:

**a** Players who like to talk about hands they don't have

**b** Players who routinely put chips on top of strong hands as they lay on the table, but don't do that with weak hands

**c** The facial expression of other players as the community cards hit the table

Don't forget about your tells. Don't give your hand away by unconsciously communicating the strength – or weakness – of your hand to other players.

■ **Even taking an innocent drink** *can be used against you if someone realizes that you only do so when you're bluffing.*

# Record keeping

Many experienced players learn to keep a logbook. The notes in the logbook should contain statistics on wins, losses, casinos, and any additional comments that might help during a future visit to a casino or card room.

# Where to play

POKER IS A GAME *that is played in many places, ranging from the kitchen table on Friday nights with a group of friends to high-stakes games in Las Vegas with a bunch of professionals. About half of the states in the US have some type of legal poker in card rooms, in casinos, or on Native American lands. The other half of the country also plays, but they do it illegally in fraternal halls, at social clubs, and in church basements. A game's location can help you determine the skill level of the players. For instance, in casinos and card rooms the skill can be very high, whereas games in social clubs will be closer to the amateur level.*

## Countries that have legalized poker

- Antigua
- Aruba
- Australia
- Austria
- Cambodia
- Canada
- Costa Rica
- Czech Republic
- Denmark
- Dominican Republic
- Egypt
- England
- Finland
- France
- Germany
- Greece
- Honduras
- Hungary
- Ireland
- Italy
- Macedonia
- Mariana Islands

- Namibia
- Nepal
- Netherlands
- New Zealand
- Panama
- Peru
- Poland
- Romania
- Russia
- Scotland
- Slovenia
- Solomon Islands
- South Korea
- Spain
- St. Kitts
- Swaziland
- Sweden
- USA – not all states: (see list *opposite*)
- Turkey
- Wales

**INTERNET**

www.european-poker.com/tournaments

*This interesting site about European poker includes listings of clubs in which poker is played, tournament schedules, a discussion area, player profiles, and a picture gallery of tournament players. It also has an interesting player ranking system with current results and top money winners listed.*

## States that allow poker in casinos or card rooms

- Arizona
- California
- Colorado
- Connecticut
- Delaware
- Florida
- Georgia
- Illinois
- Indiana
- Iowa
- Kansas
- Louisiana
- Michigan
- Minnesota
- Mississippi
- Missouri
- Montana
- Nebraska
- Nevada
- New Jersey
- New Mexico
- New York
- North Dakota
- Oklahoma
- Oregon
- Puerto Rico
- South Dakota
- Texas
- Washington

## A simple summary

✔ Poker is considered the most popular card game anywhere. There are basically two major types of poker: stud and draw. The game itself is played in homes, in card rooms, and in casinos everywhere. It is considered a true American card game.

✔ Card rooms and casinos have very stringent rules and procedures to which you must adhere.

✔ Strict betting order, special ante requirements, and the calling of hands is very regimented at card rooms and casinos. You need to know all the rules before you play.

✔ The most popular poker games are five-card draw, five- and seven-card stud, Texas hold 'em, and Omaha.

✔ Poker is considered a game of 50 percent skill and 50 percent luck, so you need to know a lot about people in addition to the mechanics of how to play.

✔ Each specific poker game has its own unique strategy for almost every round. Learn the difference between a good potential hand and a mediocre one.

✔ Twenty-nine American states and 42 countries around the world have card rooms and casinos where poker can be played. Today it's considered an international game.

# Chapter 12

# Other Table Games

THE OLD BIG SIX WHEEL can still be found in most casinos, but it seems that every time I enter a casino these days, after even a short absence, I find a new table game. Let It Ride was one of the first of the new table games introduced within the last 10 years. Now you might also see crapsjack, single dealer craps, three-card poker, and Spanish 21. The casino wants players to experience and enjoy table games as well as slot machines, and they keep trying new ones in the hope that some of them will catch on.

## In this chapter...

✓ Big Six Wheel

✓ Let It Ride

✓ Pai Gow poker

✓ Caribbean stud

✓ Spanish 21

✓ Three-card poker

PLACE A BET ON THE BIG SIX WHEEL AND ENJOY ONE OF THE SIMPLER TABLE GAMES

# Big Six Wheel

THE BIG SIX WHEEL, *also known as the Wheel of Fortune or the Money wheel, is a throwback to the old carnival spin-the-wheel game. In casinos you will find these games in strategically located spots; for example, they'll often be right in front of you when you are leaving the casino floor – casino management is trying to get one last bet from you before you leave. This game is one of the biggest long shots of any game in a casino. The house edge starts at 11 percent, and goes as high as 24 percent. This is not a good game for the player.*

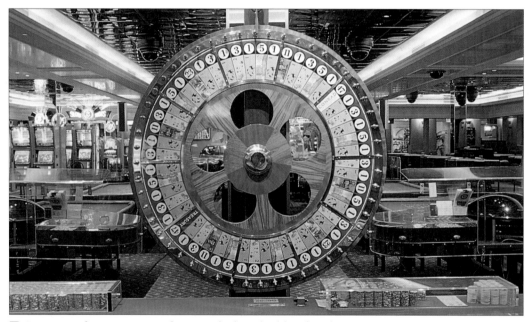

■ **Once popular as a carnival game,** *the big wheel has found its way into the casinos where it attracts first-time casino goers happy to wager their money on a game they recognize and understand.*

## How the game is played

The wheel itself is normally 6 feet (1.8 meters) in diameter and is mounted on a pedestal with 54 individual sprockets in nine groups. There is a table layout in front of the dealer, with six to seven betting spots. The spots are normally marked with $1, $2, $5, $10, $20, joker, and, sometimes, a house symbol. The player places the desired bet (or bets) on the required spots and the dealer spins the wheel. Note, though, that only one of the seven spots will result in a win, and the betting spots are not evenly distributed on the wheel. (See the "Big Six Bets" chart opposite.)

## BIG SIX BETS

| Symbol | No. of symbols on wheel | Payout | House Edge |
|---|---|---|---|
| $1 | 24 | 1 to 1 | 11.11% |
| $2 | 15 | 2 to 1 | 16.67% |
| $5 | 7 | 5 to 1 | 22.22% |
| $10 | 4 | 10 to 1 | 18.52% |
| $20 | 2 | 20 to 1 | 22.22% |
| Joker | 1 | 40 to 1 | 24.07% |
| House symbol | 1 | 40 to 1 | 24.07% |

## Playing strategy

The main thing to remember on the Big Six Wheel is that there is no strategy. The one nice thing about the game is that low wagers are allowed – normally $1. It's a fun game to watch, but it's too expensive to play. Because the Big Six Wheel has one of the highest house advantages in the entire casino, I recommend that you not play it at all.

# Let It Ride

THE GAME LET IT RIDE is relatively new; it was introduced to the playing public at the Eldorado Casino in Reno in 1993. Let It Ride is based on five-card stud poker. It's played at a table that is similar in size and shape to a blackjack table, and it accommodates a total of seven players. The game is very popular with the house because of its 3.5-percent edge. (In fact, the game was originally designed to lure slot players to a table game.) Let It Ride offers a more relaxed and much slower game than blackjack, craps, or regular poker.

The appeal of Let It Ride lies in the fact that you're not playing against the dealer or other players as you do in regular poker. Instead, you're only trying to obtain a hand with a pair of 10s or better. Additionally, you are allowed to take back two-thirds of your bet if you decide your hand is not good enough. It's an easy game to play: Your goal is to obtain a good poker hand using the three cards that are dealt to you, along with the two cards that are shared by the entire table.

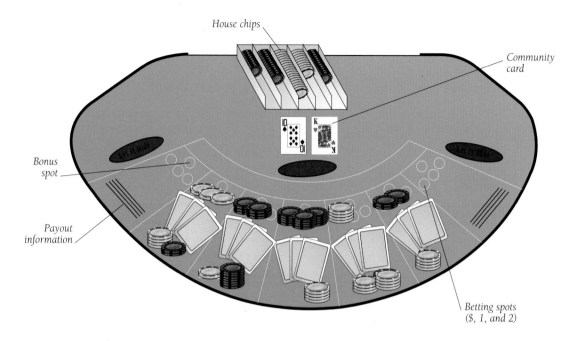

House chips

Community card

Bonus spot

Payout information

Betting spots ($, 1, and 2)

■ **Let It Ride is played on a blackjack-style table** *with the players' positions clearly defined and a description of the various payouts described in each player's "box."*

## How the game is played

To play, you start by placing three equal bets in the circles in front of your seating position. The circles are marked "$," "1," and "2." If the table minimum is $5, each bet must be $5. The dealer will deal three cards, face down, to each player, and then deal himself two *community cards*, which are also face down.

After the cards are dealt, you're allowed to look at your three cards and decide whether to let your first bet (the one marked "1") remain as a wager – you can let it ride (hence the name of the game), or you can take it back. The dealer will then turn up one community card. At this point you analyze four cards and make the decision as to whether you should let your second bet ride (marked "2") or take it back. After the dealer turns over the remaining community card, he'll turn over each player's cards one at a time and then pay winning hands or take losing ones.

### Trivia...

*A Shuffle Master dealing machine is used by the dealer to deal out the cards in Let It Ride. This device automatically shuffles and deals out three cards to each player. Interestingly, the manufacturer of Shuffle Master designed the game Let It Ride to help sell their shuffle machines.*

**DEFINITION**

**Community cards** *are those that all players can use in making up a hand. For instance, if two 8s are turned up as community cards and you have another 8 in your hand, your hand will consist of three of a kind. All players in the game use the same community cards to help form their poker hands.*

*It's important to note that players are not allowed to see or discuss their hands with other players because it might help them to know, for example, that the card they need has already been obtained by another player.*

In this game, even a bad hand of, say, a 4, 6, and 8 in unmatched suits can win. If the dealer turns up a pair of 10s or better, the entire table wins. Also, if the dealer turns up a pair of 4s, 6s, or 8s, and these are the same as the player's cards, it makes three of a kind – and a winning hand. On the other hand, a strong hand can sometimes turn out bad. For example, say you receive three cards to a flush and the dealer's first flop matches your suit. If you've let all three bets ride and the second community card does not match, you lose all three bets. So, as you can see, good poker strategy can be very helpful in this game. The payouts for each hand vary from a low pair of 10s up to a royal flush (see the following payout schedule chart).

## LET IT RIDE PAYOUT SCHEDULE

| Hand | Payout |
|---|---|
| Royal flush | 1000 to 1 |
| Straight flush | 200 to 1 |
| Four of a kind | 50 to 1 |
| Full house | 11 to 1 |
| Flush | 8 to 1 |
| Straight | 5 to 1 |
| Three of a kind | 3 to 1 |
| Two pair | 2 to 1 |
| Tens or better pair | 1 to 1 |

## Playing strategy

The object of the game is to make a good five-card poker hand with your three cards and the two community cards. When playing Let It Ride, you have to know when you have a winning hand. That might sound easy (all you need is a pair of 10s), but it becomes important when you are deciding whether to leave your remaining two bets or to draw them back.

*Remember that you can remove your second wager even if you let the first one ride. Each bet is independent of the others.*

# Let It Ride strategies to play by

When analyzing your first three cards, take back your bet unless you hold:

**a** A pair of 10s or better.

**b** Three of a kind.

**c** Three to a flush, with one high card (10 or better).

**d** Three cards to a straight flush.

**e** Three to a royal flush.

On your fourth card, take back a bet unless you have:

**a** A pair of 10s or better.

**b** Two pair.

**c** Three of a kind.

**d** A four-card flush.

**e** An open-ended straight, including a 10 or higher.

**f** Four-card straight flush.

**g** Four-card royal flush.

**h** Four of a kind.

Patience is the key to this game. You might get hand after hand without winning. But unlike regular five-card stud, you'll get a bonus when you finally get that powerhouse hand. If you use the above strategies, you'll be able to stay in the game for a longer period of time, which will enable you to get that good hand in due course. So don't think about ace-high hands or stay with a small pair, hoping for another match or another pair. Instead, stick to a good, sound, proven strategy. Familiarize yourself with the odds for obtaining a good hand. The chart opposite, "Ranking hands and odds of drawing it," will give you some idea of how often a specific hand will appear.

**INTERNET**

**www.thewizardofodds.com/java/lir.html**

*You can visit this site if you want to practice Let It Ride on the computer instead of in the casino. It has $10 bets, but you start with a $1,000 bankroll. As you play each hand, the site will give you feedback on how you did. It also has an "advice" button. This is a good site to visit when you are first learning the game.*

## RANKING HANDS AND ODDS OF DRAWING IT

| Hand | Odds |
|------|------|
| Royal flush | 649,750 to 1 |
| Straight flush | 65,000 to 1 |
| Four of a kind | 4,150 to 1 |
| Flush | 700 to 1 |
| Straight | 250 to 1 |
| Three of a kind | 46 to 1 |
| Two pair | 20 to 1 |
| Pair of 10s or better | 6.15 to 1 |

## The bonus game

The designers of Let It Ride have added a bonus side bet to make the game more interesting and exciting. The house offers high payouts for those rare premium poker hands when you make this side bonus bet. However, there is a high price to pay for this bonus play: The house edge for this $1 side bet is a little more than 25 percent! You can only bet $1 – no more, no less. At different casinos you might find some differences in the payouts (see the "$1 bonus payout" chart below), but as you can see, the rewards for this $1 side bet can be very high. Remember, you don't have to make this bonus bet to play Let It Ride. If you do want to play the bonus bet, you must make your wager before the hands are dealt.

## $1 BONUS PAYOUT

| Hand | Bonus payout |
|------|------|
| Royal flush | $20,000 |
| Straight flush | $2,000 |
| Four of a kind | $400 |
| Full house | $200 |
| Straight | $25 |
| Three of a kind | $5 |
| Two pair | no bonus |
| Pair of 10s of better | no bonus |

The dealer, not the players, will turn over each hand to determine winners and losers. Remember, in this poker game you are not playing against other players, or even against the dealer; rather, you are trying to make a hand against the odds. You can think of Let It Ride as a deviation from other games, such as slot machines and roulette. Play it for fun, but play it using the suggested strategy. Don't get wild and think you can bluff in this poker game.

# Pai Gow poker

THE GAME OF PAI GOW *poker combines Chinese dominoes, known as Pai Gow, and the American game of poker. It was introduced to California card rooms in 1986, and was so popular that Nevada casinos began to offer it the following year. The object is to make two hands of poker that beat the banker's two hands. In card rooms, players take turns being the banker and financing the game with their own money; in casinos, on the other hand,*

■ **A straight flush** *and a pair of aces would be a dream come true for any Pai Gow poker player.*

*the house is normally the banker (but players are offered the option to be the banker). Players like the game not only because poker know-how is required, but also because of the large betting variations that are allowed and because of the way in which the cards themselves are handled – all factors that make it a game of high skills. The house advantage is 2.3 percent.*

## How the game is played

Pai Gow poker is played on a blackjack-sized table, with six players and one dealer. A standard deck of 52 cards, plus a joker, is used. The dealer deals seven seven-card hands and three dice are rolled to determine which hand goes to which player. The player splits the seven cards into two hands of five and two. This is known as setting the hand. The five-card hand is known as the back, or highest hand, and the two-card hand is the front, low, or second-highest hand. The poker value of the five-card hand must always be set higher than that of the two-card hand.

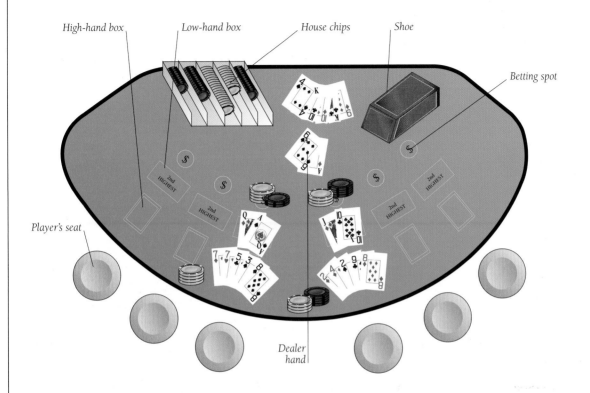

High-hand box    Low-hand box    House chips    Shoe

Betting spot

Player's seat

2nd HIGHEST

2nd HIGHEST

2nd HIGHEST

2nd HIGHEST

Dealer hand

■ **Each player at the Pai Gow poker table** *has two boxes in front of them: the five-card hand is placed in the high box and the two-card hand in the low box. The player must beat the dealer with both hands.*

## Game objective

After the players have set their hands, the dealer turns over their cards and sets them according to the specific house rules. The objective of the game is to beat both of the banker's hands. To win, your two-card hand must be of a higher poker value than the banker's two-card hand. Your five-card hand must also have a higher value than the banker's five-card hand. If one of your hands matches the banker's hand, it is called a copy. The banker wins all copies. This automatic copy win gives the banker (casino) a natural 1.3-percent edge over the player. If you win one hand but lose the other, it is considered a push, or tie, and no chips change hands.

## Playing strategy

The objective of this game is to beat the dealer on both the front and back hands. The most critical factor in winning at Pai Gow poker is the proper setting of the low and high hands. This is where skill comes in. You set two hands: the front (two-card) hand and the back (five-card) hand. The addition of the joker allows you to use it as an ace or any other card you need to complete a straight or flush, which is very helpful at any time.

*The back hand must be higher in value than the front hand. It's important to understand that if you set the front hand with a higher value than the back hand, your hand is considered "fouled" and you automatically lose your bet.*

Because the front hand has only two cards, there are no straights or flushes possible. The highest hand is a pair, and a pair of aces is the highest possible two-card hand. The back hand is made up of five cards and is rated the same as any poker hand. To win both hands, you should try to make both hands reasonably strong. If you try to make the five-card hand the strongest, it will generally be at the expense of your two-card hand. Likewise, strengthening the two-card hand lessens the power of your five-card hand. Remember: The object of the game is not to tie, but to win both hands.

**INTERNET**

**www.thewizardofodds. com/java/paigow.html**

*Practice and sharpen your skills at Pai Gow poker at this free site. Using realistic cards, the Wizard of Odds site allows you to set your front and back hands yourself, but also has an "advice" button that will set the hands properly and automatically.*

# Caribbean stud

DEVELOPED IN THE LATE 1980S *aboard Caribbean cruise ships, Caribbean stud poker became so popular with players that the game moved to the land-based casinos of Las Vegas in 1992. In this poker game, you're only trying to beat the dealer, not any of the other players. This "us against the dealer" feeling encourages a bit of camaraderie between players, who are all pulling together to beat the dealer. Another nice aspect of this game is the bonus payout for winning the bet hand against the dealer.*

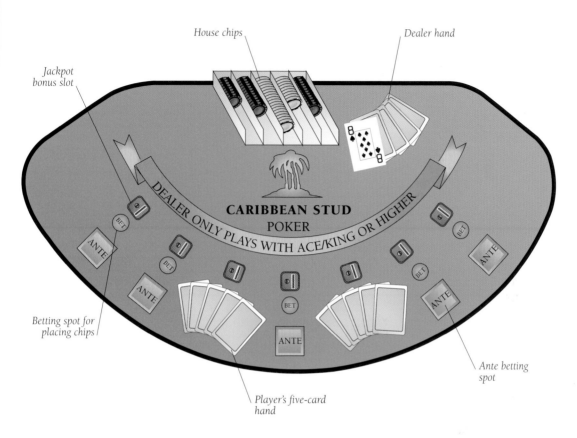

*House chips*

*Dealer hand*

*Jackpot bonus slot*

**CARIBBEAN STUD**
POKER

DEALER ONLY PLAYS WITH ACE/KING OR HIGHER

*Betting spot for placing chips*

*Player's five-card hand*

*Ante betting spot*

■ **Caribbean stud poker** *usually has seven players plus the dealer. Each betting area has three distinctive features: an ante bet, a bet box, and a slot for the optional progressive jackpot bet.*

## How the game is played

Played on an oval blackjack-style table with up to seven players, one dealer, and a standard 52-card deck, the game does not resemble a regular poker game at all. The table layout consists of three distinctive betting spots: the first, a rectangle, is labeled ante; the second, a circle, is labeled bet; and the third, a drop slot, is there for the optional progressive jackpot bet. Regardless of the number of players, everyone always plays one-on-one against the dealer. Unlike regular poker, in Caribbean stud poker you do not have to worry about the other players' cards. If your neighbor has a pair of aces, you have queens, and the dealer has a pair of 10s, both you and your neighbor win.

The round starts with each player putting a bet in the ante rectangle. If any player wants to play the optional progressive jackpot bet, he can put a dollar in the drop slot. A meter above each table indicates the amount of the ever-growing progressive jackpot, based on input from these side bets. The dealer presses a button, all the dollar coins drop into a lower box, and a red light shows which players are eligible for a jackpot.

Dealing from an automatic shuffling machine, each player (and the dealer) receives five cards, all face-down. The dealer turns one of his cards – normally the last one – face up, which can help players decide if they want to play or fold their hands. Players are not allowed to show each other their cards, and only one hand is allowed for each player.

*If a dealer suspects that players are trying to see other players' cards, he calls the round "dead," and all hands are thrown in without being played.*

**INTERNET**

**www.thewizardofodds. com/java/csp.html**

*Practice your game on this effective site, which offers a tutorial with some basic strategy, details about payoffs, and some statistics on possible outcomes for specific hands. This is a good place to go when you are first learning the game or want to strengthen your skills.*

To continue to play, you must either double the size of your ante bet by making an additional wager in the bet box or fold the hand and lose your ante bet. For players to win both their bets, the dealer has to "qualify," meaning his hand has to contain an ace–king or better. If the dealer does not qualify, the players remaining in the round receive even money for their ante bet, and push on their bet wager. If the dealer does qualify, he turns over each player's hand and compares cards. If the dealer's hand is stronger, the player loses both the ante and bet wagers.

*If the player beats the dealer, the ante is paid off at even money, but the bet wager is paid off at house odds.*

Once all the players have made their decisions, they are required to place their cards face down on the table. The dealer then removes all the ante bets from those players who dropped out. Next, the dealer turns over his remaining four cards and adjusts them to the best possible poker hand. Review the "Bet wager house payout" chart opposite to see what the reward is.

## BET WAGER HOUSE PAYOUT

| Winning hand | House payout |
|---|---|
| Ace–king | 1 to 1 |
| One pair | 1 to 1 |
| Two pair | 2 to 1 |
| Three of a kind | 3 to 1 |
| Straight | 4 to 1 |
| Flush | 5 to 1 |
| Full house | 7 to 1 |
| Four of a kind | 20 to 1 |
| Straight flush | 50 to 1 |
| Royal flush | 100 to 1 |

## Playing strategy

With only about 45 hands per hour, this is a much slower game than blackjack or some of the other new table games. Furthermore, the house edge is a little high: 5.3 percent, or about the same as double-zero roulette.

Following are some basic playing strategies:

*a* Don't wager on any jackpot bets.

*b* Unless you get an ace–king, fold against any dealer up-card.

*c* Bet any ace–king hand with a jack–8–3 or better against any dealer up-card.

*d* Bet any ace–king hand if your hand contains the dealer's up-card.

*e* Bet any pair or better.

*f* Never attempt to bluff.

## Progressive bonus

When the dealer doesn't qualify, you don't win the bet bonus, no matter how good your hand is. However, this is not the case if you originally opted for the progressive jackpot side bet. With this bet, when you get one of those powerhouse hands you win a bonus award, regardless of what the dealer has – even if the dealer doesn't qualify. The payouts vary from state to state and from casino to casino, but the following "Progressive jackpot payout" chart shows what you can typically expect on a strong hand.

## PROGRESSIVE JACKPOT PAYOUT

| Hand | Jackpot payout |
| --- | --- |
| One pair | $0 |
| Two pair | $0 |
| Three of a kind | $0 |
| Straight | $0 |
| Flush | $75 |
| Full house | $100 |
| Four of a kind | $500 |
| Straight flush | 10 percent of the meter |
| Royal flush | 100 percent of the meter |

# Spanish 21

THE GAME OF SPANISH 21 was introduced to Nevada casinos in 1995 by a casino management employee who was looking for a version of blackjack that might increase participation and spice things up with some new entertainment. He developed a variation of the "traditional" 21 using what is called a "Spanish deck," with 48 cards in it. The four 10s are removed from each of the six decks used for this game. (By 10s, I mean the index 10 cards; the jacks, queens, and kings are still included.) This game is rarely found outside American casinos.

■ **Without the 10s,** *the chances of getting 21 with your original hand are 25 percent less than in regular blackjack.*

# How the game is played

Like most new table games, Spanish 21 uses a table similar to the one used in blackjack, with six players and six decks (with all the 10s removed). The kings, queens, and jacks remain; however, with 25 percent of the 10-value cards removed, the house gains a very large advantage. So as not to scare off players, some liberal bonuses have been added. These bonus rules include the following:

(a) A player may double on any number of cards.

(b) Late surrender is allowed on the first two cards; the player can turn in a hand by forfeiting half of the original bet, but only if the dealer does not have a blackjack.

(c) A player's 21 always beats a dealer's 21.

(d) The double-down rescue allows the player to take back the doubled portion of his bet and forfeit the original wager.

(e) A player can double after splits.

(f) A player can resplit as many as three times, making four hands, including aces.

(g) A player can draw and double down after splitting aces.

(h) A five-card 21 pays 3:2.

(i) A six-card 21 pays 2:1.

(j) A seven- or more-card 21 pays 3:1.

(k) A 21 consisting of a 6, 7, and 8 of mixed suits pays 3:2.

(l) A 21 consisting of a 6, 7, and 8 of a matching suit pays 2:1.

(m) A 21 consisting of a 6, 7, and 8 of spades pays 3:1.

(n) A 21 consisting of three 7s of mixed suits pays 3:2.

(o) A 21 consisting of three 7s of a matching suit pays 2:1.

(p) A 21 consisting of three 7s of spades pays 3:1.

(q) Three suited 7s in addition to the dealer having any 7 face up pays a free bonus.

# Extra bonus

There's a super bonus to be made by going after the three suited 7s in a player's hand, when the dealer also shows any 7 up card. Most casinos offer a free "super jackpot" of $1,000 for any $5 bet, and $5,000 for bets of $25 and over. (But check the table rules where you play; they might vary on this bonus play.) In addition, casinos that offer this bonus will reward all your fellow players $50 if this unique hand occurs. This hand will certainly add some excitement to this different table game.

*Because the 10s are removed from the deck in Spanish 21, you can expect to see a blackjack about once every 24 hands (versus getting a 10–ace every 20 hands in regular blackjack).*

# Playing strategy

Even though this game is very similar to blackjack, there's another playing strategy that must be used in Spanish 21. The reason is simple: In Spanish 21, there are 25 percent fewer 10s in the deck. Review the "Spanish 21 basic strategy" chart opposite before playing this table game. And keep in mind that the game was developed to thwart card counters; therefore, keeping track of the cards will not help. The game edge will remain above 0.8 percent, regardless of the skill of the player.

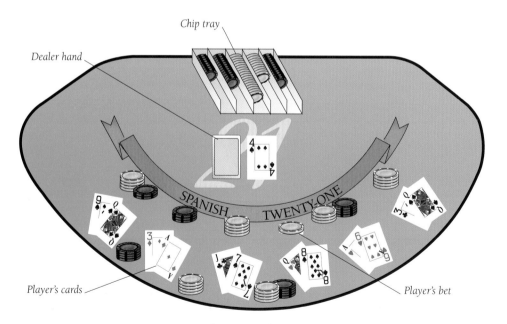

*Chip tray*

*Dealer hand*

*Player's cards*

*Player's bet*

■ **Spanish 21 is a popular new game** *that provides a change to traditional blackjack. Though the 10s are removed, the rules of play and the payoffs can make the game surprisingly lucrative for the player.*

## SPANISH 21 BASIC STRATEGY

| Your hand | Dealer's up-card | Action |
|---|---|---|
| 5 through 9 | all | Hit |
| 10 or 11 with 5+ cards | 2–7 | Hit |
| 10 or 11 | 2–7 | Double |
| 10 or 11 | 8–A | Hit |
| 12 through 14 | all | Hit |
| 15 or 16 | 2–6 | Stand |
| 15 or 16 | 7–A | Hit |
| 17 through 21 | all | Stand |
| A–3 through A–6 | all | Hit |
| A–7 through 21 | all | Stand |
| 2–2 | 2–7 | Split |
| 3–3 | 2–7 | Split |
| 6–6 | 2–7 | Split |
| 7–7 | 2–7 | Split |
| 8–8 | all | Split |
| 9–9 | 2–9 | Split |
| A–A | all | Split |
| Other pairs | all | Play as hard hands |

# Three-card poker

*IT SEEMS THAT POKER is constantly being reinvented. I've been able to find 120 different games of poker, or at least that many games that are called poker, but now I have to add three-card poker as a new game on my list. This is another simple poker game, but it's played with only three cards! You can play three-card poker against the dealer or against the odds. This fun game is spreading across America faster than a pit boss calling for cocktails.*

Like many other new table games, three-card poker is played on a blackjack-type table with up to seven players, one dealer, and a single standard 52-card deck. The ranking of hands is a little different from regular poker, though, because only three cards are used to make up a hand. Review the chart, "Three-card poker ranking hands," on the next page for the high- and low-ranking hands.

# THREE-CARD POKER RANKING HANDS

Straight flush (ace–king–queen is the highest straight flush)
Three of a kind
Straight
Flush
Pair

## How the game is played

The object of the game is to get a better three-card poker hand than the dealer or to receive a hand that results in at least a pair or higher. Before the dealer deals any cards, you have to make a decision to bet against the dealer's hand, wager that your hand will be at least a pair or better, or wager both ways. If you decide to bet against the dealer's hand, you make a wager in the ante spot. If you think a pair or better is coming your way, you place your bet in the pair plus spot.

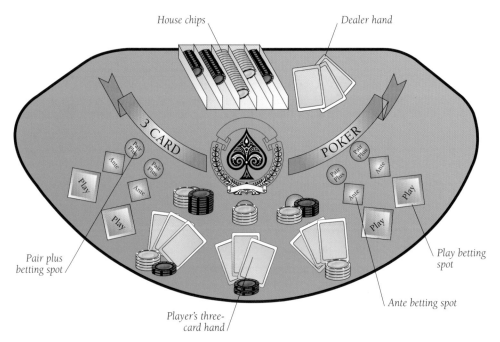

House chips

Dealer hand

Pair plus
betting spot

Player's three-
card hand

Play betting
spot

Ante betting spot

■ **Three-card poker** *is a fast-paced game that combines elements of Caribbean stud with Let It Ride – the latter game's influence clearly visible by the three betting spots on the table layout.*

All the players are dealt their three cards, all face down, and the dealer gets his three cards, also face down. If you decide to stay in the game after reviewing your hand, you have to make another wager in the play spot. If you want to fold, place your cards face down on the table. The dealer will take your cards and the ante bet, plus the pair plus wager, if you bet both. When all the players have made their decisions to play or fold, the dealer turns his cards over and checks for at least a queen or higher. If the dealer does have a queen or higher, the hand is said to qualify. The dealer then turns over the players' hands to determine if anyone has a higher poker hand than the dealer's queen. You win even money for your ante and play bets if you beat the dealer, but you lose both if you don't.

*The good news is that if the dealer can't qualify with a queen or better, the dealer pays all players who remained in the game even money on the ante bet and returns the play wager as a push.*

**INTERNET**

www.thewizardofodds.
com/game/threecard
poker.html

*Click here to find out the rules of play, the basic strategies, and useful tips on both the ante and pair plus game.*

## Bonus hands

In contrast to Caribbean stud poker, where the player's premium hand doesn't count if the dealer doesn't have a qualifying hand, the player's premium hand does make a difference in three-card poker. It doesn't matter if the dealer qualifies or you beat the dealer's hand; in this game you are always eligible for a bonus payout for a premium hand. If you end up with a straight, a straight flush, or three of a kind, you get a bonus.

## THREE-CARD BONUS PAYOUTS

| Hand | Payout |
|---|---|
| Straight | 1 to 1 |
| Three of a kind | 4 to 1 |
| Straight flush | 5 to 1 |

If you don't want to play against the dealer, you have the option of playing on the pair plus spot. Here your objective is to obtain a hand with a simple pair or better. On this wager, there is also a bonus payout. The higher the hand, the higher the payout. Again, it doesn't matter what the dealer has; you are only playing against the mathematical odds of obtaining a specific hand.

## PAIR PLUS PAYOUTS

| Hand | Payout |
| --- | --- |
| Pair | 1 to 1 |
| Flush | 4 to 1 |
| Straight | 6 to 1 |
| Three of a kind | 30 to 1 |
| Straight flush | 40 to 1 |

## Playing strategy

Following are some strategies for playing three-card poker:

*a* Play like the dealer does. If you have a queen or better, make a wager in the play spot; otherwise, it's best to fold.

*b* When it comes to the pair plus bet, you can expect to win only about 25 percent of the time. Consider this pure-luck bet an optional one. If you see other players winning a lot on this wager, bet it. If not, skip it.

*c* The dealer will qualify with a queen on about two-thirds of the hands, and four out of every ten ante hands will win an ante bonus.

A straight is harder to get than a flush with only three cards, which is why a straight is ranked higher than a flush in this game. Because you can either play against the dealer, as in blackjack, or against the mathematical odds, as in video poker, three-card poker is a unique poker variation that can be interesting and fun to play. However, the overall house advantage is somewhat high – they have a 3.4 percent edge.

# A simple summary

✓ Most new games favor the house more than the traditional games of craps, blackjack, and baccarat. Learn which ones are fun and which ones to stay away from.

✓ The Wheel of Fortune, or Big Six Wheel, is an old carnival game that should be avoided because of its high house advantage.

✓ Let It Ride is a slow and relaxing poker game in which you don't play against other players or the dealer. Instead, you're simply trying to get a pair of 10s or better.

✓ Pai Gow poker combines an old Chinese domino game with American poker. In this game, you want to arrange seven cards into two different hands, with the five-card hand stronger than the two-card hand. Both hands must beat the dealer or it is a push.

✓ Caribbean stud is not a regular poker game, but one that requires each player to beat the dealer. Starting with the betting, you have two choices to make: ante or the optional progressive bonus wager. After seeing one of the dealer's cards, you can bet double your ante or fold.

✓ Spanish 21 offers a lot of bonuses to compensate for the fact that all the 10s are removed from the deck. A strategy that differs from the one used in regular blackjack is required to win at this game.

✓ Three-card poker allows for three betting options: play against the dealer, play against the odds, or bet both ways. The game requires the dealer to qualify with a queen or better. If the dealer does not qualify, everyone remaining in the round wins one bet and pushes on the other.

# PART THREE

# MACHINE GAMES

MODERN PEOPLE LOVE machines, gamblers love machines, and casino management especially loves machines. Some *machines*, like slots, have been around for almost 100 years, but video poker machines are fairly new. Keno is about 70 years old, and bingo, as we know it today, is less than 100 years old. Lotteries have been around for centuries, but modern lottery machines have been used only since 1964.

Players like machines because they are less intimidating than table games and are usually *easy to learn* and play. Management likes them because of the low operating costs and the high financial returns. Learning how to play machine games and play them successfully should allow you to enjoy all your visits to a casino.

# Chapter 13

# Slot Machines

W HEN IT COMES TO THE MODERN SLOT MACHINE, the man who is given all the credit is Charles Fey, a German immigrant mechanic who lived in San Francisco in 1898. He designed and built the 5¢ Liberty Bell slot machine. Fey rented his machines to saloons on a 50–50 split in an attempt to keep his invention secret. Although his venture turned out to be very profitable, his secret didn't last long. A Chicago businessman named Herbert Mills obtained one of Fey's machines, made some changes, and within 5 years had marketed his own machines all across America. It was Mills who came up with the symbols that have become the standards for slot machines the world over. The lemon, plum, cherry, and bar symbols that he designed are still in use today.

## In this chapter...

✓ Types of machines

✓ What are the true odds?

✓ Managing your game

✓ Playing to win

IF YOU CAN FIND THE LOOSE SLOT YOU MAY BE ONTO THE MONEY

# Types of machines

ALTHOUGH THE SLOT MACHINES *we play today come in a large variety of shapes and types, they all boil down to two basic types: straight slots and progressive slots. Straight slots have preset payoffs that never change. The only variation in the payoff on a straight slot machine occurs when multiple coins are inserted, thus increasing the payoff at a fixed ratio. A progressive machine, on the other hand, is one in which the jackpot becomes progressively larger as more and more coins are dropped into the machine. The jackpot continues to increase at a fixed percentage rate, based on the accumulation of coins played over a long period of time. Megabucks is an example of a progressive slot machine.*

As you venture through a casino you will see many slots of different names, sizes, and shapes, which can be quite confusing. To help alleviate some of this confusion, I'm going to lead you through the various types of slot machines you will normally encounter in any major casino.

## Trivia...

*You can see Charles Fey's original Liberty Bell slot machine (and many other antique slots) at the Liberty Belle restaurant on South Virginia Street in Reno, Nevada.*

## One-line, three-reel machine

Let's start with the traditional one-line, three-reel machine. This modern version of the slot machine that was invented by Charles Fey more than 100 years ago is quickly fading away. To win the prize on this type of machine, you must line up the proper symbols on one pay line.

■ **The days of the mechanical slot** *machine are now over, but some casinos retain these traditional machines and power them electrically.*

## Three-line, three-reel machine

With this type of slot, you win by lining up the proper symbols on any of three lines. The payoffs are geared proportionately. This means that the same symbols that would win you 20 coins on a one-line, three-reel machine would only pay ten coins on the first line, 20 on the second line, and 40 on the third line on a three-line, three-reel machine. Note that it takes additional coins to play the three-line machines.

## Five-line, three-reel machine

This slot pays off on three lines, as well as diagonally in a crisscross fashion. Thus, you have a five-line play. The payoff schedules are set in fixed proportion to the number of coins played.

## Low-level machines

Low-level, or sit-down, machines are just that – they have a built-in chair, enabling you to sit comfortably with the machine at elbow level. You will often find similar types of low-level machines at the bars in casinos. These machines come in all the same standard types: one-line, three-line, and five-line.

## Stand-up machines

You can either sit on a stool or stand to play stand-up machines. These slots work in the same way as the low-level machines. The more coins you insert, the larger the number of active lines, and the higher the payout.

**INTERNET**

**www.iplayslots.com**

*This large site contains a lot of slot machine information, as well as offering a free e-mail newsletter. The site provides tips, strategies, online play, information on where to buy a vintage slot machine, a casino slot guide, books, and even advice on how to get slot comps.*

## Pay for play

One slot that sometimes confounds the novice player is the pay-for-play type, or full coin play. This is a good example of why you should always read the payout instructions before inserting coins. You need to know exactly what you're doing. Generally speaking, there are two types of pay-for-play machines. On one type of machine, you simply insert one coin, and you only qualify for the wins associated with that coin. In other words, one coin will allow you to win on one line. When you insert a second coin, you qualify for both the first and second coin wins, or the first and second lines. The final coin allows you to cash in on any winning lines. The other type of pay-for-play machine allows a bigger return on a win for each additional coin inserted. For example, if a winning combination of symbols occurs with three coins, the payout will be three times as much as it would with one coin. You will often see a confused-looking player with three sevens on the line and nothing in the tray because he only played one coin. So remember, it pays to read the machine payout chart.

## High-tech machines

High-tech machines are only different from other slots in appearance: they might have more bells and whistles, but they pay about the same. The main difference with these is that they cater to the specific preference of the player. The novelty of an Elvis Presley or a Star Wars machine is quite an interesting development, and they do appeal to a wide audience. Payoffs are all pretty much the same on a percentage basis, ranging anywhere from a low of 75 percent (which Nevada law requires) to the upper 90-percent range, which competition forces on casinos.

## Progressive jackpots

Some slots are tied to banks, or carousels, of machines so that a coin that is played in one of the slots will increase the jackpot of all the machines in that carousel. In fact, in Nevada there are machines that are tied together statewide. These are known as Megabucks. With these, even when there is no one playing a machine in one particular casino, you know the jackpot is still progressing because someone at another casino or in another city might be playing at that time.

■ **Today,** *most slot machines function at the press of a button despite having a handle for old times' sake.*

The Megabucks machines in Nevada, where the jackpot starts at $5 million are located at more than 125 casinos in various locations around the state. They are linked by computer.

■ **In January 2000,** *Cynthia Jay, a cocktail waitress in Las Vegas, invested $27 in the Megabucks machine at the Desert Inn Resort before lining up three lucky Mega logos. She won $34,959,458.*

# What are the true odds?

AN INTERESTING PHENOMENON with slots is that the odds do change, depending on the denomination of the bet. Playing at a higher wager level in any other game (such as blackjack, craps, or roulette) makes no difference to the odds, but it does at slots! It is a fact that the 25¢ machines pay out more than the 5¢ ones. Dollar slots pay more than the 25¢ machines, and $5 machines have even higher payout rates. There is a reason for this. Management knows that each machine requires a given amount to operate. Every machine takes up the same amount of floor space, and they all require the services of a mechanic and a change person.

If the casino takes in more money on the dollar machine than on the 5¢ machines, they can afford to be more generous with their payoffs. And they are. Research shows that the higher the denomination, the higher the payout.

One recent report gave the following rates:

- 5¢ payouts = 92.5%
- 25¢ payouts = 94.1%
- $1 payouts = 95.9%
- $5 payouts = 98.4%

## The real payouts

In the state of Nevada, the Gaming Commission requires that slot machines pay out a minimum of 75 percent. The New Jersey Casino Control Commission directs Atlantic City casino slots to pay out at least 83 percent. However, the actual payback percentages for those particular states are much higher. In New Jersey it's about 91 percent, and in Nevada it's on the order of 95 percent. This means that, on average, for every $1 you play at slots in Atlantic City, you'll lose 9¢; in Las Vegas you'll lose 5¢ on every dollar. Other states and countries set their own standards for machine payouts.

## Trivia...
In 1986 Megabucks was introduced to Nevada casinos. The jackpot started at $1 million. Terry William won the first Megabucks jackpot – $4,988,842.14 – at Harrah's, Reno.

## Expected results

However, a 95-percent payout will not be the result every time you play. The numbers are usually based on an annual return. In other words, the machine is required by law to return the amount (75 percent in Nevada) that was put into it over a given period of time. When the machine is programmed at the manufacturer, it must be set to return at least that much.

# The percent difference

It's important to recognize the value of playing a high 98-percent machine versus, say, a lower 93-percent one. Consider the following scenario: You start to play a 98-percent machine with $100, and after cycling the entire amount, you get $98 in return (in theory). You put in $98 and get back $96, and so on, until after 20 pulls you end up with $60. But when we look at the 93-percent machine, the results are considerably different. We again start at $100, and this time we get back $93; we then put in $93 and get back $86, and so on, until after only 14 rounds we end up with only $2. Thus, the 5-percent difference in payout between the two machines can be a very big difference.

*Always play on slot machines with the highest return rate possible.*

# Where, oh where?

So, where do you find high-payout machines? The best-paying slots can be found in the most competitive gambling areas, such as Nevada, Atlantic City, Mississippi, Colorado, and Midwest non-Native American casinos. You won't find low 90-percent payout slots in casinos with lots of competition. Those casinos want all the customers they can get, so they have high payouts on a lot of machines. You should forget about most casinos located in isolated areas and on cruise ships – you can expect low returns in those places.

*Believe it or not, casinos love big jackpot winners. Remember that when they give out $50,000, in return they get $250,000 worth of publicity.*

# Finding those loose ones

Today you can go on the Internet and find out lots of information on slot returns and where the *loose* machines can be located. There are also newsletters and monthly magazines that list slot machine payout percentages by state, area, and, in some cases, individual casinos. *Casino Player* and *Strictly Slots* magazines each publish a list of slot payout results every month, and even have special annual reports on slot payouts for the entire United States and some Canadian gambling areas. My advice is to obtain this valuable information and use it when considering where you want to play the slots.

An important detail for you to know is that all gambling income, for you and for the casinos, is subject to taxes. Therefore, slot returns are considered public information in most cases.

> **DEFINITION**
>
> A **loose** *slot machine is one that pays out more often than others, which are known as tight machines. But the terms loose and tight can be very subjective. One machine can be loose for a given period of time, and later it might be tight. Some (loose) machines are set to return 98 percent of what is played in, whereas others (tight) are set at 80-percent return.*

# Managing your game

THERE IS AN OLD EXPRESSION: *"Winning is not that difficult in a casino; what is difficult is leaving with your winnings." That saying holds true for playing slots as well as any other game. What can you do to ensure that you leave a winner? Consider some of the following tips and techniques when playing.*

## Playing what you can afford

Play the highest-denomination machines that fall within your budget. The higher the denomination, the higher the percentage of the payout. Therefore, if you can afford it, you should play the dollar slots in the best locations (those that advertise high returns, and those that are listed in various publications as being the best). If the dollar slots are too steep for you, drop down to the quarter machines, or to nickels. Once you know where the loose machines are located, you need to decide which denomination machines to play based on your bankroll and comfort level.

■ **As a beginner, pick a machine that you enjoy playing** *rather than risk your budget trying to find the loose slots – that will come later once you've made a profit and become more confident with your game.*

## Coin denomination

As I said earlier, playing at higher wager levels has no impact on the odds in any game except slots. Quarter machines will pay out more than nickels. Likewise, dollar slots are looser than quarter machines, and $5 machines will be even looser. Remember this when you are getting ready to play.

# PLAY PER HOUR

The following figures will give you an idea of how much of a bankroll is needed for each type of machine (based on a three-coin maximum bet, with ten spins per minute, at a 90-percent payout rate):

- Nickel machine: $9.00 per hour
- Quarter machine: $45.00 per hour
- One-dollar machine: $180.00 per hour
- Five-dollar machine: $900.00 per hour

## Making a plan

In making your plan, you should decide that each session is to be approximately an hour long. Then, figure the total number of sessions for your trip. You can find this by dividing the amount of your total bankroll by the number of days of your visit. Then divide your daily allowance by the number of sessions per day. For example, if you arrive in Las Vegas with an $800 gambling bankroll and plan to stay for 4 days, you can wager $200 per day. Say you decide you want to play three sessions each day. This means you can afford to lose up to $65 per session. Thus, using the information given in the preceding table, you can see that you will want to play the 25¢ slots.

Once the proper machine denomination has been determined, the best strategy is for you to start out slowly by playing flat-pay machines in the best locations. As you increase your bankroll with winnings, you can advance to progressive and higher-denomination machines.

*Always read the machine's payout table prior to inserting any money, and always insert the maximum amount of coins. Remember, the maximum amount of coins to be played is sometimes determined by the number of pay lines.*

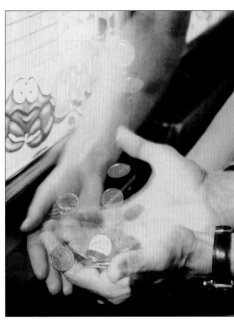

INTERNET

slots.casino.com

*All Things Slots with Gayle Mitchell includes an introduction to slots, basic game rules, tips, and a Question to the Pro section.*

The biggest mistake you can make when playing slots is not getting up and leaving the machine when you're winning. To avoid this mistake, smart players will use the credit meter to help keep track of where they stand. Play the coins in your hand, not the ones on the credits. Also, make sure the credit meter is activated by observing whether or not the button is lit.

Once you have accumulated a profit from playing only the best machines in the above manner, it's time to move up to a higher-denomination machine or to the progressives. When you do, you should play in the exact same way you did on the lower-denomination machines.

## Playing technique

Every slot player has some special technique they use to "win" at slots. Some techniques are born from disciplinary purposes, and others are just old habits acquired over years of playing. Following are some for you to consider on your next slot visit:

(a) Dollar players should run one full rack of coins through the machine ($100 worth of coins). On a three-coin maximum bet machine, there will be one coin left over at the end. Hold on to that coin. Press the CASH OUT button and put all the coins into a bucket or back into the original rack. Immediately walk to the cashier's window and cash out!

(b) You should always know if you are up or down; it helps in keeping your plan in place. Putting the coins you've won back into the slot from the bucket is not a good idea because it causes you to lose sight of where you stand.

(c) To stay ahead, don't play with the credits that are accumulating in the machine. It's the only way for you to keep score while you're playing.

■ **When you cash out,** *change your coins into dollar bills so that you don't put your winnings back into the machine.*

**d** Only play three-reel machines. Normally, the odds are 8,000 to 1 for hitting a jackpot. These odds go up to 160,000 to 1 on four-reel slots, and soar into the millions to 1 for five-reel slots.

**e** Join all the slots clubs offered by the casinos. Joining is free, and you will get back some of your investment in the form of comps.

**f** Play in slot tournaments. Normally, the entry fee is reasonable, and the wins are high. Ask about tournaments whenever you visit a casino. They are fun and inexpensive.

*Play slot machines to have fun, and don't expect to win much. But if you do get a big win or jackpot, take the money and run — otherwise, you won't get to enjoy it.*

# Playing to win

TODAY'S MODERN CASINO *slot machines are all-electronic, offering a multitude of betting options and CD-quality sound. They come in a variety of sizes, types, and shapes, including sit-down, stand-up, one-line, two-line, three-line, five-line, three-reel, four-reel, five-reel, and big-bertha types. If this is not enough for you, there are also video slots that will take up to 25 coins and feature multiwin lines. With these new machines you don't have to pull a handle; you can just push a button (but there is also a handle, to keep traditional players happy with familiar equipment).*

## The random number generator

The reel spins on all new machines are controlled by a computer chip called a random number generator (RNG). It makes absolutely no difference if you pull the handle, push the button, or insert one or five coins – the RNG will control the entire reel outcome. When a casino orders a slot machine, it tells the manufacturer what percentage it wants that specific machine to pay back, and that amount is then programmed into the RNG. The casino can change the payback percentage, but in order to do so, it must go back to the manufacturer to get a new RNG programmed with the new amount. In addition, paperwork must be filed with the state commission, listing serial numbers, dates, and lots of other information. For these reasons, most casinos seldom change their payback percentages.

RNGs are programmed to produce a higher number of stops, reels, and symbols on progressive jackpot machines than on regular or non-progressive machines. Because of this, you're better off concentrating on regular machines.

## Look for these places

The standard places for loose slots are always changing. You might not find them near the front door or near the end of the aisles anymore, as these spots are now reserved for mid-paying and tight slots. Some casinos are changing loose slots locations to elevated carousels and areas that are highly visible from all angles because players are more likely to play where they see winners. Remember, loose machines are few and far between, and there are more mid-pay and tight machines scattered around than loose machines. Here are a few tips for finding those loose slots:

■ **Whether you have to pull a handle** *or push a button, stand up or sit down, once you've found that loose machine you're almost guaranteed a win.*

*a* Pick the area near the change booths: this is often a popular location for loose slots. Players who are waiting for change are enticed by the sound of coins dropping into the coin tray and seeing excited winners collecting their money.

*b* Seek out the machines near the coffee shops; the winning sounds are designed to entice diners to eat quickly and get out there and win some money.

*c* Take your time and walk around, observing the slot action. One method for finding winning machines is to view the payout window on machines. See what past players cashed out for before they left.

*d* Start with machines that you have won on before. For example, you might have had good luck in the past with Double Diamonds or Blazing 7s. Past experience will give you some idea what these machines are all about.

*e* Since tight machines are normally placed on either side of a loose one, when you do find a machine that is paying off, don't play the ones on either side of it.

The task of locating that loose slot still remains for the smart player. Not all slots in a specific area will be loose, but a bit of work on your part will help you to locate those that are.

**INTERNET**

www.slot-secrets.com

*You'll find everything you wanted to know about slots at this site. It explains in detail machine externals, internals, contains slot math, advanced math, and a lot more.*

## Avoiding the tight slots

Note that tight slots are normally placed near the craps and blackjack tables and roulette wheels. This is because slot players who hit jackpots make a lot of noise, which distracts the table players, and neither the players nor the management want that. Another area that casinos place tight machines is near the sports book. Sports bettors are easily distracted by the clanking of coins into the coin tray, and if it becomes too annoying, most sports bettors will go elsewhere. Also, casino management knows that table gamblers frequently drop coins into slot machines as they leave the table games. These players are not long-term slot players, and the casino knows they would be more likely to take the money and run instead of continuing to play. Therefore, only tight machines are available to those types of bettors.

■ **Check out the location of the machines** *before playing: You'll increase your chances of finding a loose machine if you play the ones on elevated carousels and avoid those near the gaming tables.*

## Follow the money

There are two psychological methods employed by casinos to separate you from your money. When you change bills for coins or tokens, you lose sight of the real value of what you are playing with. Also, when you exchange your bills for credits, your money becomes a number on the credit meter. Most machines now have bill acceptors to change your bills into slot credits. Although it seems more convenient to play the credits (that's the idea), it's really more advantageous to you to insert the coins yourself. It does slow play, but it should remind you that it is money and not a number that you see on the credit window.

Large jackpots are normally paid by the change person; also, some machines pay partial jackpots, and the slot staff will pay the balance. When these conditions occur, it is important that you never leave your machine until you have received your total winnings.

## A simple summary

✔ Slots have been around since Charles Fey invented the Liberty Bell machine in San Francisco more than 100 years ago.

✔ There are more types of slot machines available to today's player than ever before. Knowing the types and how they pay out will help you plot a winning strategy.

✔ The odds on the machines change depending, in many cases, on the coin denomination. Use good money-management techniques and pay attention to your comfort level to determine your level of play.

✔ Loose machines are there in the casino. It's your job to seek them out. Read all the information available to help you in the task of finding them.

✔ Make a plan when visiting a casino. There are techniques to employ in managing your bankroll. Use them to help you become a successful slot player.

✔ Always remember that you are playing with real money. Don't lose sight of that fact just because you changed your dollars into credit numbers on a slot machine.

# Chapter 14

# Video Poker

O N THE RIVER BOATS OF THE MISSISSIPPI RIVER and in the saloons of the Old West in the 1800s, draw poker and five-card stud were the standard gambling card games. By the 1900s, Americans across the country were playing these same poker games on Friday night with friends and family. However, you really had to have played a lot of poker and understood the game completely before you would venture into a card room to play poker. That notion might have been true until video poker was introduced in the late 1970s. Here was a new, simple, and entertaining computerized game that you could play alone without being intimidated by dealers and other players. It immediately became a very big hit with casino patrons across the land.

## In this chapter...

✓ A different game

✓ What are the true odds?

✓ Types of machines

✓ Playing to win

THE PRESSURE'S OFF WHEN IT'S JUST YOU AGAINST THE VIDEO POKER MACHINE

# A different game

VIDEO POKER IS FAST AND FUN *but requires a lot on the part of the player. To play it you have to think! Unlike regular slot machines, video poker is an interactive machine game because you choose which cards to keep and which to discard. It's based on five-card draw poker, which is relatively easy to learn and understand. You have a great amount of control in this game. You can pick the right machine, select the amount to wager, and have an excellent edge against the house when you play skillfully.*

## A little history

The first video machines were introduced in Las Vegas in 1976. These early machines were limited on payouts, but did have a $1,500 royal flush payout on the dollar machines if all five coins were inserted. Once the casino operators and manufacturers increased the payouts (to levels like eight or nine coins for a full house, for example), players started to take notice and the game's popularity began to improve. Today casino managers are moving old slots out and installing new video games as fast as possible. Video poker is not only popular with patrons, it's also one of the best games in the casino for a player.

## How to play

Video poker machine play is different from regular slot machines. At first the procedure seems similar. You insert a coin or coins (almost all video poker machines take multiple coins), push the "play" or "deal" button, and five cards appear on the viewing screen. Here is where it changes from a normal slot machine play. You select which cards to hold. You can hold all five or none. It is entirely up to you. There are five buttons on the front of the machine; when pushed, "hold" will appear above those cards selected. Your objective is to get the best or highest hand possible.

■ **Playing video poker** *is all about pressing the right buttons: from selecting your hand to dealing the winning combination of cards.*

You then push the "deal" button and new cards appear, replacing the ones you did not hold. If a winning combination results, the machine will award you units based on the payout chart. After the credits are awarded, the "player paid" sign will appear on the screen. The units will equal the value required to play the machine. For example, a machine that requires 25¢ to play would record each unit as 25.

With that hand over, you bet how many units or coins to play on the next hand and again hit the "deal" button. When you have finished playing a session, simply press the "collect" button, and the machine will pay you by dropping all the credited coins into the tray. The object of the game is to end each round with a winning combination.

## The skill needed to play

As in any other game, you need to know some video poker concepts to be successful. First, you need to know how to play basic five-card draw poker. Reading and understanding the chapter on poker will be an important aid in this area. You should also know that, since you are playing one-on-one with a machine, there are some important differences compared to the live game of five-card draw poker. For example, in video poker three of a kind is the same regardless of its card ranking. That means three 5s is the same as three 8s. In addition, you should have a working knowledge of what the chances are of getting a particular hand as well as the value of going for a higher hand and what it means in payouts.

## RANKING OF HANDS

You should be aware of what the ranking order is in video poker and what the odds are of receiving a particular hand during the original draw.

| Original dealt hand | Odds of receiving |
| --- | --- |
| Royal flush | 1 in 655,000 |
| Straight flush | 1 in 73,000 |
| Four of a kind | 1 in 4,200 |
| Full house | 1 in 700 |
| Flush | 1 in 500 |
| Straight | 1 in 250 |
| Three of a kind | 1 in 50 |
| Two pair | 1 in 21 |
| High pair | 1 in 8 |
| Low pair | 1 in 3 |
| No pair | 1 in 2 |

## Differences in video and live poker

There are many differences between the two games. Some are minor while others are very significant. Study the list and make sure you understand each point.

1. Bluffing, "check and raise," sandbagging, and other strategies of live poker do not apply or work in video poker.

2. Regular live poker includes several stud varieties, as well as high-low games, that do not relate to video poker at all. The game of draw poker is the only one that applies to both video and live poker.

3. Video poker games are available 24 hours a day, 365 days a year. Sometimes you may not have enough players to make up a live poker game. Video poker needs no other players.

4. Hand rankings are very similar and yet can be different. Every video poker game will pay more for a straight than for three of a kind. Some pay the same for straights and flushes, and straight flushes are not always worth more than four of a kind. In live poker, four 6s are worth more than four 3s, but in video poker they are always worth the same.

5. You can't lose with a good video poker hand. If you end up with four of a kind, you are going to get paid. You can't lose out to another player getting a straight flush as in live poker.

6. There is only one decision point in video poker. Regular live poker frequently has several betting rounds, and sometimes several decisions per round. In video poker, you make your one choice before the draw. After the draw the game is over.

7. In video poker, you know at the beginning what any winning hand is worth. In regular poker, three of a kind may or may not be a winner, and it could cost a lot of money to find out. This is not the case with video poker.

8. In video poker, you know at the outset what any hand costs. The amount you put in a machine is the most you can lose. You rarely know this in live poker.

9. A good psychologist would play well at regular live poker, but a good mathematical mind will do well playing video poker.

10. Strategy charts or crib sheets can't be used at live poker tables. However, strategy charts can be very useful at video poker, and most casinos allow you to use them.

11. You can call "time" in live poker, which will allow you a few more minutes to make a decision; in video poker you don't have to worry about time at all.

Royal flushes get a big bonus. In regular live poker, a king-high straight flush is very marginally inferior to a royal flush. Either hand would win every pot every time in live poker. In video poker, the difference between these hands is huge, especially if a progressive bonus payout is involved.

 There is no reason to hold a *kicker* in video poker, but it can be an important card in live poker.

> **DEFINITION**
>
> A **kicker** is an unpaired poker card used to determine the better of two near-equivalent hands. It's usually a high card like an ace or king.

# What are the true odds?

THERE ARE A TOTAL OF 2,598,960 *totally different hands that can be dealt to you in video poker, but don't be alarmed by that number. When reviewing the mathematics we find that a player, after drawing additional cards, will get a royal flush once in about 40,000 hands and a straight flush in about 9,000 hands. That results in about a 63-percent chance of getting at least one royal flush and about a 27-percent chance of getting two in the same 40,000 hands.*

> **Trivia...**
>
> Las Vegas, Nevada, is the best place to play video poker. It has the most video poker machines with the best payouts of any location in the world.

Now you ask the question how long does it take to play those 40,000 hands? If you play 500 hands an hour, which is reasonable, then it takes about 80 hours of play to reach 40,000 hands. That could range from 2 weeks or 2 months depending on how often and how long you play each session.

> **DEFINITION**
>
> The 9/6 and 8/5 numbers are used by the gaming industry and players to identify its payout schedule. The first number tells you what the payout will be for a single coin played if a hand ends with a full house. The second number tells you what the payout will be for a flush.

## Payout schedule

Video poker machines are identified by name and payout schedule. For example, you might see a Jacks or Better **9/6** machine sitting side by side with a Jacks or Better **8/5** machine.

Regardless of the payout schedule, all video poker machines play the same way, but one will pay more for the same hand than the other machine. You can tell the difference by looking at the payout schedule on the front of the machine. You always want to play the video poker machines with the highest payout schedule.

## Understanding the odds

You might wonder what the real difference is between a 9/6 versus an 8/5 machine. A 9/6 machine, with maximum coins played and with perfect strategy, will return 99.5 percent. Under the same conditions an 8/5 will return only 97.3 percent. Over the long run, that small percent of 2.2 will have an effect on your overall win-rate. The chart below shows the differences between other various types of machine.

## ODDS BETWEEN DIFFERENT MACHINES

| Machine type | Payout | Machine type | Payout |
|---|---|---|---|
| 10/7 (double bonus) | 100.2% | 8/5 | 97.3% |
| 9/7 | 100.7% | 7/5 | 96.3% |
| 9/6 | 99.5% | 6/5 | 95.2% |

**Note:** These percentages assume a royal flush is hit one time during the period of play.

## The varying hands

How often a specific hand appears will vary depending on the type of machine you are playing. Deuces Wild will be different from Joker Wild, which will also be different from Jacks or Better. Listed in the chart below is a 9/6 Jacks or Better machine to give you an idea of the payout, along with the frequency of receiving specific hands.

## FREQUENCY OF HANDS (9/6 Jacks or Better machine)

| Hand | Payout | Frequency |
|---|---|---|
| Royal flush | 4,000 | 1 in 40,390 |
| Straight flush | 250 | 1 in 9,148 |
| Four of a kind | 125 | 1 in 423 |
| Full house | 45 | 1 in 86 |
| Flush | 30 | 1 in 90 |
| Straight | 20 | 1 in 89 |
| Three of a kind | 15 | 1 in 13 |
| Two pair | 10 | 1 in 7 |
| Jacks or better | 5 | 1 in 4 |

**Note:** The above figures are based on playing the maximum coins (5).

# Types of machines

THERE ARE MANY TYPES *of video poker games: Jacks or Better, Bonus Poker, Double Bonus Poker, Deuces Wild, Joker Wild, All American, and others. The payout schedule can differ for each variation. Some games offer more than 100-percent potential payback over the long run. You have to use the correct playing strategy for each one in order to obtain a positive result. Keep in mind that there are only a few video poker games where you can achieve this. The most popular video poker game is Jacks or Better. It has a 99.5-percent payback, giving you a good rate of return and allowing you to gain the necessary experience to move on to other more complicated games.*

## Jacks or Better

This is the best game when first starting to play video poker. In fact it is a good all-around machine to play any time. As discussed earlier, you can identify a good-paying machine by reviewing the full house and flush payouts on the first column on the payout chart. On a 9/6 machine you will be paid nine coins for a full house and six for a flush.

*Don't play the low payout 7/5 machines you'll find at airports, laundromats, or grocery stores. The house odds are just too high.*

The next factor to look for is the royal flush payout. You want to play on nonprogressive machines that award at least 4,000 coins for a royal flush. This means that if you play the maximum five coins (and you should always play the maximum) and get a royal flush, you will get 4,000 coins back.

*The royal flush payout is the bonus that makes video poker a winner. If you can't or won't play the maximum coins on a given video poker machine because of its cost, go to a machine with a lower denomination.*

■ **Tempted** *to play video poker machines in stores and laundromats? Don't be – they have low payouts!*

## Joker Wild

This game is played with the standard 52-card deck, with a joker thrown in as a wild card. This wild card can be used as a substitute for any other card or can be used to create a five of a kind. The machine will automatically compute the best hand when a joker is present, usually about 10 percent of the time. Because of the added bonus of the wild card, the minimum rank for a winning hand is two pair.

## Deuces Wild

The standard 52-card deck is used, with all four deuces (2s) designated as wild cards. Because of the added bonus of the four deuce wild cards, the minimum rank for a winning hand is three of a kind.

*Never discard a deuce in a Deuces Wild game. (Believe me, it can and will be done if you're not paying attention.)*

## King of the Decks

In this game, five decks of the standard 52-card decks are used. If you get five kings of clubs, you will win the progressive jackpot. Because of the added bonus of the increased number of potential pairs, the minimum rank for a winning hand is two pair.

*Games with more than one deck will always reduce the player's odds, so consider other games before playing King of the Decks.*

## Progressive machines

Another video machine you will find is an 8/5 Jacks or Better progressive. These machines have a lower payout for a full house and flush; however, this can be overcome if the progressive jackpot is high enough. On a 25-¢ machine, if the jackpot is above $2,240, it's worthwhile to play. If it's below the $2,240 level, go back to the standard 9/6 machines.

*On progressive 9/6 Jacks or Better machines when the jackpot raises above 6,500 coins, the payback reaches a 100-percent return making this an excellent machine to play.*

## The best machines

The three best machines you can play are the 9/6 Jacks or better, 10/7 Double Bonus, and full-pay Deuces Wild. When you insert the maximum coins and use perfect strategy, these machines will pay out 99.5 percent, 100.2 percent, and 100.8 percent, respectively. Look for these machines and play them.

# Playing to win

THE ONLY WAY TO TRULY BEAT *a video poker machine is to receive a high-paying royal flush. You must play both the correct strategy required and the maximum coins to make this hand; otherwise you'll play a losing game. Don't overlook the idea of playing the maximum coins each time. The casinos know that players won't always do this. That is one of the big ways casinos make money. You should always play the maximum number of coins, as this is the only way to get the big payoff when you get a royal flush.*

## Using the payout schedule to select your machine

Selecting the best machines is one of the cornerstones of winning at video poker. One of the first things to do is review the payout chart. This is a must. You want machines that will give you the most for your money. Remember, all machines are not the same. They might look alike and may even sit side by side; but they could have different payout charts. Start by playing only machines that return your original bet for at least a pair of jacks or better. Next, read the first payout column on the face of the machine and look to see what a full house and a flush will pay out. For example, if it pays nine for a full house and six for a flush, it's a Jacks or Better 9/6 and has a higher payoff than an 8/5 machine that only pays eight for a full house and five for a flush.

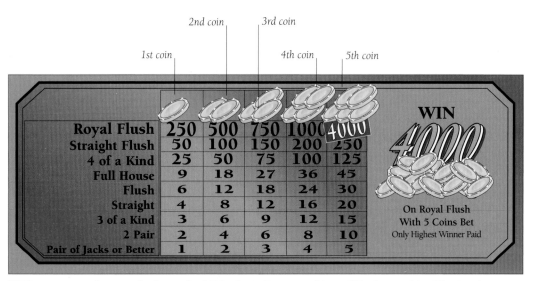

| | 1st coin | 2nd coin | 3rd coin | 4th coin | 5th coin |
|---|---|---|---|---|---|
| Royal Flush | 250 | 500 | 750 | 1000 | 4000 |
| Straight Flush | 50 | 100 | 150 | 200 | 250 |
| 4 of a Kind | 25 | 50 | 75 | 100 | 125 |
| Full House | 9 | 18 | 27 | 36 | 45 |
| Flush | 6 | 12 | 18 | 24 | 30 |
| Straight | 4 | 8 | 12 | 16 | 20 |
| 3 of a Kind | 3 | 6 | 9 | 12 | 15 |
| 2 Pair | 2 | 4 | 6 | 8 | 10 |
| Pair of Jacks or Better | 1 | 2 | 3 | 4 | 5 |

WIN
4000
On Royal Flush
With 5 Coins Bet
Only Highest Winner Paid

■ **The payout chart** *on the front of a 9/6 Jacks or Better machine will look something like the above; always read what the full house and the flush payouts are before selecting a machine.*

## Basic strategy

As I have said throughout this chapter, the strategy for video poker is different from that for live poker. The chart listed is considered basic strategy. To use it, simply go down the list under "initial hand" until you find the hand you received on the initial draw. Reading across under the "decision" column, you'll find what action will give you the best chance of improving your hand. Make a copy of the chart, take it with you to the casino, and use it while playing. It is legal and perfectly all right to use in a casino.

# BASIC STRATEGY 9/6 JACKS OR BETTER

| Initial hand | Decision |
|---|---|
| 4 of a kind | keep all (*see note 1*) |
| 4 card royal | draw 1 |
| Full house or flush | keep all (*see note 2*) |
| Three of a kind | draw 2 |
| 4 card straight flush | draw 1 |
| Straight | keep all (*see note 2*) |
| Two pair | draw 1 |
| High pair (Jacks or better) | draw 3 |
| 3 card royal | draw 2 |
| 4 card flush | draw 1 |
| Low pair | draw 3 |
| 4 card straight (1 high card) | draw 1 |
| 3 card straight flush | draw 2 |
| 2 card royal (ace, no 10) | draw 3 |
| 3 high cards (J, Q, K, no ace) | draw 2 |
| 2 high cards | draw 3 |
| 2 card royal (10, no ace) | draw 3 |
| 1 high card (J, Q, K, or ace) | draw 4 |
| Mixed low cards | draw 5 |

**Note 1:** Hold all five cards with four of a kind; machines have been known to malfunction and void a hand.

**Note 2:** Hold any hand (cards) where you are a winner (flushes, straights, high pair, etc.).

**Note 3:** There are small differences in strategy when playing different types of machine. I suggest you review some of the information on the Internet and study the books about video poker recommended in the Appendices for these changes.

## Learning basic strategy

For fast and accurate play, you must commit to memory the strategy for the game you are playing. You need to be able to handle 98 to 99 percent of the hands correctly without resorting to any reference guide. A reference guide is one of the laminated strategy cards available that you can set right on the machine to assist you in playing the 1 or 2 percent of the hands that you might need help with.

## Strategy for other games

With so many different machines available and new ones popping up all the time, it's impossible to identify and lay out all the strategies for every machine in this one book. I suggest you review the strategies for the various games on the Internet and in the video poker books listed in the Appendices.

■ **Video poker machines are usually grouped together,** *so remember the strategies you've learned to help you recognize a better-paying video poker game and you'll already be way ahead of most players.*

## Player speed

The speed of playing video poker will vary depending on the experience of the player. The inexperienced player can probably play a machine at about 300 to 400 hands per hour. An experienced player can easily average 400 to 600 hands per hour. An extremely fast player can probably play one machine at 700 to 1,000 hands per hour. Expert players can play two machines at a combined 1,200 to 1,400 hands per hour. High speed is one objective you want to work toward as you gain experience playing video poker.

## Money management

*Money management by itself will not make you win more hands, but it will allow you to play more hands.*

**INTERNET**

www.gambling.
jaxworld.com

*This is an excellent site with lots of video poker tips about bankroll requirements, playing speed, and card recognition. In addition, the site has strategy guides for Jacks or Better, Deuces Wild, and Joker Wild.*

A reasonably experienced player can expect to play about 500 hands an hour. You should see one royal flush every 80 hours of play. Keep in mind that this represents an average only. You could get two royals or none during that same period. To be in range of hitting a royal you need to play about 40,000 hands.

**DEFINITION**

*Cash earned or awarded in proportion to the amount wagered in a machine is called* **cash back**. *Points are accumulated from using a players slot club card. Some casinos give comps while others award cash. In order to woo players, casinos may also mail invitations to visit them and include extra vouchers such as 2-for-1 $5 betting coupons or discounts on food, shows, and hotels. This will add a small percentage to your overall win rate.*

To do that on a 25-¢ machine, you'll need a bankroll of at least $1,000. This will give you about a 60-percent chance of success. It's interesting to note that in 50 to 60 hours of play you will cycle about $37,000 through a video poker machine. You should now see why it's so important to use your player slot club card whenever you are playing.

By using a players slot club card and getting the benefits from the casino by way of *cash back* or comps you will be able to see a return of more than 100 percent most of the time. By pacing yourself, playing the right machines, and using the correct strategy you'll have the makings of a successful money-management program.

## Becoming an expert

When you are first starting to play video poker, I advise you to stick to one type of machine or game, since each one requires its own particular strategy. For example, there are some differences between the strategy for Jacks or Better and those for Deuces Wild. Don't overload yourself. Specialize and learn one game well before moving on to other types of machines.

There also should be no question in your mind that your skill at video poker is what determines if the house wins or you win. Video poker is a game of skill. What skills do you need to become a winner? Have a decent bankroll, select the right machine, play skillfully, and manage your funds properly. How do you gain all these skills? By reading and rereading the material just presented and by playing video poker machines. In addition *Strictly Slots* magazine has monthly articles on video poker by some of the best industry experts.

# A simple summary

✔ Poker has been played for many years, but video poker only came about in the late 70s.

✔ Video poker is similar to, but different from, slots because it is an interactive game. It is also different from live poker, and knowing all the differences is very important to the player.

✔ A big difference in video versus live poker is what the payout is for every hand. In live poker it's always an unknown, while video poker payouts are fixed but vary greatly.

✔ There are lots of different types of video machines, and the player needs to know how each one is played.

✔ There is a basic strategy to video poker that a player needs to know and memorize. Different games and machines will vary in how to play each of them. A good player will review and study the different strategies before playing any of them.

✔ As with all gaming, a good money-management program on the part of the player is important in improving the financial outcome when playing video poker.

# Chapter 15

# Keno

KENO IS CONSIDERED ONE OF THE OLDEST gambling games, its history going back almost 2,000 years to the Han Dynasty of China. The original game required players to pick 10 Chinese characters out of a total of 120. Chinese laborers who came to the US in the mid-1800s brought the game, which came to be called Chinese lottery, with them.It thrived in many towns in the West but was difficult for Americans to understand and play. In 1936, the game was revised by reducing the total (now Arabic) numbers to 80, and adding racehorse names to the numbers to make it "legal" in Nevada. It's new name was "racehorse keno." That 80-number lottery game is now known simply as keno.

## In this chapter...

✓ How the game works

✓ Some game knowledge

✓ Types of keno tickets

✓ Playing strategy

KENO HAS EVOLVED INTO ONE OF TODAY'S MOST POPULAR CASINO GAMES

# How the game works

MOST PLAYERS ENJOY *the game of keno because of its simplicity, convenience, and leisurely pace. It can also be exciting because of its big payoffs, which can reach as much as $250,000 for a $2 bet. And it's simple to keep track of: You can walk into any casino restaurant in Las Vegas, Reno, Atlantic City, Michigan, Minnesota, or Wisconsin and look up at the keno flashboard, conveniently located for your viewing.*

## DEFINITION

*A casino employee who combs the casino, collecting keno tickets and delivering winnings, is called a* **keno writer** *or* **runner**. *The term also applies to those who write tickets behind the counter in the keno lounge.*

## Trivia...

*In 1951 the United States Congress passed a law taxing off-track betting on horse races. Since the game's original name, racehorse keno, might be construed as off-track betting, the name was shortened, and since that time the game has simply been known as keno.*

To help further your participation in the game, *keno writers* or *runners* constantly make the rounds, calling for new players and checking other players' keno tickets. For convenience, they will offer to take your tickets to the keno lounge to have them posted, allowing you to continue your meal or drink without interruption. The keno lounge itself is large, with comfortable seating and cocktail waitresses moving through, taking orders for free drinks. The keno area is also one of the quietest areas in the casino. The house provides all this grand service because they can well afford it – the return on keno is almost 40 percent, which makes for a very nice profit for the casino.

Keno is very similar to the lottery games found in most states in the US and around the world. In both types of games, you pick specific numbers and hope they will come up in the drawing. Like lottery games, keno has a very low betting requirement – sometimes as low as 50¢ per game.

*The big difference between keno and lottery games is that in keno there are many different ways to play specific numbers. The game has a total of 80 numbers to select from, but only 20 will come up during each game.*

## Trivia...

*In 1963 the aggregate keno payout limit in Nevada was limited to $25,000. In 1979 it was changed to $50,000. In 1989 the Nevada Gaming Commission eliminated the cap, and casinos are now free to set their aggregate limits as they choose. Nowadays, some keno winnings might be as high as $250,000.*

## The gooseneck machine

Originally, 80 numbered wooden balls were pulled by hand through a wooden gooseneck device. Nowadays, lightweight Ping-Pong balls are forced from a large plastic bubble or bowl through the gooseneck, allowing 20 balls to pop up, revealing the numbers for that game. No human hands touch the balls, ensuring independence and fairness. The numbers appear on an electric flashboard, which can be seen throughout the casino. In some US states and in Britain and Australia, computers are beginning to be used to randomly select the keno numbers.

## Marking your ticket

You play the game by marking an X on your ticket using special crayons that are provided by the casino. You can mark from 1 to 15 spots, and sometimes more. You can also play various combinations of numbers. When you give your ticket to a keno writer, you will receive a computerized, marked, duplicate ticket stamped with the ticket number, date, and game played. This is your official receipt, and the only one that can be used to collect winnings.

■ **Using the gooseneck machine** *ensures the game is played with complete impartiality, as at no time do human hands come in contact with the balls.*

If you have a winning ticket, you have to present it before the next game starts. If you don't, your chance to collect will be gone. There are some exceptions to this time limit, particularly when you play multigames.

*Be sure to ask the keno staff what your time limit will be in multigame situations. You don't want to lose out on a winning ticket because you ran out of time.*

## Ticket prices and payouts

All game prices and payouts are contained in rate-card brochures that are published by the casino and located in the keno lounge and in many of the casino restaurants. These brochures will list the games that are offered, along with some basic selections. Many casinos offer special games for very small wager requirements, some as low as 50¢. You can play a lot of keno for a long time with a total budget of $20.

It's important to remember that the house advantage in keno will vary from 25 to 40 percent, which makes it one of the highest-odds games in the entire casino. The casino industry explains this high advantage by noting that the overhead for the game itself is the highest of any casino game. Plenty of floor space is devoted to the game, there are a large number of runners and writers, and relatively small bets are the rule. It would not be profitable for a casino to run keno at a much lower "take."

Not all keno games are created equal; it pays to look around. A recent survey of 21 Las Vegas casinos, all with keno games, found ten different payouts for the $5, five-spot play. The payouts ranged from a low of $2,400 to a high of $5,500, all for the same win. If you become a serious keno player, you will want to review the payout or rate-card brochures from all the casinos before you begin to play.

The following box contains a sample of a typical payout chart from a keno brochure:

### MARK 6 SPOTS

| Catch | Play $1 | Play $2 | Play $5 |
|-------|---------|---------|---------|
| 3 | $1 | $2 | $5 |
| 4 | $8 | $16 | $40 |
| 5 | $50 | $100 | $250 |
| 6 | $1,500 | $3,000 | $7,500 |

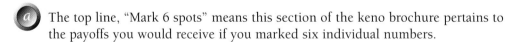

ⓐ The top line, "Mark 6 spots" means this section of the keno brochure pertains to the payoffs you would receive if you marked six individual numbers.

ⓑ "Catch" refers to how many of your chosen numbers match what the house draws.

*c* "Play $1" means you can bet $1 on your ticket for the six numbers. As the table shows, you can also bet $2 or $5. In fact, you can bet more if your bankroll allows; ask the keno runner for help with playing above the brochure's listed amounts.

*d* As the payoff table shows, if you play six numbers and catch five of six, the payout will be $50. If all six numbers appear, a $1 ticket will return $1,500.

*A keno payoff is usually on a "for" basis rather than a "to" basis. This means that if you collect $8 for matching four numbers, you've already paid $1 for the ticket, so you're actually winning $7. Even so, it is standard keno terminology to say you "won $8."*

Winnings listed in keno brochures will show total aggregate payout. This aggregate payout limits the total payout liability of a casino during any one game. Therefore, no matter how many winners there are, the casino will only pay the aggregate, or total, limit; if there is more than one winner, the players split the total winnings evenly.

Keno operators are required to complete tax form W2-G on all permanent residents of the United States (aliens get a different form) on all net wins of $1,500 or more.

*Keno operators do not withhold any part of the win. You, the winner, are responsible for paying any taxes that are due.*

# Some game knowledge

THE GAME ITSELF IS SLOW – *about five or six games an hour – which is a very leisurely pace compared to other games found in the casino. This allows you plenty of time to review numbers and analyze your ticket to ensure its correctness before playing a game. With a total of 80 numbers available, only 20 come out, which means that 75 percent of the numbers will not appear. This gives the house a big edge over the player. Unlike bingo, where numbers are called until there is a winner, the game is over after all 20 numbers have been pulled, regardless of whether there are any winners.*

# How to play

You can find blank tickets, crayons, and payout brochures in the keno lounge and throughout most restaurants in the casino.

Here's how to get into the game:

**1** Using only the special crayons provided, mark an X over each of your chosen numbers on the ticket. Each number is called a "spot"; so, if you choose four numbers, the ticket is called a "four-spot" ticket, and if you pick eight, it's an "eight-spot" ticket. For new players, I suggest limiting yourself to picking three, four, or five numbers at most.

**2** Mark the price, number of spots played, and number of games you want to play in the *conditioning* area of the ticket. You'll find the conditioning area in the right margin or special boxes on the ticket.

**DEFINITION**

*The casino term for a player's marked choices, which are listed along the top or right margin, is* **conditioning**.

**3** Present your ticket to a keno writer or runner.

**4** Make sure you get the computerized ticket back, with all your picks posted correctly.

**5** Check the keno flashboard or monitor – if your numbers are among the 20 drawn, you have a winner. Any keno employee will be glad to help you check your ticket.

# Turning in tickets

You must turn in your winning ticket before the next game begins. If you play more than one game at a time, you must turn your ticket in after your last game and before the next one begins. If you play between 10 and 20 games, you might have 48 hours to collect. When you play more than 21 games, you normally have one year to collect. However, in all cases, you must read your keno rate-card brochure to make sure you're aware of your time limits. All casinos have different rules and time limits.

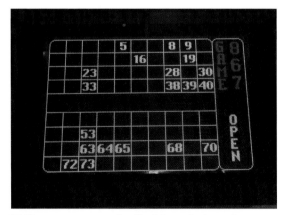

■ **Keep an eye on the flashboard:** *Apart from showing you the winning numbers, it will also tell you how long you have until the next game starts.*

# Types of keno tickets

**THERE ARE A VARIETY** *of ways to play keno, in addition to just marking a few of your favorite numbers on your ticket. Some ways are very simple, while others can be more complicated but give you a better chance of winning. The following sections detail the various types of keno tickets that are available to you in most casinos.*

## Straight ticket

A single ticket with "straight" X-marks posted with various numbers on the ticket is called a straight ticket. The numbers that are played can range from 1 to 15. Straight tickets are the easiest to mark, to write, and to calculate winning results for.

■ **The straight ticket** *is the easiest for the new player to understand. This is a 3-spot ticket. Note the conditioning area at top.*

Since 1936 when the game we know today as keno came into play, no one in the state of Nevada has ever hit a straight 15-spot ticket.

*You should not play any ticket above a 10 spot, if you do then only play as a way ticket.*

## Way ticket

A ticket marked with two or more sets of numbers is called a way ticket. For example, if you want to play a three-3-spot ticket, you mark the 4, 5, and 6; then you mark the second group, 24, 25, 26; finally, you mark the third group, 44, 45, and 46. You put Xs on each of the numbers, and then circle each of the three groups of three. You mark the ticket on the right margin as "3/3," indicating that you are waging on three sets of three numbers each. What you now have is a 3-way-3 keno ticket.

**KENO**

| MARK NO. OF SPOTS OR WAYS PLAYED | NO. OF GAMES | TOTAL PRICE |
|---|---|---|
| *3/3* | *1* | *3 00* |

| | | | | | | | | | |
|---|---|---|---|---|---|---|---|---|---|
| 1 | 2 | 3 | ⊗X | X | X | 7 | 8 | 9 | 10 |
| 11 | 12 | 13 | 14 | 15 | 16 | 17 | 18 | 19 | 20 |
| 21 | 22 | 23 | X | X | X | 27 | 28 | 29 | 30 |
| 31 | 32 | 33 | 34 | 35 | 36 | 37 | 38 | 39 | 40 |
| 41 | 42 | 43 | X | X | X | 47 | 48 | 49 | 50 |
| 51 | 52 | 53 | 54 | 55 | 56 | 57 | 58 | 59 | 60 |
| 61 | 62 | 63 | 64 | 65 | 66 | 67 | 68 | 69 | 70 |
| 71 | 72 | 73 | 74 | 75 | 76 | 77 | 78 | 79 | 80 |

■ **A 3-way-3 ticket** *is made by marking three sets of three numbers and then circling each group of three. Keep an eye out for fractional rates.*

*The advantage to this is that you are given credit for hitting all three numbers if any one in the group comes up.*

Another reason to play a way ticket is fractional rates: some casinos will let you play for as little as 50¢ per way, instead of the usual $1 you would have to play on a straight ticket. The payouts on way tickets are the same as they are for playing the same numbers using multiple keno tickets.

## Split ticket

A ticket that utilizes two or more groups of numbers, separated from each other in some manner, is called a split ticket. The most commonly used methods for a split ticket is to draw a line between the groups or to circle one group. There is no real advantage to a split ticket; it simply allows you to play two or more games on the same piece of paper. One disadvantage to the split ticket is that you cannot use the same number more than once.

**KENO**

| MARK NO. OF SPOTS OR WAYS PLAYED | NO. OF GAMES | TOTAL PRICE |
|---|---|---|
| *2/5* | *2* | *4 00* |

| | | | | | | | | | |
|---|---|---|---|---|---|---|---|---|---|
| 1 | 2 | X | 4 | 5 | 6 | X | 8 | 9 | 10 |
| 11 | X | 13 | 14 | 15 | 16 | 17 | 18 | 19 | 20 |
| 21 | 22 | 23 | 24 | X | 26 | 27 | 28 | 29 | 30 |
| 31 | 32 | X | 34 | 35 | 36 | 37 | 38 | 39 | 40 |
| 41 | 42 | 43 | 44 | 45 | X | 47 | 48 | 49 | X |
| 51 | 52 | 53 | 54 | 55 | X | 57 | 58 | 59 | 60 |
| 61 | 62 | 63 | 64 | 65 | 66 | 67 | X | 69 | 70 |
| 71 | 72 | 73 | 74 | X | 76 | 77 | 78 | 79 | 80 |

■ **Playing a split ticket** *won't increase your chances of winning; in fact, the odds are lower as you are unable to use the same number twice.*

## KENO

| MARK NO. OF SPOTS OR WAYS PLAYED | NO. OF GAMES | TOTAL PRICE |
|---|---|---|
| 1/3  1/4  1/7 | 1 | 3ºº |

# Combination ticket

A combination ticket is a versatile and complicated ticket that combines unequal groups of selected numbers to form various combinations, or ways. The final result is really a ticket that combines many different types of tickets into one, and plays them simultaneously. The alternative would be to mark separate tickets and pay $1 for each.

For example, let's suppose you want to play the top three numbers as a 3-spot, the bottom 4 numbers as a 4-spot, and the whole ticket as a 7-spot. After marking your seven numbers, draw a thick line separating the three top numbers and the bottom four. Then, on the right margin of the ticket, you write, "$3"; below that write, "1/3," which is shorthand for one 3-spot; below that write, "1/4," which means one 4-spot; and below

■ **A combination ticket** *is a complicated ticket that is formed, as the name implies, by combining different types of ticket into one.*

that write, "1/7" for one 7-spot. Below that you would write "$1," indicating that you are betting $1 on each of those combinations. This is actually three separate wagers, and if you win you will be paid off as if you had submitted three separate tickets. This type of ticket allows the player to spread money over more combinations.

# King ticket

A ticket that contains a single circled number is called a king ticket. This single circled number is combined with other groups of circled numbers making a way ticket – it is never played alone. This combination gives you the most versatile of all tickets. A king gives you more "ways" to catch a group of numbers.

■ **The king ticket** *gives you a variety of combinations, and provides you with one of the best and most powerful ways to win at keno.*

King spot

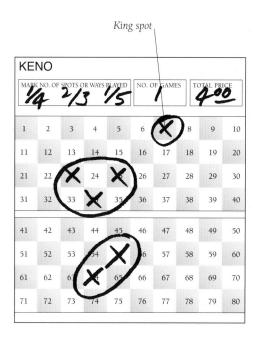

# Special ticket

In addition to all the normal options that are available to you when playing keno, casinos present special offers, bonus games, progressive jackpots, and other interesting and unusual games in the hope of drawing you to their facility. Late at night, when the casino is nearly empty, special "night owl" games are run for customers who might be coming off the swing or graveyard shift. These include special reduced rates with bigger payouts. The only problem with these specials is that the house odds are increased, unknown to the player.

■ **As well as being an interesting** *and diverting game in its own right, keno allows you to sit down, relax, and take some time out from some of the more stressful games in the casino.*

# Playing strategy

KENO IS A GAME OF CHANCE. *Numbers come and go, and sometimes numbers repeat themselves for no good reason. Other times, specific numbers will not show up for long periods of time. The best advice of all is not to "fall in love" with any specific number. Each casino, each day, and each session should be treated as a new and separate event from your last one.*

*If you are not sure what numbers to play, many casinos have a quick-pick option. With this option, the computer selects the numbers for you. All you need to do is decide how many numbers you want.*

## Playing favorite numbers

Lots of people will pick their favorite single number, or perhaps two numbers that represent a birthday. These are not good selections. A one-spot win pays 3 to 1, but the real odds are 4 to 1. The same is true for a 2 spot: Casinos will pay you 12 to 1 on a 2-spot win, which might sound good, but the true odds in this case are 16 to 1.

## Playing the 3 spot

When it comes to the 3 spot, things start to look better. If you hit two of the three numbers, you get your money back. Hitting all three will win you a payout of 42 to 1 (and maybe a little more, in some places). A straight 3-spot ticket can be profitable. For example, using a bankroll of, say, $60, you can bet $3 on 3-spot tickets for a total of 20 games.

**INTERNET**

www.thegamblersedge. com/keno/kenoodds.htm

*This site shows the number of spots you can play, up to 15. You'll see both the probability of each numerical outcome and the odds against that outcome.*

*Hitting a few 2-spot wins will get you some funds back, but hitting just one 3-spot in any one of the 20 games will get you $126 to $132 back, which doubles your initial investment.*

Also, it will take 3½ to 4 hours to get through 20 games, which can add up to a leisurely and fun afternoon of gaming.

## Playing way tickets

Most casinos will allow you to wager half the normal rate when you play 3-ways or more. Why would a casino let you do that? Because playing those types of tickets gives them a better chance to get your money before you get theirs.

When you first begin to play, watch five to ten games, and plot the 20 numbers drawn for each game. Or you can ask the keno writer for the results of the last ten games. He will normally print them out for you. This will give you some idea of which numbers seem to be repeating. Just like any mechanical device, the keno gooseneck and balls are subject to fair wear and tear. You might find a biased game with repeatable numbers. If so, you might want to consider playing those numbers during the next session.

## Some general playing strategies

You might not always win when playing keno; that's why they call it gambling. So think in advance about what you are going to do when the time comes to play. Establish your plan, including what you will budget, and stick to it. Don't go to the extreme and play or bet foolishly. Consider the following tips:

1. More often than not, keno numbers tend to run in groups. Therefore, it is better to group your numbers, rather than mark just straight tickets.

2. Be alert for short-term streaks, which seem to appear frequently. Go to the keno lounge and ask for a printout of the last 10 games. Study the numbers that have been drawn and look for any trends.

3. When you are first starting to play the game, limit yourself to three or four numbers.

4. Bet a maximum of ten numbers, and then only bet them as a way ticket.

5. A good rule to follow is this: Don't bet on a ticket that won't pay out for at least the price of five new games if you win.

### Trivia...

*Recently, a Canadian casino was "hit" for a fair amount by a player who noticed the machines always produced the same numbers in the morning. Basically, the machine would start from a given spot, and then produce random numbers from there on. However, unbeknown to the programmer, the casino turned the machine off every night when it closed. So in the morning the Random Number Generator (RNG) would always start off from the same base, instead of keying off something truly random. The player discovered the secret, but eventually got too greedy. He hit too many jackpots, and the casino uncovered the problem.*

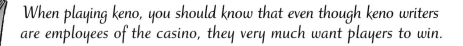

*When playing keno, you should know that even though keno writers are employees of the casino, they very much want players to win.*

If you are having trouble trying to figure out a play, such as a special way or some other combination, the runner will be happy to help. They are always courteous, friendly, and helpful, hoping you'll remember them with a tip if you become a big winner later on.

# A simple summary

✔ Keno has been around in one form or another for thousands of years. The Chinese are given credit for inventing the original game, called Chinese Lottery, which they brought to America in the mid-1800s. The game was changed considerably in the 1930s so that it would be easier for Americans to play.

✔ The game is a simple and leisurely one, requiring you to pick only 20 of 80 numbers. It can be played in the quiet of the keno lounge or from almost any other area in the casino.

✔ You, the player, should mark your ticket using only the special crayons provided. Tickets with errors that are not corrected before the start of the next game will be read as issued. Winners are only paid upon presentation of computerized marked tickets.

✔ Keno writers are available for your convenience. Ask them for help if you're not sure of how to mark or price your ticket. They will also post your ticket at the keno lounge for you.

✔ There are lots of different ways to play the game, but in no case will they change the house advantage. However, playing different ways does help increase your chances of hitting some or all of your numbers.

✔ Have a plan before you begin to play. The plan should not only tell you what types of games you will play, but also what your budget will be for that keno session.

✔ Always go to the keno writer booth on complex, combination, and king tickets to make certain that they are correctly "conditioned."

# Chapter 16

# *Bingo*

THERE IS A SAYING: "Bingo is more than a game . . . it's a way of life." You'll find that motto to be true as you experience the game. Bingo can be traced back to 16th-century Italy, when the state-run lottery (Lo Giuoco del lotto d'Italia) was inaugurated. Lotto migrated from Italy to France in the late 1700s, in a form that was similar to the bingo we know today, with a playing card, tokens, and numbers that are read aloud. Today bingo is actually a form of lottery, but the cards cannot be purchased or played outside the bingo hall, and the player must be present to hear the numbers that are drawn and cover them on the card.

## In this chapter...

✓ The game

✓ What are your chances?

✓ Improving your odds

✓ Playing better bingo

✓ Where can you play?

BINGO: A GAME RECOGNIZED THE WORLD OVER

# The game

*BINGO CAN BE PLAYED* in casinos, veterans' halls, on cruise ships, and even in church meeting halls. On Indian reservations all across America, Bingo has become a game with very large jackpots, and a very big business. No matter where it is played, the game is basically the same. The only difference you will encounter will be the equipment used to house and draw the balls, and the materials used to record your individual results.

## Bingo balls

In Bingo, 75 numbered Ping-Pong balls are housed in a metal cage or a glass-plastic blower, which is spun around to ensure random selection of the balls. After a ball is selected, the caller announces the number and places it in a separate rack so that number cannot be called again during that specific game.

## The card

A standard bingo card has 24 numbers, out of a total of 75 possible game numbers (in the UK and Australia they play with 90 numbers). Across the top of the five columns are the letters B, I, N, G, and O. In the center of the card is an empty, or free, space. The numbers 1 through 15 are listed under B; 16 through 30 fall under I; 31 through 45 come under N; 46 through 60 are listed under G; and 61 through 75 fall under O. Players cover each number as it is called by the caller.

■ **Bingo cards** *may vary slightly from venue to venue and country to country, but the aim is basically the same: to mark off the winning numbers as they are called out.*

Bingo cards can be either the paper throwaway type or the permanent type: hard-plastic or cardboard with sliding windows over each number. With the throwaway type, each card will have different numbers for every game, whereas the permanent cards can be used over and over, for all the games.

# WINNING CARD PATTERNS

The most basic bingo patterns are straight horizontal, vertical, and diagonal lines. Another simple and popular winning pattern is the "blackout," or "coverall," which requires you to cover the entire card. Letters such as H, C, or T, and special patterns such as "corners," "outside square," or "checkers" are also common patterns you will see during any given session. The caller usually starts off with simple patterns, and then moves on to more elaborate patterns (or to his or her favorite patterns). The caller always identifies the column letter first, followed by the number, as each ball is selected. For example, typical calls will be read as follows: G-55, I-24. The free square is automatically covered, regardless of the pattern selected. Below are an assortment of winning patterns that can be selected for a particular game.

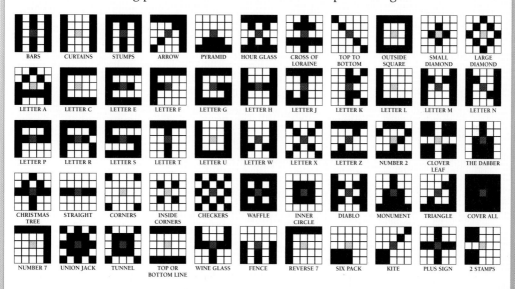

BARS · CURTAINS · STUMPS · ARROW · PYRAMID · HOUR GLASS · CROSS OF LORAINE · TOP TO BOTTOM · OUTSIDE SQUARE · SMALL DIAMOND · LARGE DIAMOND

LETTER A · LETTER C · LETTER E · LETTER F · LETTER G · LETTER H · LETTER J · LETTER K · LETTER L · LETTER M · LETTER N

LETTER P · LETTER R · LETTER S · LETTER T · LETTER U · LETTER W · LETTER X · LETTER Z · NUMBER 2 · CLOVER LEAF · THE DABBER

CHRISTMAS TREE · STRAIGHT · CORNERS · INSIDE CORNERS · CHECKERS · WAFFLE · INNER CIRCLE · DIABLO · MONUMENT · TRIANGLE · COVER ALL

NUMBER 7 · UNION JACK · TUNNEL · TOP OR BOTTOM LINE · WINE GLASS · FENCE · REVERSE 7 · SIX PACK · KITE · PLUS SIGN · 2 STAMPS

*When playing different patterns, use a pencil or pen to outline the specific game pattern you are playing. Placing a pattern outline on the bingo page will help you remember which specific pattern you need to win. This can be very important, particularly when you are playing an exciting jackpot game.*

## Selecting cards.

If you select a single card, you will have a total of 24 numbers to play, plus the free spot in the center. This means that out of the 75 numbers that could be called, 51 will not help you.

You can normally select as many cards as you want to play, but you will be charged a fee for each card you play. Also, playing multiple bingo cards can be very difficult, particularly for a newcomer. You have to check each card to find out if you have a called number and if it is in the correct pattern – all before the next number is called.

> *When you first start to play bingo, don't play more than one or two cards. Consider this early period as your learning time.*

### The best cards

Once you are comfortable playing with one or two cards, you can increase the number to better your chances of winning. Optimally, you can play four cards, which will enable you to cover all 75 numbers. To do this, you'll need to have all 15 numbers under each letter of bingo on your cards. To accomplish this, pick out two cards. Examine them to see if any duplicate numbers are present. If so, eliminate one of the cards. Keep doing this until you get two cards without any duplicate numbers. Then, use the same method to select a third card. With the fourth card, the process is very simple: all you have to do is find a card with a total of three missing numbers. You now have accounted for all 75 numbers, and the more numbers you cover, the better your chance of winning.

When you have your four cards, you no longer need to be concerned about certain numbers coming up more than others. You don't worry if some balls are weighted more than others, or if any balls have holes or cracks in them. No matter what number is called, you'll have it. Your chances of winning a straight bingo, four corners, or even a coverall are much greater because you have 75 numbers on your four cards.

> *Don't play in any bingo parlor or hall that will not let you pick your own cards.*

**INTERNET**

dir.clubs.yahoo.com/ games/bingo/index.html

*This fun site for bingo lovers links to 20 bingo club sites. There are clubs for bingo-holics, phone numbers for each club, and chat rooms.*

■ **You may be more likely to win some serious prizes** *once you've got the hang of playing four or more cards; but remember, no matter how large the stakes, bingo is essentially a game played for fun.*

## Things that help

I suggest that you get to the bingo area at least 30 minutes before any games begin. Bingo players are known as a serious group, and many will reserve seats for every session. If you get there early, not only will you be able to select a seat that will allow you to see the flashboard clearly, you'll have time to select your individual cards.

Get any required drinks or food before any game begins. Make sure that you have a marker, or *dauber*, and some other type of marker to help indicate the different patterns on your cards as each different game is played. A typical session will include 10 to 15 individual games and can last for 2 to 3 hours.

It's important that you pay attention to the pattern that's being played. You only need the numbers that form the pattern to win the game. Some patterns are much easier than others to complete.

**INTERNET**

**www.bingobugle.com**

*The site for the newspaper Bingo Bugle, which claims to be the largest gaming publication in the world, includes online games, links, a local game finder, bingo astrology, and an advice column for bingo players called "Aunt Bingo."*

# What are your chances?

TO FIGURE THE ODDS OF ANY GAME, *you have to know how many game cards have been issued. If 200 people are each playing five cards, there are 1,000 cards in play. Thus, with one card, you have a 1 in 1,000 chance of winning. If you play five cards yourself, your odds increase to 5 in 1,000.*

Coverall is the most popular jackpot game. To win at coverall, all 24 numbers on one card must be called. It's inevitable that someone will cover all the numbers; so, the important thing (which leads to the big payoff) is that you do it with a minimum amount of called numbers.

*The big prizes for coverall will normally require that the game be completed in 50 numbers or less. If no one gets bingo in 50 draws, a smaller consolation prize is normally given as additional numbers are drawn.*

## Random cards

When you pick three random cards, you will find an average of 23 duplicate numbers. When you include the three free spaces, you end up with 26 missing numbers on the three cards. This adds up to a total of only 49 different numbers on the three cards. So, now you know one reason you have not been winning on those 50 number coverall games: you have been playing bingo with only 49 numbers. So, you should pick cards carefully rather than take them at random. It will greatly increase your chances of winning.

### Trivia...

*Edwin Lowe, the originator of the game "Lowe's Bingo," sought the services of Carl Leffler, a mathematics professor at Columbia University. Lowe wanted Leffler to increase the number combinations for his game. So, in 1930, Professor Leffler devised 6,000 bingo cards with nonrepeating number groups. It is said that after successfully completing the task, he went insane.*

## Favorite numbers

Try not to pick your favorite number on each card you are playing. For example, let's say your favorite number is 17, so you pick four cards that have 17 on them. You can expect 17 to come up only once in every 4.5 games with 500 cards out. With 1,000 cards in play, your number will come up once in every five games. Thus, using the four-card selection method previously discussed, you know it's all right to pick one card with your number, but no more than one.

# Improving your odds

BECAUSE BINGO IS A GAME OF CHANCE, *it can be very difficult –
but not impossible – to improve your chances of winning any specific game.
The following sections detail a few things that can help improve your odds.*

## Tracking numbers

One method of tracking numbers is to keep a separate sheet of paper,
recording all numbers that have been called during one entire session.
After at least five sessions, you will begin to see some numbers more
than others. Then, on your next bingo visit, try to select cards with those
numbers that come up more frequently. This can be a long and
tedious process, but some serious bingo players have been
known to use this method regularly, and to good effect.

### INTERNET

**www.bingoseek.com**

*This very large site features a
search engine with more than
1,100 different bingo-related
links, including directories,
bingo news, overseas bingo,
online bingo, general bingo
information, bingo suppliers,
bingo cruises, and more.*

## When to play

If you like to play bingo but
never seem to win, try playing at
the most unpopular times of the
day, and on the least popular days
of the week. There will be fewer
players, so you'll stand a much
better chance of winning. Ask the
staff at the casinos and bingo
halls when their slow times are; it will help you to know
the specific days and times when it's not very crowded.

## Trivia...

*The most cards played by
one player in a single game
was 346. The individual was
playing in Pacific Beach,
California, on November 16,
1973. The numbers were
drawn at roughly 30-second
intervals.*

■ **The more people** *playing
alongside you in the bingo hall
or casino, the more competition
you'll be up against for the
winning prizes, so plan to avoid
the most popular times of day.*

# Playing better bingo

*BINGO EXISTS IN A WORLD all of its own. You can play it for fun, you can become a serious player, or you can totally emerge yourself in it. I recommend that you use it as a source of fun and entertainment, a place to meet people and have some enjoyable experiences.*

## ETIQUETTE

Following is some friendly advice for bingo players. It deals with the bingo rules of etiquette that will help make playing a more enjoyable and friendly experience for all.

1. Don't jump ahead in line for your bingo cards or refreshments. Be polite and wait your turn.

2. If someone attends bingo every week and prefers to sit in the same seat each time, don't be rude or upset if he or she asks you if you wouldn't mind moving. Let her have her "special seat," and you sit somewhere else.

3. Don't hog an extra chair for your belongings. If someone else needs that chair, give it up.

4. Don't spread your bingo cards and belongings all over the table so no one else can sit there. Leave space for others.

5. Be a good player and keep your conversation down during bingo play; this will allow others to hear the numbers without having to ask that they be repeated.

6. Don't be angry if someone else wins a game. Consider it their lucky night, and wait for yours.

7. Don't yell at the caller or ticket sellers. Remember, at local bingo halls these people volunteer their time so you can enjoy the bingo event. (You can yell at the casino, though, because they pay the callers.)

## Money management

Never spend more than you can win! This sounds simple, and you probably can't imagine how you could overspend. But the concept is not really based on a dollar-per-dollar criterion; instead, a standard dollar rule for bingo should be based on a 30 to 1 ratio. For example, if the prize is $50, you shouldn't spend more than $1.65 for all the cards you select. You don't want to end up paying for cards with your winnings.

# Where can you play?

IN ADDITION TO CASINOS, *you can play bingo at many other places around the around the world. Veterans' clubs, schools, churches, grange halls, and fraternal groups often use bingo as a fund raiser. Some facilities will house a maximum of 100 players; others will seat many more (such as the Foxwoods Native American casino in Leyland, Connecticut, which has a bingo hall that seats 3,000). In Britain, bingo clubs can be found all over the country, some of which have been specially built in recent years while others are converted theaters or dance halls. You will also find this fun game in South Africa, Asia, Australia and New Zealand. There is no question that bingo is popular worldwide.*

■ **These bingo players** *in the Himalayas demonstrate the global appeal of the game; they also reveal how a spacious hall or electronic display board are not essential requirements for a fun game of bingo.*

■ **This large, modern** *bingo hall with its brightly colored walls and plush furnishings is typical of many of the bingo clubs found in the UK.*

## Native American bingo

Native Americans on reservations have used bingo as a source of revenue for many years. They have bingo halls that will accommodate large numbers of players. They also have very large jackpots, which help in attracting hordes of bingo lovers.

## Bingo and cruising

The *Bingo Bugle* newspaper has been sponsoring a World Championship Bingo Tournament and gaming cruise for the last 12 years. They offer $200,000 in prize money, days and days of bingo, and the World Champion title for the finalist.

## Casinos

Many gambling casinos around the country and the world offer bingo on a regular basis. It is interesting to note that although Nevada has been known in the past to give away more prize money than it takes in (to lure potential gamblers), bingo in casinos is on the decline.

**INTERNET**

**www.bingo-directory.com**

*The Bingo Directory Yellow Pages of Bingo Halls is the most comprehensive and up-to-date listing of bingo halls in the United States and Canada. All bingo hall listings are verified every 6 months, making this directory perfect for traveling players.*

## Bingo halls

Throughout the United States, with the exception of Utah, there are scores of places that are devoted strictly to bingo.

*By reviewing some of the Internet sites and your local newspaper ads, you can find a bingo hall almost anywhere.*

Many of these halls will rent the facility and equipment out in total for fund-raising groups. The facility will take a commission, and the rest goes to the fund-raising group. Bingo is a great way to raise funds; people enjoy paying when they know they'll have fun and that their money is going for a good cause.

## A simple summary

✔ Bingo has been around for many years and is very popular in North America, as well as in many other parts of the world. It can be played in a variety of venues: from casinos to cruise ships to church halls.

✔ Bingo is played with 75 Ping-Pong balls. A specific pattern is selected by the caller from a wide range of available patterns, and balls are drawn until a player completes the pattern and calls "Bingo!"

✔ Bingo is a game of chance, but through careful card selection, a player can have a better chance of winning than if he selects the cards at random.

✔ Playing bingo for fun and following the accepted rules of etiquette and some money management techniques should result in a more pleasant experience for you and your fellow players.

✔ You can play bingo in the United States and Canada and in many countries around the world. Use the Internet to find halls and casinos that have bingo near you or your travel destination.

## Chapter 17

# Lotteries

L OTTERIES HAD A PROMINENT PLACE in the early history of America. In 1612 the Jamestown (Virginia) Colony was supported in England by a lottery that raised £29,000. Lotteries became the US government's standard method of raising funds for public works and higher educational institutions like Yale and Harvard. Despite these notable successes, in 1890 Congress banned lotteries due to the mishandling of funds and it wasn't until 1964, when New Hampshire authorized a lottery as a new revenue source for local education, that a second revolution of lotteries began. New York followed in 1966, New Jersey in 1970, and ten other states by 1975.

## In this chapter...

✓ Types of games

✓ Which one to play

✓ How to play

✓ What are the odds?

✓ Tips on playing

THE LATEST LOTTERY UPDATES HAVE LONG BEEN OF PUBLIC INTEREST

# Types of games

THE THREE MOST COMMON lottery games
are instant scratch-off, daily number, and a weekly
super jackpot game. To win the grand prize in a typical
lottery, you must buy a ticket and correctly match the
six numbers drawn randomly from, say, 49 numbers
(this is called a 6/49 game). The odds of your ticket
winning the jackpot in a 6/49 game are 1 in 14 million.
The weekly super jackpot lottery games are, by far, the
most popular, accounting for nearly 75 percent of
worldwide lottery revenues.

<table>
<tr><td>

**DEFINITION**

A **lottery** is a game of
chance whereby a small
series of numbers are selected
from a large amount
of numbers in a given
lot. Subscribers or players
who have selected the
correct numbers drawn
are declared winners.

</td></tr>
</table>

■ **All over the world, lottery balls** *are spun and drawn for daily or weekly lotteries, while ticket
holders watch TV screens or scour the newspapers to find out if their lucky numbers have come up.*

## Scratch-off games

Many states and countries have scratch-off games that are paid off on the spot. These instant games are launched regularly covering a variety of themes, designs, and play styles. To play these games you simply purchase a ticket at your market or lottery outlet store, scratch off the coating on the ticket and match the required symbols or numbers. You are normally paid on the spot if you win. If the winning ticket is over a designated amount, you might have to present or mail the ticket to the lottery headquarters to collect your prize.

## Daily lottery games

Many states and countries also have daily lottery games with prizes considerably lower than the big lottery jackpots. Some examples are Pick-3, Daily-4 or Fantasy-5. In these type of games you only need to pick three, four, or five numbers to win. The odds are greatly reduced, but they're still considered long shots. In a Pick-3 game you select one number out of 999 possibilities. For example, if you select 246, your odds are still 1 in 1,000 that number will come up. In a Pick-4 game you would have a 1 in 10,000 chance of winning.

### Trivia...

*Instant scratch cards, as they are called in the UK, have sold over £43 million per year since they were first introduced in 1994. They are the biggest impulse buying item sold throughout the UK.*

## Super lottery jackpots

The big jackpot games often go by the name of Lotto, Super Lotto, Powerball, or National Lottery. This is the type of game that produces the "instant" millionaires. This game is normally played once a week, but in some states and countries you will find it played twice a week. It is a very low-cost game normally costing little more than a dollar per ticket depending on where you live. If no one wins the big jackpot it normally rolls over to the next drawing and the prize total increases in value.

■ **Buying a lottery ticket** *takes only a few seconds and for many people is part of their daily or weekly routine.*

# Which one to play

TODAY, WELL OVER HALF *of the states in the US have lotteries. Some of the less-populated states have joined together to form joint lotteries with games like Powerball. In addition to the ones in the US, there are over 50 countries throughout the world that use lotteries to raise funds. In most of these countries the lotteries are at the national level, like the National Lottery in Great Britain. Canada has both national and provincial lotteries. It's been estimated that worldwide over $70 billion a year is wagered on lotteries games alone.*

Trivia...

*In the late 1700s there were more than 2,000 authorized lotteries functioning in the American colonies.*

## US lotteries

The lottery stands out in the gambling industry by virtue of several unique features. It's the most widespread form of gambling in the US, and the only form of gambling that's a virtual government monopoly. At the present time 37 states, the District of Colombia, Puerto Rico, and the Virgin Islands all offer lotteries. Due to their generally good financial success you can expect more states to have lotteries in the future.

Trivia...

*It's a fact that it's against the law to operate a lottery in the state of Nevada.*

## Multistate lotteries

Powerball is a multistate lottery designed to generate funds for some of the smaller-sized states. Twenty states and the District of Columbia presently participate in this joint program. In addition to picking all six numbers, there are eight other ways to collect prizes ranging from $1 to $100,000.

*The odds of winning a little something from a Powerball game have been rated as 1 in 35. The odds of hitting the super Powerball jackpot are estimated to be 1 in 80 million.*

## Foreign lotteries

It's illegal for US citizens to participate in a foreign lottery using the US Postal Service. A federal statute prohibits mailing payments to purchase any ticket or chance in a foreign lottery. You can use private mailing sources such as FedEx or UPS. First-time offenders convicted of knowingly violating the US postal anti-lottery statute can face penalties of up to a $1,000 fine and 2 years in prison.

■ **The sight of an old woman** *selling tickets on a bench in the town square is still very much a part of Spain's lottery tradition, despite the fact that anyone can enter the Spanish lotteries online.*

Most foreign lottery solicitations sent to the US and other countries do not come from the official government lottery agencies. Instead, they come from "bootleggers" who seek inflated fees to play these lotteries. Typically, when you pay the required fees you never see any lottery tickets issued by the government-operated lottery. You are left to rely on various forms of entry "confirmation" issued by the bootleggers. This is not a good way to play in a foreign lottery.

# How to play

*TWO FACTORS THAT MAKE THE LOTTERY so inviting to players are the low cost of a ticket and the simplicity of the game. You don't need to study odds, strategy, or a complex set of variables to win. You just put up your money, pick a few numbers, and take your chances. We know it's a long shot, but sometimes life itself is a long shot, so we play. There are really very simple steps you need to follow to get a winning ticket.*

1. **Choose your numbers** Normally the play slip has a number of boxes on it. You select your six numbers by marking them on the official slip. If you want to pick another six, you can normally use the same slip. You can also let the computer terminal randomly choose your numbers. To do this, you simply mark the "Quick Pick" or "Lucky Dip" box on your play slip or ask the retailer for a "Quick Pick" or "Lucky Dip" ticket.

2. **Pay the retailer** You pay for the amount of games you wish to play. Normally you can play one game or multiple games or even select future games.

**3** **Get and check your ticket** The retailer will enter your selections into the terminal and give you a ticket. It will have your chosen numbers and the draw date printed on it. You should check that the numbers you have selected and the day or days you wish to play are all correct.

*Keep track of your ticket. You will need it to claim your prize. Normally the ticket is the only proof required to be declared a winner.*

**4** **Look for the winning numbers** If six numbers on one of your selections match the six numbers that are drawn – in any order – you are a jackpot winner. You can also win a prize by matching five, four or even three out of the six total numbers. Sometimes there will be a seventh "bonus number" drawn. The bonus number gives you the chance to win the second highest prize.

## COUNTRIES WITH LOTTERIES

Whether bought at a newsstand, from a sole vendor on the street, or online, lottery tickets are still the most popular and accessible form of gambling for millions of people all over the world.

- Argentina
- Australia
- Austria
- Belgium
- Benin
- Brazil
- Canada
- China
- Christmas Island
- Cook Islands
- Cyprus
- Czech Republic
- Denmark
- Estonia
- Fiji

- Finland
- France
- Germany
- Gibraltar
- Greece
- Hong Kong
- Hungary
- Iceland
- Ireland
- Israel
- Italy
- Jamaica
- Japan
- Korea
- Liechtenstein
- Malaysia
- Netherlands
- New Zealand
- Northern Mariana Islands
- Philippines
- Poland

## Game objective

The objective of playing the lottery is to select a combination of numbers or symbols that match those selected, through a random process, by the governing agency. Each governing agency selects the total amount of numbers to be used in its various games.

## Collecting your winnings

You normally have 180 days from the closing date of the game to present the ticket to be declared a winner. There are some exceptions so check the rules. You can go back to where you bought the ticket and get a slip of what numbers were drawn, but again, you must have your ticket to claim a prize. Some states have special telephone numbers you can call to check winning numbers. Today many lottery agencies have Internet sites with current and past numbers on it. Don't lose or forget your ticket. And don't give up – check your ticket and recheck it, you just might be a winner!

- Portugal
- Singapore
- South Africa
- Spain
- Sweden
- Switzerland
- Taiwan
- Thailand
- Trinidad & Tobago
- Turkey
- United Kingdom
- Uruguay
- Vietnam
- Yugoslavia

### Trivia...

In 1994, the UK started a national, government-run lottery to compete with the various privately run games that existed in that country. By July 1995, 30 million people were betting £100 million a week on National Lottery tickets.

■ **Here, a woman buys** *a lottery ticket in Ho Chi Minh City; Vietnam's traditional paper lottery game has recently been updated to an online system with daily televised draws.*

Every lottery agency has millions of prize monies resting in bank accounts waiting for winners to collect them. People win and for many reasons don't collect their prize. Maybe someone was visiting a relative in another state and bought a ticket, but didn't check it because they left the state before the numbers were announced. People misplace tickets then forget about them altogether. Keep track of all your tickets.

### INTERNET

**www.lottery.com**

*All the current US states with lotteries are listed on this site. Every lottery number including current and past number results can also be found here. Winners' stories, the highest jackpot results, and the latest lotto news are also shown. You can even watch a video of the current and past Powerball weekly drawings.*

### Trivia...

*The National Lottery in the UK is unique among European lotteries because it is run by a private company rather then the state. Surveys have also found that 70 percent of the UK population have played the tax-free lottery at one time or another.*

## Record keeping

You should keep records of all your lottery playing. Just like other games you can reduce your taxable winnings by the amount of your losses. Keep losing tickets and record each play so that you will have good documentation in case you are audited. Good record keeping will also tell you how you have been doing, that is, whether you are having a good or bad year at gambling.

## THE TAX MAN COMETH

In the US, all lottery winnings are considered regular income and therefore you will be taxed on it. The lottery agency is going to withhold anywhere from 30 to 35 percent for taxes when they award you the big prize. Depending on how high your win might be in other games, taxation will vary from state to state. Remember, all winnings are required to be reported on your income tax return forms every year. The lottery agency will normally issue you a W2-G IRS form when awarding your winnings. A copy will also be sent to the IRS. Americans shouldn't be fooled by the Canadian or British lottery winnings being tax free. It's only tax free for Canadians and UK citizens. When you come home to the US you will pay taxes on all your winnings.

# What are the odds?

*LOTTERIES HAVE THE WORST ODDS of any form of gambling, with a chance of approximately 1 in 14 million when playing most lottery jackpot games. However, they also promise the greatest potential payoff to the winner with prizes regularly amounting to tens of millions of dollars.*

## Jackpots

Lotteries have several interesting factors. If the jackpot is not won on a given draw, it's normally rolled over into the jackpot for the next drawing. These rollovers can create jackpots in the millions of dollars. In addition, lotteries are pari-mutuel games, which means that there can be multiple winners on any game.

■ **Winner takes all?** *Unfortunately, most lottery jackpots are paid out over a few years rather than in one lump sum.*

Winning ticket holders will have to share equally the grand prize. Finally, a jackpot is usually paid out over 20-plus years. The advertised jackpot is naturally the undiscounted sum of 20-plus annual payments.

## Successful wins

The odds of success in lotteries do not seem that important to players. When interviewed, they don't seem to know the real odds of a lottery ticket. Researchers have found that once people believe that a low probability event can occur, they tend to overestimate the chances of it really occurring. The fact is that a small number of people do win and win large amounts, however, the overwhelming majority of players lose.

# Tips on playing

*IT'S REALLY NOT THAT SIMPLE* to *improve your odds of winning the lottery. In fact the tips I've listed and the ones I've heard about cannot help you select those winning numbers. There's no question that luck is the major factor when it comes to picking the right numbers in the lottery.*

## A few tips for better lottery playing:

**Trivia...**

*There is a joke about the padre who prayed very hard to win the lottery so he could help the poor of his church. One night after weeks of not winning, he was praying and asked aloud why he hadn't won. A voice came out of the heavens and said to him. "Buy a ticket." The moral here is, to win the lottery you must buy a ticket, if you don't you can never win.*

**1** **Game selection** You should choose to play the lottery game with the lowest odds, in other words the game with the smallest amount of numbers. Many states have various lottery games, ones with high jackpots and very high odds, as well as games with fewer numbers. The games like Pick-3 or Daily-5, which have only three or five numbers to choose from have much better odds for the player.

**2** **Number selection** Choose lottery numbers that have the best chance of being drawn. Most people would not bet on a horse without first studying its record. This is called "handicapping," which is the study of what has happened in the past to see how it can have an effect on the future. With the lottery, you analyze past numbers to help determine which numbers have the greatest probability of being drawn. Even though the numbers are chosen at random, randomly drawn numbers are known to form patterns that are predictable.

*You should know that research indicates the six consecutive numbers of 1-2-3-4-5-6 have never been drawn in any US or international lottery game.*

**Trivia...**

*Fate will always be your partner when it comes to winning the lottery.*

**3** **Probability** Play that which is most likely to happen. If something rarely happens in lottery drawings (such as a winning ticket with 1-2-3-4-5-6 on it), or if something has never happened before in the history of the lottery, common sense tells you not to expect it to happen just because you bet on it.

■ **No one can predict which numbers will be drawn,** *but there are ways of choosing your numbers wisely, like spreading your selection out between the high and low numbers and not sticking to birth dates.*

4 **Everything doesn't even out** Many people play a number because they think it's "due." They have the mistaken notion that in lotto, everything has to even out. That simply is not true. During one period in the New York lottery, number 45 did not show up in 100 drawings.

5 **Favorite numbers** Picking numbers from birth dates or anniversaries starts you out with a disadvantage for winning a game. This is because the month and day birthday numbers are limited to the digits 1 to 12 and 1 to 31. Your selections exclude the numbers above 31 and bias your ability to hit in over one-third of lottery numbers available.

**INTERNET**

**www.lottery.co.uk/results**

*Review this site for UK lottery results. They list all the past and current National Lottery winning numbers.*

6 **Number spread** Try and spread your selections evenly between high and low numbers. This will help statistically to balance your entry.

7 **Patience** When playing a given set of numbers that you have played for a long time, stick with them. Patience is known to pay off. Be sure you review past results to insure your numbers didn't come up some time in the past when you were away and didn't play.

■ **Beating the odds of 1 in more than 76 million,** *the Kainz family from Chicago won over $181 million by picking all six winning numbers in the May 2000 draw of the Illinois Big Game Lottery.*

**Software** There are a lot of computer products on the market with claims that cannot be relied on. No lottery analysis software can predict exactly which lottery numbers will be drawn in the next game. They will pick numbers for you but so will the lottery machine itself. They're fun, but don't bet on them.

## If you win

One of the most important tips you should note if you win a big lottery prize is to write or rewrite your will. Consult an attorney to write one as soon as possible. Future payments from a lottery prize will be treated just like any other asset, and if you die without a will, the state's laws for distributing your assets, including lottery prizes, may be very different from what you want. If your will has already been written, you may want to change some things in light of your new prosperity.

## A simple summary

✓ Lotteries are a very old form of gambling. Today, half the states in the US and over 50 other countries around the world have lotteries.

✓ Though the odds are very high, the cost of a ticket is very little; and that is what draws lots of players.

✓ The object is to select a given amount of numbers that exactly match those drawn by the lottery agency.

✓ Prizes can range from a low of $5 to millions of dollars.

✓ In the US, taxes must be paid on all lottery winnings; however, in some countries like Canada and the UK, lotteries are awarded tax free.

✓ Like other gambling games, spending some time "handicapping" past results can help in picking future winning numbers.

# PART FOUR

Chapter 18
*Horse and Dog Racing*

Chapter 19
*Sports Betting*

HARD WORK HAS ITS REWARDS ON AND OFF THE COURT

# SPECTATOR SPORTS

BETTING ON HORSES, DOGS, and people has brought great fun, excitement, and entertainment to gamblers for many generations. Knowing how to pick winners can also bring great *financial rewards*. Betting on sporting events is a billion-dollar-a-year business all around the world.

Sports betting is one area where the bettor can gain an advantage over the house. However, doing a lot of research and analyzing a great deal of information is essential for success. This research and analysis can take a huge amount of time and effort on the part of the gambler, but that's what's needed to be a winner. By picking one sport and concentrating on one area of that sport, you can become an expert and a *winning bettor*.

# Chapter 18

# Horse and Dog Racing

HORSE RACING GOES BACK THOUSANDS OF YEARS and is known as the "Sport of Kings." The Greeks turned horses into racing animals around 2500 BC, beginning with chariot races, and later moving on to horse races with riders. And horse racing has been popular in one form or another in Britain since the Roman invasion. But it wasn't until the 17th century that James I of England established a racetrack of the type we are familiar with today. The first official regulated race in North America took place in 1665, at Hempstead Plain, in New York state.

## In this chapter...

✓ Horse racing

✓ Before and during the race

✓ Betting the ponies

✓ Harness racing

✓ Dog racing

THOROUGHBRED RACEHORSES, LIKE THEIR CANINE COUSINS, ARE SUPREMELY FIT SPEED MACHINES

# Horse racing

TODAY THERE ARE BASICALLY
*three kinds of horse races:* **thoroughbred**, *steeplechasing, and harness. Thoroughbred racing is popular in many countries around the world, including Germany, Italy, Canada, France, Russia, Scandinavia, South Africa, India, and Japan.*

Steeplechase racing is found in many places in Britain and other European countries, but it's only found on a limited basis in the US. Harness racing, as we know it today, was originally developed in the United States, but has now spread to many other parts of the world.

■ **Horse racing is enjoyed by millions** *of people around the world, at the tracks, on TV, and in casinos. And invariably that enjoyment is heightened by betting on the races' outcomes.*

## Racetracks

There are 134 racetracks in the US, spread out over 35 states. In addition to the primary tracks, many others with limited racing periods are located at state and county fairgrounds. And there are hundreds of other racetracks all around the world, including some 59 throughout Great Britain, and 350 in Australia. Some tracks are familiar to the general public, such as Churchill Downs (home of the Kentucky Derby) and Epsom Downs in England (where the Derby is run every year). If you can't get to a racetrack, in the US you can go to a casino sports-book area in Nevada or Atlantic City and see and bet on races from all over the country viewed on satellite TV. A similar experience can be had in Australia at the TAB (Totalizator Agency Board) or in the UK by going to a betting shop. At all these locations, "betting the ponies" is accomplished in basically the same way.

### Trivia...

Britain's famous thoroughbred race, the Derby (pronounced "DAR-bee"), was instituted by the 12th Earl of Derby in 1780. Since 1784, the Derby has been run annually on the first Wednesday in June at Epsom Downs racecourse, outside of London.

## Racing oversight

Horse racing is more honest than many people suspect. Information about all horses' past performances is readily available to anyone who wants it. There is an American organization called the Thoroughbred Racing Protection Bureau, which is constantly on the lookout for any wrongdoing. Every race is supervised by track stewards. In addition, there is a lot of publicity associated with racing, and there are many journalists who are ready and eager to pounce on any suggestion of illegal practices – that'll keep them honest!

# Before and during the race

ALTHOUGH THE ENVIRONMENT *surrounding horse racing is fun and exciting, the race itself is very short. But everything that leads up to the actual running can be a long and very interesting process. Hardcore horse bettors spend a lot of time analyzing the before part of a race.*

These bettors want to know what lines, or parentage (the sire and dam), the horse came from; what jockey will be riding and what his record is; how the weather is; whether the track is "slow," "fast," or "muddy"; details about the races the horse has run in the past; what time the race will be run; and from which post position at the gate the horse will start. In some countries, studying this data is known as *handicapping*, and it is supposed to enable a bettor to best determine which horse will win.

### DEFINITION

**Handicapping**, *sometimes called studying the form, is the technique of collecting information about a race and using it to predict the outcome of the race.*

267

# FACTORS AFFECTING HANDICAPPING

Although predicting the winner of a race is not an exact science, betting on horse races is a game of skill – so the more you know, the better your chance of picking the winner. Taking into account the following variables can help increase your skill at predicting a winner in a specific race.

1. **Fitness** As with humans, horses must be in top condition to run their best. Handicappers will look for horses with recent race dates, which can be an indicator that the horse is in peak condition.

2. **Class** What class of competitors has the horse raced against recently? If its performance has been just adequate against a weaker class, it may not have the ability to win against a higher class of thoroughbreds. See if a horse is dropping or going up in class. Types of class include the following:

   - **Maiden races** Races for horses that have never won a race.
   - **Claiming races** A race for which any horse can be brought in to race for a specific amount of money. So, good horses are never entered in a claiming race. Note that these races also have the cheapest purses.
   - **Allowance races** The race is restricted to horses who have not won more than one race other than maiden or claiming races.
   - **Handicap races** Top horses are entered, but weights are added to each horse to help equalize the field.
   - **Stakes races** Races for high purses with better horses. These often have names such as the Golden State Derby or the Kentucky Derby.

3. **Distance** A horse is usually only good at short distances (under a mile [1,600 m]) or long distances (over a mile [1,600 m]), not both. Consider a horse only if it shows good past performance at the distance that is being run in the race you are betting on.

4. **Post position** Different tracks favor different post positions, but generally, far outside positions (10 and up) will produce fewer winners. Inside posts are usually favorable, but are not enough by themselves to help a weak horse.

5. **Running style** One of the most important and yet least understood and utilized techniques in handicapping is identifying the running style for each horse in the field. Horses usually fall into one of three categories: pace-setters, stalkers, and closers. If there are a few pace-setters, go with one of them. Seek out a stalker if pace-setters are either numerous or nonexistent in the race, and if there are no closers. Closers are

preferable when an abundance of early speed exists, but they are in general the riskiest bets.

- **Pace-setters** A front-runner or a horse that wants to stay within 2 lengths behind the front-runner or leader
- **Stalkers** A horse that is never more than 4 lengths back from the leader
- **Closers** A horse that is never closer than 5 lengths from the leader

6 **Trainer** The trainer can be an important factor in handicapping. Although a good trainer doesn't guarantee a win, you're probably safe discarding a horse that comes from a low-ranking trainer.

7 **Jockey** Don't underestimate the importance of the jockey. If the rider doesn't have an acceptable record, eliminate the horse.

8 **Present form** Horses tend to enter a period of peak performance, and then gradually slide down. Look at the most recent races to see if the horse is still at peak. If not, chances are it won't return to peak for this race.

■ **A good jockey** *is just as important as a good horse, and the best of these diminutive figures reap incredible fame and fortune for their efforts.*

9 **Consistency** A good recent history isn't enough unless the horse is consistently superior. Was that recent win luck or part of ongoing excellent performance?

10 **Weight** Some handicappers feel weight is an important factor, whereas others think 10 lb (4.5 kg) will hardly affect a horse that weighs more than 1,000 lb (450 kg).

11 **Speed figures** These are objective measures of how fast a horse ran each of its races. The higher the number, the faster the horse ran. The *Daily Racing Form* numbers are known as the Beyer Speed Figure. Note that these numbers can be useful, but they should always be considered in conjunction with other factors.

## Experience at handicapping

Horse racing is a game at which many players can and do make a living. It's difficult, but remember that it's a game of skill, not one of chance. Conversely, there are those who say that studying all these factors will only give you a hunch as to which horse might finish in the money. If all that studying leads only to a hunch, some argue, why not just bet based on the color the jockey is wearing or on the name of a horse? Regardless of how you choose to bet, though, betting on the horses can be fun – both before and during a race.

*Experience will give you the edge when it comes to picking winners.*

# Betting the ponies

AT A RACETRACK *or at a casino sports book, the smallest bet you can make is $2. For this $2, you can bet that a particular horse will come in first (win), second (place), or third (show). You can also bet **across the board**. In this case, you are wagering on all three results: that the horse will win, come in second, or finish third.*

**DEFINITION**

*To bet **across the board**, a bettor picks a particular horse and bets that it will come in first, second, or third. If the horse does come in on any one of these positions, the bettor wins the payout for that position, and all the positions after it. For example, if the horse wins, the bettor receives all three payouts: win, place, and show. If the horse comes in third, however, the bettor only receives the show payout monies.*

To bet across the board, you must bet a total of $6: You'll bet $2 that the horse will win, $2 that the horse will place, and another $2 that the horse will show. If the horse wins, you are paid the odds on each wager – for winning, placing, and showing. If the horse comes in second, you win both the place and the show odds. If the horse comes in third, you win the show wager only.

## Basic bets

The following bets are your basic win-type wagers. These are not exotic types of bets that require a lot of checking. You are only betting on those horses who will finish first, second, or third.

● **Win:** You pick one horse to come in first in the race.

- **Place:** Pick a horse to finish either first or second; if it does, you receive the money from the place and show wagers.

- **Show:** You pick a horse to finish first, second, or third in a particular race. Your horse must come in at least third (show) in order for you to collect a payout. In this case, you only receive the money from the show pool.

**INTERNET**

**www.stretchcall.com**

*Click on "Site search" and type in the word "bets." A list of relevant options will appear. Select "The Starting Gate" for an excellent betting tutorial, descriptions of payoffs, and some information on reading the daily racing program.*

Be aware that the specific bets you can make, and what they are called, vary from country to country. Familiarize yourself with the bets available in the country in which you will be placing your wagers. For example, in the UK and Australia they have a bet called "each way" that is similar to the American bet "across the board."

## More exotic bets

There are a number of additional bets you can place in horse racing. All are variations of the three basic bets. The following are all examples of exotic bets.

- **Daily double:** You bet on the first and second races (or, at some tracks, the last two races). You pick a horse in both races, and both must win for you to collect.

- **Exacta:** You pick two horses in the same race: one to win and another to place. They must finish in the order in which you chose them.

- **Exacta box:** You pick two horses to finish first and second in any order. You are betting only a $1 exacta box, but since you are betting two ways to win, this bet costs $2.

- **Pick 3:** You wager on three horses to win three different races.

- **Pick 6:** You must pick the winners of six consecutive races. This is a real long shot.

- **Quinella:** You pick the winners in the second and fourth races.

- **Superfacta:** You select the first, second, and third place horses in the last race of the day.

- **Trifecta:** You select the correct first, second, and third place finishers in any one particular race.

- **Trifecta box:** You wager on three horses for first, second, and third places, in any order. A $1 trifecta box will cost a total of $6 because there are six different ways you can win this wager.

## Picking favorites

About one out of every three races is won by the favorite. (The favorite is the horse on which the crowd bets the most money.) By simply betting on favorites, you can increase your odds of picking winners. Around 80 to 90 horses will race in nine or ten races each day, and there's often only one favorite per race. Just knowing this gives you an advantage, and should help you to pick about three winners per visit. Betting favorites is an easy method to use when it comes time to bet on a horse. Be careful, though: the public will sometimes create false favorites, long shots with little chance of winning. The odds should be high for these horses, but because so many people are betting on them, the odds drop considerably.

*As a general rule of thumb, very few horses that go to the post at odds of 10 to 1 (also written 10/1 or 10:1) pay off. Don't bet on them.*

Who will end up in the winner's circle doesn't depend on past performance; it depends entirely on what happens in a specific race, on a given day, at a given track, at a stated time, under specific conditions. Winning payouts at racetracks are very different from casino-game payouts. The most obvious difference is that with horse racing, the payouts are not determined until after the race. First, the track takes its percentage, and then the state takes its cut, and then the total of all bets is calculated by a machine known as a *totalizator*.

Trivia...

*Jockey racing silks originated in Newmarket, England, in 1762, as a method for distinguishing between horses during races. The US registry of silks designs is maintained by The Jockey Club in New York, and all owners who race in New York must register their silks there. In other states, the racing commissions have jurisdiction, but because many owners intend to race in New York, they apply to The Jockey Club before finalizing their designs. Thus the Jockey Club is officially and unofficially the arbiter of style when it comes to silks design.*

**DEFINITION**

*The **totalizator** is a sophisticated adding machine with inputs based on the state and track commissions, winning-horse prize monies, and other considerations. All the money that is bet on a particular horse is added to the equation. That information is then reported on the tote board in front of the grandstands as the win, place, and show payoffs.*

■ **It ain't over 'til it's over:** *Many a race is won right on the finishing line, and this phenomenon has given rise to the phrase "pipped at the post."*

## Some general rules

At most tracks, the traditional minimum bet is $2. Each track usually allows 30 minutes between races. However, with satellite broadcast races, there's almost always a race about to start somewhere, no matter what time of day it is. Before you begin betting on all these races, though, you should know that wagering on *pari-mutuel* events, such as thoroughbred, harness, quarter horse, and greyhound races, is not like wagering at a casino. Pari-mutuel wagering means that you and other bettors wager into common pools – not against the track.

## Strategy

There are two ways to become a good handicapper: by finding and using information that is not readily available to other players, and by developing a greater ability to evaluate the available information than other players.

*When you are learning to become a serious track bettor, you need to study the game in great detail. Review the books and web sites that are recommended in this chapter, and go to the track and practice handicapping before you make your first bet.*

## Placing your wager

Here is a simple four-step betting procedure to follow:

**1** **Pick your horse** You can rely on luck, or you can consider such factors as the horse's racing history, track conditions, and other handicapping information. Start your research with the Official Program and the *Daily Racing Form*.

**2** **Decide how much to wager** The odds for each race are shown on the large tote boards located in the infield, as well as on television monitors. The odds are constantly changing because they're determined by the amount that is wagered on each horse. Odds reflect what the crowd thinks of a particular horse. If the odds are low, say 3 to 1, a large number of people at the track think that horse will win. If a horse's odds are high, say 40 to 1, very few people think it will win. The less money wagered on a particular horse, the fewer people there are to split the winnings if that horse wins, and the larger the payoff will be.

> **DEFINITION**
>
> **Pari-mutuel**, *which is French for "to wager amongst ourselves," means that when you place a win, place, or show bet, your money goes into a pool. After a race, the pool is typically divided between the winners, the racetrack, and other entities, such as the horse's purse, the state, breeder's and owner's awards, and the jockey club. The track has no interest in the outcome of any race – they get their cut regardless of who wins.*

**Place your wager** The window clerk will need the following information when you place your wager:

- The track
- The race number
- The amount you want to wager
- The horse number
- The type of wager

(For example, "At Santa Anita, in the fourth, $2 on number 5 to win.")

**4** **Watch and win** From the track or the TV monitor, watch your horse run for the money. After the race has been declared "official," you can collect your winnings at any window.

## Where your money goes

Horse racing is a form of pari-mutuel wagering. The difference between pari-mutuel wagering and other forms of wagering is that with pari-mutuel wagers, you compete against other players, not the house. In casino-style wagering, the winners' money comes from the house. Therefore, the only way the house can make money is for players to lose. That's why all games in a casino are set up to favor the house. With pari-mutuel wagering, however, the people who select winning horses win money from the people who select losing horses.

## TRACK OR HOUSE EDGE

Between 17 and 20 cents of every dollar that is bet at the window goes to the track or house. This is the "vigorish," or vig, and it costs the player 17 to 20 percent at the racetrack or the sportsbook.

After the race, the track totalizator posts the results of the betting. It will look like the following table:

|  | Horse no. | Win | Place | Show |
|---|---|---|---|---|
| 1st place | 2 | 5.80 | 3.60 | 2.80 |
| 2nd place | 5 |  | 8.20 | 4.50 |
| 3rd place | 3 |  |  | 2.60 |

# Harness racing

SINCE ITS INTRODUCTION *at Midwestern state fairs, harness racing has become a popular spectator sport. With tracks in 15 US states as well as in 24 other countries, including Australia, the sport is seen by millions every year. In this type of racing, the horse pulls a driver and a cart, called a sulky. The horse must trot, not gallop, run, or canter. Hence the term "trotters," often used for harness-racing horses. Horses used in harness racing are called "standardbreds."*

## Handicapping harness racing

When it comes to handicapping the trotters, you'll find that the process is very similar to the one used in thoroughbred racing. You'll need to look at the class, speed, distance, post position, and the size of the track, as well as the age, weight, and sex of the horse. *The Daily Racing Form* and the racing program will provide all this information, just as in thoroughbred racing.

In 1976, the traditional sulky cart was redesigned by an aerodynamics engineer. The weight of the driver's legs and the sulky itself were moved from the horse's front feet to under the horse's chest. Since then, the horses' speeds have improved substantially.

■ **Once only run at county fairs,** *harness racing is now an exciting sport seen by millions of paying fans every year.*

# Dog racing

*SOMETIMES CALLED THE "SPORT OF QUEENS," dog racing, or greyhound racing, involves the racing of greyhounds around an enclosed track in pursuit of an electrically controlled and propelled mechanical hare. Dog racing is a 20th-century outgrowth of the older sport of coursing, in which dogs hunted by sight rather than by scent.*

In 1919, in Emeryville, California, Owen Patrick Smith demonstrated an electrically controlled mechanical hare, and introduced greyhound racing as we know it today to the world. In that same year, he opened the first oval dog track in Emeryville.

By the mid-1920s, the sport had spread as far east as Florida. By the 1990s, dog racing was a popular pastime in 15 American states, with 51 greyhound dog tracks. Dog racing is also popular in Australia, Belgium, China, France, Greece, Holland, Ireland, Italy, Mexico, Puerto Rico, South America, Spain, and the UK.

**INTERNET**

**nga.jc.net/ngatop.htm**

*The official site for the National Greyhound Association lists racing records, sire standings, race results, meet information, and information on buying a greyhound or obtaining a greyhound as a pet. It also has a small photo gallery.*

■ **Perhaps** *there is no need for the mechanical hares to be as elaborate as this one. The dogs will chase it whatever it looks like.*

■ **Dogs love to run,** *and in particular they love to chase small, furry things moving at high speed. So what harm does it do to have a little wager on the side . . . ?*

# Dog tracks

Dog racing in the US comes under the supervision of state commissions. Normally, eight dogs compete in each race, and there are usually 10 to 13 races in a program. Dog tracks in the United States are made of sand and loam, and are normally quarter of a mile (400 m) long, while some races are five-sixteenths (500 m) or three-eighths of a mile (600 m). Before the race starts, the mechanical hare, or "lure," is set in motion in view of the greyhounds, who are confined in a starting box (or trap box). When the lure is about 20 feet (6 m) beyond the starting box, the dogs are released.

*As the race progresses, the lure is controlled so that it remains in front of the pack.*

If any of the dogs interfere with the lure at any point short of the finish line, the race is automatically declared null and void. Most races are now held at night, under lights, when more people are available to attend, which has greatly improved its popularity.

> ## Trivia...
> The National Greyhound Racing Club in England, founded in 1928, is the governing body of UK races. The club declared that race distances should range from 230 to 1,200 yards (210 to 1,110 m). Usually no more than six greyhounds run in a race in the UK.

# Handicapping races

Pari-mutuel betting is an essential feature of dog racing in most countries. Today, more than $3 billion a year is spent betting on greyhound races in the US alone. In the early years, a lot of hanky-panky went on, such as doping and dog substitution. But new regulations put a stop to those practices. Now greyhounds are registered at birth, their paw prints are put on file, and they must wear an identity disk at all times. Bettors like dog racing because each greyhound races twice a week, demonstrating their form over a considerable period of time.

> ## INTERNET
> ### www.thedogs.co.uk
> *Gone to the Dogs, the official British Greyhound Racing Board's web site, features the excellent "Guide to Betting the Greyhounds" pages. There's also a lot of good information about handicapping races.*

There are some differences in handicapping greyhounds versus handicapping horses. As in horse racing, with greyhounds you should consider class, form, speed, and trap draw (post position). In addition, you should consider a dog's age. As a rule, a male dog will reach his peak at 2½ years old, and a bitch will reach her peak around age 3. This is just a loose rule, though; some dogs reach their peaks when they are as young as 2, and then fail to improve any further. In handicapping, the weight of the dog can also be a factor. A heavier dog will get better traction, whereas a lighter one might "glide." Also note that there is a class system for dogs: A, B, and C, with A being the highest. You should find out if the dog is moving up or down in class. Finally, the trap draw is of vital importance in dog racing. It can be an important factor when it comes to making your final selection.

## Adopting a greyhound

There are dozens of groups around the world that have formed to promote the adoption of racing greyhounds. Rather then put down these fine animals after retiring from racing, these groups promote adoption. Greyhounds make excellent house pets and are reported to be very gentle around people and particularly children. You can find information about adopting greyhounds, as well as a list of agencies, at the Greyhound Project's web site (www.adopt-a-greyhound.org).

## A simple summary

✔ Horse racing can be found all around the world. Betting on thoroughbreds, steeple chasing, and harness racing is a multibillion dollar business in the United States and in other countries.

✔ The US has well over 100 racetracks in 35 states, providing thoroughbred and harness racing in addition to a limited amount of steeplechase racing. Steeplechase racing is more popular in the UK than in most other countries.

✔ Handicapping a race can be fun, but it can also be time-consuming. Analyzing all the factors will help you select the horse who is most capable of winning a specific race.

✔ With only a $2 minimum bet at the track, you can play a lot and not lose too much. You can also win a lot – if you know what you're doing.

✔ As with other gambling games, there are some basic bets and some long shots. Learn the difference. The main objective is to overcome the house vig of between 17 and 22 percent.

✔ Harness racing at night is very popular. Handicapping the trotters is basically the same as handicapping thoroughbreds, but there are some differences.

✔ Dog racing is a popular spectator sport and can be handicapped just like horse racing.

# Chapter 19

# Sports Betting

IF YOU ENJOY WATCHING BASEBALL, football, basketball, hockey, golf or tennis, or some other sport, you might want to consider wagering on your favorite team or player. However, your options will be somewhat limited, at least legally. At present there are only three ways you can make a bet legally on sports, and I'll talk in detail about these in this chapter. I'll also cover some of the sports you can bet on, how you can bet on them, and some sports betting strategies to improve your odds and help you enjoy your favorite sports even more.

## In this chapter...

✓ What is sports betting?

✓ What sports can you bet on?

✓ How to bet

✓ Sports betting strategy

IT'S NOT JUST TEAM SPORTS – MAYBE YOU'LL HAVE A STROKE OF LUCK BETTING ON GOLF

# What is sports betting?

SPORTS BETTING IS WAGERING *on professional or college football, basketball, baseball, soccer, rugby, hockey, boxing, golf, and some special auto and tennis events like the Indy 500 and the Wimbledon tennis championship. Where you live in the world will determine which sports you can wager on. In addition to wagering on the result, you can bet on many special or proposition bets, like what team will score the first goal and what will be the total points scored in a game. Some* sportsbooks *in the US (known as the* TAB *in Australia) will allow you to bet on international games like World Cup soccer. However, they normally only allow wagering on sports in the US. Bookmakers offer many betting options when it comes to wagering on sporting events.*

> ### DEFINITION
>
> A **sportsbook** *or* TAB *is a gaming facility designed and operated to accept wagers on races and sporting events. The how, when, and where you can make a sports bet depends on the laws of the state or country you are in when placing your wager.*

### Trivia...

*With millions of dollars wagered on all kinds of sporting events every year in Nevada, the so-called "big three" – football, baseball, and basketball – attract almost 92 percent of all betting action.*

## United States sportsbooks

In the US you can go to the state of Nevada, the only state with legalized sports betting. Secondly, you can call an 800 telephone number for an International sportsbook and make a wager with them. The third way to make a bet is via the Internet. Any other means of betting, at least in the United States, is illegal.

Presently, in the state of Nevada, there are over 130 licensed sportsbooks. You must be physically located within the state of Nevada to make a wager in one of these facilities. No bets can be accepted if made by interstate telephone. Sportsbooks in the US only accept wagers on sporting events that are listed on the boards inside their facility. These events, known as "board games," consist of major league baseball, NFL, NBA, and NHL games. College football and basketball games are also covered but for major division 1 schools only.

THE BETTING LOUNGE AT THE MIRAGE CASINO IN LAS VEGAS

## International sportsbooks

A sports bettor can establish an account, normally for a minimum of $1,000, in an offshore bank with an international sportsbook to make legal telephone wagers directly. You simply dial a special toll-free telephone number to be connected to an offshore sportsbook and tell them what you want to bet on. Most of these sportsbooks have operations in the Caribbean, with a few others located in England. As we go to press, I have found about 50 sportsbooks operating overseas with more expected over the next few years.

## Internet sports betting

Modern technology has made sports betting an in-home event. New Internet sports-betting sites seem to be coming online almost every week. There are many advantages of betting on the Internet. You can wager 24 hours a day, 7 days a week; you can do it right from your own home; and you can place wagers of as little as $5. The US federal and state governments have not been able to regulate or control Internet betting, at least not yet; therefore, you can still bet legally using your own computer. What will happen in the future for Internet betting remains to be seen. In the meantime, Internet sports betting is very much alive and accepting bets daily.

**Trivia...**

*In September 1995, in the storybook European country of Liechtenstein, the first lottery was started on the Internet. That specific event is considered the beginning of Internet gambling as we know it today.*

## Overseas bookmaking

Each country has different laws. In the UK sportsbooks are called betting shops or offices and are licensed by local governments. Currently, there are some 8,500 licensed betting offices (bookmakers) throughout Great Britain. You can make a wager on any sporting event such as football (soccer), rugby, tennis, and horse or dog racing in any betting shop throughout the UK. Football pools is by far the most popular component of sports betting in the UK, although this is not usually done in a betting shop. Bookmakers will also take different types of wagers besides sports bets. Events like who will be the next British prime minister or president of the United States, and who will win an Oscar for best picture, actor, or actress, all have odds and can be wagered on at any betting office throughout the country.

As in the UK, in Australia and Germany you place a wager in a betting shop. In France it is illegal to bet on sporting events. In Japan they bet heavily on motorboat, motorcycle and bicycle racing. Become familiar with what is legal and common where you live. Sports betting is one of the games that a skilled player can make great gains at and even one where you can make a living playing.

**Trivia...**

*Recently, British patrons placed bets with bookmakers totaling $350,000 on the outcome of the US presidential elections in the year 2000. Not surprisingly, both candidates were pretty evenly backed, with Bush just ahead. One bettor – believed to be living outside Britain – put £10,000 ($16,000) on a Bush win.*

# What sports can you bet on?

YOU CAN WAGER ON MOST *professional and college sporting events, with one exception: In Nevada you cannot bet on sporting events that take place within the state. In addition to the ones mentioned earlier, boxing is a major betting sport. Major golf and tennis events, along with some miscellaneous sporting events such as the Indy 500, are posted to the game board but not on a regular basis. Also you must be 21 to make a wager in a sportsbook in the state of Nevada.*

## Trivia...

*In the UK you can bet on almost anything, including when Elvis will show up and whether he will arrive in a UFO or not. In Nevada, you can only take bets on sporting events. Any other type of bet would be considered a publicity stunt and not taken seriously.*

## Baseball

Betting on baseball is only done with the professional American and National League teams. You will not find college teams posted to any game boards. Also in baseball, the starting pitcher is what decides the odds for a specific game, not the team itself. Normally, if you bet with a sportsbook, you limit your bet to the starting pitchers scheduled for that day. If a pitcher is withdrawn you are given the option of canceling your bet, which I recommend. Since betting on baseball is so dependent on starting pitchers, it would be wise to study pitchers and their records thoroughly as part of your handicapping program.

■ **In US Major League baseball,** *you might fancy a bet on home-run hero Mark McGwire and his St Louis Cardinals . . .*

## Football

All college division 1 and professional football games can be wagered on. The postseason playoffs and all bowl games appear on the game boards of the sportsbooks. From the first week in September until the Super Bowl in late January, there are over 250 pro football and more than 600 college games you can bet on each season. In both college and pro football the point spread is the normal criterion for betting on games. (I'll explain more about the various odds criteria used in sports betting later in the chapter.)

## Basketball

Similar to betting on football, in basketball you have the point spread, for both collegiate and pro teams. College basketball requires a lot of scrutiny since there are so many teams and so many games. Higher scores, coaches' relationships with players, and other variables can each have an effect on a team's play. On the pro side, travel is a very important factor. The team's cohesiveness and momentum also have a big impact on performance.

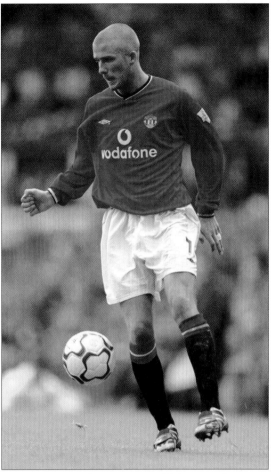

■ **. . . while in the UK,** *you could do worse than put a few pounds on all-conquering Manchester United in the Premiership, featuring sublimely skilled David Beckham.*

### Trivia...

*Sports betting can be found in at least 67 different countries around the world. Some are very small like Benin, in West Africa; others, like the UK, have enjoyed betting on sporting events for many years.*

*Pro teams seem to go on winning and losing streaks. Finding a team on a roll and starting to win big is an important item to consider when it comes time for you to bet on basketball.*

285

## Hockey

When the National Hockey League (NHL) increased in size through an expansion of teams, this sport attracted more interest and more gambling. Betting on hockey is similar to betting on baseball, where not enough points are scored to make a point-spread wager feasible and where many games end in a tie. Sportsbooks use a puck line, which is similar to the point spread, and a money line to establish hockey odds.

## Boxing

Boxing prize fights held throughout the entire world can be wagered on. The house edge can be higher than for other sports, so pick your bets carefully. Thanks to closed-circuit television, boxing still provides great entertainment and good wagering for both players and sportsbooks alike. Most, but not all, wagering is done on championship bouts. The heavyweight fights held in Las Vegas can bring lots of action and a big assortment of bets for the players.

# How to bet

*ONE IMPORTANT THING to remember about sports betting is that the sportsbook or casino doesn't make any money betting against the bettor. They make their money by providing two equally attractive betting options so that an equal amount gets wagered on both teams or boxers. Sportsbooks charge a commission on every bet made. The commission in sports betting, similar to other casino games, is known as the vigorish, or vig. To help equalize the betting, sportsbooks create a mechanism designed to make each team appear equal. They accomplish the equalization by one of two techniques: the money line or a point-spread system.*

■ **You won't find Australian Rules Football** *on the game board at Las Vegas casinos, but the sports- and gambling-mad Aussies enjoy betting on the game.*

# The money line

With the money line, or "line" as it is commonly called, a bettor is penalized for betting on the favorite. He has to bet more to win less. For example, if your favorite team is listed as 8-to-5 odds to win, you have to bet $5 to win $8. If your team wins you get back $13. (Your $5 + $8 = $13.) If you bet on the underdog, you bet less to win more. With the money line, the final score determines the winner and loser.

# Point spread

In the point-spread system, the winning bet is not determined by which team won the game, but rather by the final score. The system is designed to give extra points to the underdog, thereby, in theory, bringing both teams to a more equal balance. For example, in football, if the 49ers are favored over the Vikings by 11 points, as posted on the sportsbook board, and you bet on the Vikings, they can lose the game by 10 points but you still win the bet. The reason you win is that the 49ers have to get 12 more points than the Vikings to "cover the point spread." Another thing that can happen is for the 49ers to win by 11 points only. When the winning team matches the spread, the game is considered a tie, or "push," and you, the bettor, will get your entire wager back.

When betting the point spread, you always have to lay odds by paying $11 to win $10, no matter what team you bet on. This is the commission, or vig; and it's the method used so the book can make its money. In most sportsbooks, the vig is normally 10 percent, so if you want the 49ers to win, you must bet $110 to win $100. The point spread is used for football and basketball wagering.

# Over/under

Another kind of wager you can make on sporting events is an over/under bet. You are betting on the total number of points that will be scored by both teams during the event. You decide whether the final score will be over or under the amount posted on the sportsbook big board. For example, if the over/under posted score is 45, and the game ends with a score of 49ers 28 and Vikings 20, then you would win if you wagered over, because the total score was 48, three points higher than the over/under posted score. If the game ended at 20 to 16, with the combined score of 36, you would have lost if you bet over. If the score hits right on the O/U mark, it's a tie, or push, and all bets are returned. Football, baseball, basketball, and hockey all have over/under betting options.

There are marked differences in how you make bets from country to country and also across different sports. It's a good idea to ask for advice on making bets at your sportsbook or betting shop if you are unsure.

# Sports betting strategy

THE MOST IMPORTANT THING in sports betting is the research you do before placing any bet. The research is called handicapping, and it is similar to that used in horse and dog racing. Each sport has its own criteria for items to analyze. I'll try to list the important ones for each sport.

To overcome the bet-$11-to-win-$10 vig that the sportsbook imposes on all bets, you must win better than 52.38 percent of all your wagers to end up even.

## General betting strategies

Here are some strategies you can use to improve your odds.

*a)* To end up a winner you need to carefully weigh the pluses and minuses of the various factors (handicapping) involved in the sport you are interested in.

*b)* Select a few wagers that offer real potential for winning. Stay away from too many bets and the long shots.

*c)* Review the sports sections of your local newspaper or *USA Today* for information about teams and players.

*d)* Listen to commentaries by radio and TV sportscasters, especially ones who are former players and coaches; but be aware that they sometimes talk from the heart instead of the head.

*e)* When reviewing publications look at the statistics of pitchers, team performance, and results of playing both at home and on the road.

*f)* Pace yourself. No matter what sport you bet on, they all have long seasons. Spread your bets out so you can participate throughout the entire season.

■ **The NHL regular season** is 82 games long. That provides plenty of scope for betting – don't burn out too early.

■ **International special events, like the World Cup** *of soccer, won at home by France in 1998, are often found in Las Vegas sportsbooks. If nothing else, they at least provide the bettor with a little variety.*

*Don't make a bet just to have some action on a game.*
*If you don't like the spread or line, don't bet.*

## Bettor's advantages

Keep these choices in mind when choosing your bet.

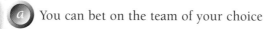 You can bet on the team of your choice

*b* You can analyze the data yourself

*c* You can pick and choose which game you want to bet on

*d* You can go with the selections of a professional sports handicapper or discard them

*e* You can decline to bet at all

**INTERNET**

**www.vegasinsider.com**

*Vegas Insider has the latest news about football, basketball, and hockey and lots of articles with the latest news on the various games.*

*Their free newsletter, delivered via e-mail daily, contains information on game odds, the line, sports highlights, and much more.*

# Handicapping

Sports handicapping takes quite a bit of work. By work I mean homework! You have to review past performances, team rivalries, home-team advantages, and much more. Here are some things to review and weigh before making a bet on your favorite team.

*(a)* Be alert to recent injuries, long road trips, home-field advantages, and weather; these apply to all sports.

*(b)* Start to specialize in one particular sport. To succeed as a sports bettor you need to concentrate in one sport and one specific area, like one league or conference.

*(c)* In baseball, identify the best pitchers along with the best team record. Look for batting order changes and be alert to winning streaks. The team that scores the most runs in the first inning will win the game 70 percent of the time.

*(d)* At football look for the best quarterback. He sets the pace. Look for teams that have a high first and third down record and the best running game. Research the best coach and the best win record at home.

*(e)* When betting basketball, the pros will play more true to form than college teams. Home teams should have a six-point advantage. Past performance and experienced players are a plus for any team. Look for team strength instead of one superstar.

■ **Big-time prize fights,** *like this one between Evander Holyfield and Lennox Lewis, are a sports-betting favorite, but be sure to find the best odds.*

*Trivia...*

*In 1991, the US Congress passed the Professional Sports Amateur Protection Act, which was designed to prohibit the spread of legalized sports betting. Instead, the measure allowed offshore betting outlets to grow by leaps and bounds and to become a major competitor for Las Vegas sportsbooks with each passing sports season.*

*Most sportsbooks don't set their own lines or odds on games. They buy lines from handicapping businesses that specialize in researching and establishing the lines of all sports.*

Las Vegas Sports Consultants, owned and operated by Michael (Roxy) Roxborough, is the largest sports-betting company. Sportsbooks and bookmakers worldwide subscribe to his service.

## Trivia...

*On November 14, 2000, during the regular basketball season, every NBA home team won its game that day.*

# A simple summary

✔ There are only three legal ways to bet on sports in the US: at a sportsbook in Nevada, on account with an international off-shore establishment, and on the Internet.

✔ In the US, UK, Australia, and other countries, you can bet on a variety of professional and, in the US, college sports. Outside the US (and occasionally in the US), you can also wager on auto, tennis, and golf sporting events.

✔ There are two ways that teams are evenly matched up for betting purposes: one is through the money line, and the other is by a point spread.

✔ In sports betting the house makes its money by charging a commission, or vigorish, on every bet.

✔ When betting, each sport is wagered on somewhat differently, and each has some special proposition bets available to the bettor.

✔ When it comes to betting strategy in sports betting, handicapping is the tool to use. Each sport should be analyzed a little differently, but for each you want to be able to make a clear judgment on what the outcome is likely to be.

# PART FIVE

CASINOS EUROPEAN STYLE

# WHERE THE GAMES ARE

GAMBLING IS NO LONGER looked on as a path to damnation. Today, casinos are considered *vacation destinations*. Casinos cater not only to the gambler but also to the whole family. It doesn't matter whether you are in Las Vegas, in Malaysia, or on a cruise ship, gambling has become an accepted form of entertainment by the general public.

Looking around the world we see more than 100 countries and 130-plus cruise ships that offer gambling. You can even gamble from your home by going on the *Internet*, a new area that's changing almost on a daily basis. It appears that, today, people not only like to gamble but like to do it a lot.

# Chapter 20

# Casinos

W ITH LEGALIZED GAMBLING IN OVER 140 COUNTRIES it's not difficult to participate in some type of gaming no matter where you are in the world. Casinos are located from Antigua in the Caribbean to Zanzibar in Africa and all points in between. The only continent without any organized gambling is Antarctica. Gambling has become big business throughout the world.

## In this chapter...

✓ Casinos around the world

✓ European casinos

✓ Asian and Pacific casinos

✓ Latin American casinos

✓ African casinos

✓ North American casinos

✓ Big people's playgrounds

FEW GAMBLERS CAN RESIST THE BRIGHT LIGHTS OF THE CASINO

# Casinos around the world

IN 1808 EMPEROR NAPOLEON *of France signed a decree authorizing a gambling establishment at the Palais-Royal in Paris. Many scholars recognize this facility as the first legal casino in the world. Similar to today's modern casinos, the Palais-Royal, located on 6 acres near the Louvre, had shops, clubs, restaurants, and cafes adjoining the casino to help entertain gaming clients. The gambling offered at that time included roulette, dice, and various card games. Later, casinos similar to the one in Paris opened elsewhere in Europe, notably in Baden-Baden and Hamburg in Germany, and in Luxembourg.*

**INTERNET**

**www.casinocity.com**

*This site has a casino directory for the entire world. You select location or type, and the site presents them in detail. You can click onto the casino site itself and get maps to its location, hours of operation, games offered, and more. The site also offers a gaming industry newsletter.*

The early French and German casinos were popular with the aristocrats and nobility. Later, in England and on the continent, "new money" from the Industrial Revolution began to appear at the casinos. Today, whether you travel for business or for pleasure, a visit to a casino can be an attractive choice for the international traveler. Many casinos are located in resort areas, and others are in major business and tourist cities. Europe, Asia, North and South America, Africa, the Middle East, Australasia, and the islands of the Pacific all have casinos with familiar games such as roulette, blackjack, baccarat, and craps. Some have games that are unique to their part of the world; others have poker games similar to those found in any card room in America. In many overseas casinos you need your passport to enter, and a small entry fee is commonly required. Later in this chapter you'll find a few interesting facts about some of the casinos around the world.

■ **By the early 19th century,** *gambling had became an official, organized, and legal activity among the aristocracy of Europe.*

# COUNTRIES WITH CASINOS

Casinos are everywhere. With over 140 countries operating casinos and the United States alone having over 500 of them, you don't need to worry about finding one to play, especially in locations frequented by tourists. Many countries view casinos as part of their tourist program.

**Europe**
Austria
Belgium
Bosnia
Bulgaria
Croatia
Cyprus
Czech Republic
Denmark
Estonia
Finland
France
Germany
Gibraltar
Greece
Hungary
Italy
Latvia
Lithuania
Luxembourg
Macedonia
Malta
Moldova
Monaco
Netherlands
North Cyprus
Poland
Portugal
Republic of Ireland
Romania
Russia
Scotland
Slovakia
Slovenia
Spain
Sweden
Switzerland
Turkey
Ukraine
United Kingdom
Yugoslavia

**Africa**
Benin
Botswana
Cameroon
Comoros Islands
Congo (Brazzaville)
Djibouti
Egypt
Ethiopia
Gabon
Gambia
Ghana
Ivory Coast
Kenya
Lesotho
Liberia
Madagascar
Mauritius
Morocco
Mozambique
Namibia
Niger
Nigeria
Republic of Congo
Réunion Islands
Senegal
Seychelles
Sierra Leone
South Africa
Swaziland
Tanzania
Togo
Tunisia
Uganda
Zambia
Zimbabwe

**North America**
Canada
United States

**Central America**
Costa Rica
Honduras
Nicaragua
Panama

**South America**
Argentina
Bolivia
Chile
Colombia
Ecuador
Paraguay
Peru
Suriname
Uruguay
Venezuela

**Caribbean**
Antigua
Aruba
Bahamas
Barbados
Bonaire
Cuba
Curaçao
Dominican Republic
Guadeloupe
Haiti
Jamaica
Martinique
Puerto Rico
Saint Kitts and Nevis
Saint Maarten
Saint Vincent
Trinidad and Tobago
Turks & Caicos Islands
US Virgin Islands

**Asia**
Azerbaijan
Cambodia
India
Israel
Japan
Kazakhstan
Kyrgyz Republic
Lebanon
Macao
Malaysia
Myanmar
Nepal
Philippines
Singapore
South Korea
Syria
United Arab Emirates
Uzbekistan

**South Pacific**
Australia
New Caledonia
New Zealand
Solomon Islands
Tahiti
Tinian
Vanuatu

# European casinos

MOST EUROPEAN CASINOS are located in resort areas and cater to business travelers and holiday visitors. The casino in the spa town of Baden-Baden, Germany, is typical of the type of casinos found throughout Europe. Built in the early 19th century, it is known as the oldest, richest, and maybe the most beautiful casino in Europe. However, perhaps the casino with the most elegant setting is the Monte Carlo Casino in the principality of Monaco. This architectural masterpiece overlooks the Mediterranean and dazzles visitors with its sculptures, reliefs, and a gold and marble atrium.

In the European Union, gambling is ranked as the 12th largest industry.

■ **Slot machines** *have had a place in the exquisite setting of the Monte Carlo Casino since the early 20th century and are as popular with gamblers as the more traditional European and American table games.*

# United Kingdom

Currently there are 120 casinos throughout the UK. The law authorizing casinos was only passed in 1960 and permits casino gaming only between 2 p.m. and 4 a.m. Some, but not all casinos offer baccarat, mini-baccarat, blackjack, roulette, Caribbean Stud Poker, craps, and poker.

All casinos in the UK are private clubs with membership required. An applicant must wait 24 hours after applying for membership before being allowed to enter and play. The minimum age is 18, and jacket and tie for men and appropriate dress for women is always required. (If you think your $125 running shoes will be okay, they won't. Casinos throughout the UK enforce a strict dress code.) Gambling on credit and tipping are prohibited.

Craps tables are only found in a few casinos in the UK. However, when you do locate a craps game, you'll find the odds more favorable than in US casinos. For example, a craps bet on 2 and 12 pays 33 to 1, not 30 to 1, and the 4 and 10 payout at 9½ to 5, not 9 to 5. You should find room at the craps table since the game is not a popular one with UK casino patrons.

*Trivia...*

*Slot machines in the UK are known as fruit machines, and casinos are limited to having a maximum of ten machines in any one casino.*

**INTERNET**

**www.british-casinos.co.uk**

*The British Casino Association site has lots of information including a complete listing of all the casinos in the UK.*

■ **The London Park Tower,** *like most of London's casinos, is situated in an area frequented by the more affluent tourist; many of the UK's provincial casinos cater more for the local player.*

## France

France has had legalized casinos since the 19th century. At present there are about 160 casinos throughout the country. Many are small, with the large ones located in the resort and spa towns. The minimum age to play is 18. Games include roulette, blackjack, punto banco, baccarat, and craps, and since 1987 slot machines have been allowed. Casino employees are not allowed access to slot machines; all maintenance must be performed by outside companies that do not participate in any way with the winnings of a casino.

French casinos have a dress code that ranges from "proper" to "casual," and an entry fee ranging from 55 to 75 francs ($10 to $15). The Casino de Divonne, a deluxe resort complex just

■ **The Casino de Deauville** is typical of France's more traditional casinos.

10 miles (16 km) from Geneva airport, is France's top money-making casino. It's almost an American-style casino with 280 slots, and 24 table games. One of France's more traditional casinos is the Casino de Deauville in Normandy, built in 1912 and popular among many visitors to Paris. It's interesting to note that 12 of France's casinos produce 60 percent of the total casino revenues because of their size and high number of slot machines. Most French casinos offer only low-stakes games.

## Germany

Germany's history of casino gambling goes back 200 years. Today there are 38 casinos in the country. As with many other countries in Europe, Germany has a dress code and a fee for casino entry. Gentlemen are required to wear jacket and tie, and women are required to dress appropriately. If you should forget to dress properly, casinos will rent men jackets to wear. The entry fee is usually in the range of 5 Deutschmarks, and the minimum gambling age is 21.

*German casinos allow other players to play, or piggy back, on your hand.*

While sitting at the blackjack table making your bets, other patrons behind you can bet on one of the four corners of your betting square. Those players are not allowed to talk or suggest how to play the hand, but if you win, they win, and if you should lose a hand, they also lose.

Most casinos, but not all, are located in spa towns or in popular tourist centers. The most famous casino in Germany, Baden-Baden, is also a world-class spa resort that just happens to have a very old and elegant casino.

Games in German casinos include blackjack, roulette, poker, and baccarat. Slots are also allowed but are normally located in a separate room or building away from the main casino. It's interesting that the machines have had their bells removed. What happens when a machine hits a jackpot? The lights flash, but it's very, very quiet.

■ **Many European casinos** *have a strict dress code, so if you're planning a gambling vacation to Europe make sure you pack appropriate items of clothing so that you can enjoy the experience fully.*

## Monaco

Monaco's four casinos are all within the city limits of Monte Carlo and under the direction of the Société des Bains de Mer et Cercle des Étrangers (Sea-bathing Society and Circle of Foreigners). The principal owners are Prince Rainier III and the estate of Aristotle Onassis.

### Trivia...
*J.P. Morgan, the noted financier and banker, was the only man who ever refused to play at the Monte Carlo Casino because the stakes were too low. The maximum bet at the time was 12,000 francs, and Morgan wanted it increased to 20,000. When Edmond Blanc, the manager, refused; Morgan shouted out, "12,000 francs! I have no time to lose such ridiculous amounts," and promptly left the casino.*

The most celebrated gambling hall in Monaco is the Casino de Monte Carlo. Ever since it was built in 1863, it has offered royalty, millionaires, and celebrities from all over the world the place to gamble and be seen. One of the early financial investors was Cardinal Pecci, who later became Pope Leo XIII. Louis Blanc, the original casino manager, started the first school for croupiers (dealers). He also designed the present-day layout for roulette. Speaking of roulette, in Monte Carlo the roulette wheels start spinning at 9.30 a.m. and are stopped at 2 a.m., whether or not anyone is playing the game.

■ **Pennies from Heaven:** *In his days as a cardinal, Pope Leo XIII was one of Monte Carlo's prime investors in the gaming industry.*

## Italy

There are only four casinos in the whole of Italy: three in resort areas and the other in Venice. The minimum age to play is 18, and a dress code of jacket and tie is strictly enforced along with an entry fee, usually about 15,000 lire ($7). Games include blackjack, baccarat, roulette, punto banco, poker, craps, video poker, and slots. Some casinos also host international bridge, backgammon, and gin rummy tournaments.

## Spain

Casino gambling in Spain was only legalized in 1977. Today there are a total of 22 casinos, 17 in the country, three in the resort towns of the Canary Islands and two in the Balearic Islands. The minimum age to gamble is 18, and proper dress is required. Spanish law prohibits casinos inside cities with populations over 300,000. Many are located in tourist resorts or even in old castles. Games include blackjack, craps, roulette, punto banco, baccarat, slots, and video poker.

■ **A taste of history:** *the billiard room of the Gran Casino in Murcia, southeastern Spain.*

## Russia

Though the gaming market is fairly volatile, with casinos opening and closing often, there are about 60 casinos in Russia today. Moscow has about 30, with 20 in St. Petersburg and the rest in the resort towns of Kosice, Novgorod, and Sochi. There's also one casino in Vladivostok. The games offered are blackjack, craps, roulette, baccarat, and slots. They do offer poker and have even hosted international poker tournaments. The minimum age to gamble is 21, and many casinos require an entry fee, usually $10. Some casinos allow only US currency to be used when betting.

# Asian and Pacific casinos

GAMBLING IS VERY POPULAR in Asia, and you'll find lots of casinos on the world's largest continent. Gambling has also proved popular in Australia and has been available in New Zealand since 1990.

## Nepal

All four hotel-casinos in this Himalayan land are five-star rated. Only foreign visitors over 21 years old may gamble in these casinos. Games offered are blackjack, roulette, baccarat, poker, video poker, and slots. Games not played in America or Europe are also offered, such as Kitty, Flush, Beat the Dealer, and Paplu. Most of these incorporate both cards and dice.

**INTERNET**

**www.casinosnepal.com**

*You can go directly to the Nepal casinos site and learn various games not normally seen in the Western world. They offer instructions on Kitty, Flush, Beat the Dealer, and Paplu.*

## Malaysia

Although Malaysia has only one casino, the Genting Highland Hotel, it is one of the largest in Asia, so big that it's divided into five main gaming areas. Games offered are roulette, baccarat, blackjack, keno, and slots.

*To discourage the local population from gambling, Malaysia's Genting Highland Hotel requires a passport and a deposit of $200 before allowing anyone in to play.*

## South Korea

At present South Korea has 14 casinos in 12 cities throughout the country. Ninety percent of the gamblers are Japanese. The minimum gambling age is 20. The government owns all the slot machines and gets its revenues from the slots and entry fees. The casino makes its money from the table games, which include blackjack, roulette, baccarat, mini-baccarat, keno, and craps.

### Trivia...

In East Asia, jade is a symbol of power. Casino employees who deal to customers are not allowed to wear any jade jewelry.

## Cambodia

This southeast-Asian country has three casinos all located in its capital, Phnom Penh. They offer blackjack, slots, baccarat, mini-baccarat, roulette, Tai Sai, and Pai Gow tiles.

## Macao

Ten casinos operate in Macao. They cater mostly to Hong Kong tourists. The legal gambling age is 18 for foreigners and 21 for Macao residents. Slot machines there are known as "hungry tigers" and are found everywhere in Macao. The grand Hotel Lisboa is almost a city under one roof and houses Macao City's largest casino with the widest variety of table games and slot machines on the island.

■ **Macao's Hotel Lisboa,** *with its 18 restaurants and 24-hour entertainment, is one of the largest and most elegant hotel-casinos in Asia.*

## Australia

Australians seem to have almost an obsession when it comes to gambling. They love to wager. There are 13 casinos scattered throughout the country along with some 350 racetracks. It seems as if every city and town has a racecourse. Some casinos are large, like the Crown Casino in Melbourne, while others are small by international standards. The games offered in these casinos are blackjack, baccarat, mini-baccarat, Caribbean stud poker, craps, poker, roulette, slots, video poker, and keno. Slots and video poker machines are known as "pokies" in this part of the world and are found not only in casinos but also in pubs and clubs throughout the country. In addition to the regular games found in most casinos, Australians also play two-up, dice track, big and small, and crown & anchor, all of which are coin and dice games.

### Trivia...

*Crown Casino in Melbourne is said to be one of the largest entertainment complexes in the world. It cost US $1.6 billion to build and has 35 food and beverage outlets seating 3,000 patrons. It also has 14 movie theaters, four nightclubs, 24 retail stores, and a 39-story hotel. It boasts 2,500 slot machines and 350 table games.*

## New Zealand

New Zealand officially approved casino gaming in 1990. There are four casinos presently operating: one each in Auckland, Christchurch, Queenstown, and Dunedin. The New Zealand Casino Control Authority has approved five additional casino licenses that will allow more casinos in the future. Sky City Casino in Auckland is a very large facility with 89 tables, 1,050 slots, and a 100-seat keno lounge. It has three separate gaming levels: Alto Casino for the general public, Sky City for members only, and a third level with admittance by invitation only. The casino games offered throughout the country are blackjack, roulette, baccarat, mini-baccarat, craps, big six wheel, Caribbean stud poker, Pai-Gow poker, keno, Sic Bo, video poker, and slots.

■ **Auckland's Sky City Tower** *houses New Zealand's state-of-the-art casino.*

# Latin American casinos

*GAMBLING IN LATIN AMERICA is very popular. At the present time there are more than 160 casinos in 13 countries. They include Argentina, Honduras, Costa Rica, Panama, Bolivia, Chile, Colombia, Ecuador, Paraguay, Peru, Suriname, Uruguay, and Venezuela.*

*Most casino staff in Latin American countries speak only Spanish. However, in most games, like blackjack, roulette, and craps, there's no language barrier since you can play successfully without doing any talking.*

## Argentina

Argentina has the highest number of casinos of any country in the area (25). The Central Casino, in Mar del Plata, is the largest, most modern, and most luxurious in all South America. With 108 roulette and 55 punto banco (baccarat) tables, it can accommodate 9,000 players at one time. Located 250 miles (400 km) south of

Buenos Aires, the resort town on the Atlantic coast is known as "the happy city" and has been a lively resort area for wealthy Argentines for almost 300 years. There is an entry fee of US $23 for this government-owned casino, and the minimum gambling age is 18.

## Chile

Chile has six casinos, most of which are small by international standards. However, the Casino Municipal Viña del Mar, overlooking the Marga-Marga Inlet on the Pacific Ocean, is the second largest casino in Latin America. This is where Chilean jet-setters come to play. The casino, located in an elegant 1930s building set in an ample beautiful garden overlooking the bay, has 200 slots and 74 table games.

## Caribbean Islands

Nineteen islands in the Caribbean have a total of 96 casinos. This is a very popular area for casino gambling, most of it done by tourists. All the popular games like blackjack, baccarat, mini-baccarat, roulette, video poker, and craps are offered. Nearly all the casinos have Caribbean stud poker, as you would expect.

The islands with casinos are Antigua (7), Aruba (12), the Bahamas (4), Bonaire (1), Curaçao (8), the Dominican Republic (13), Guadeloupe (2), Haiti (3), Jamaica (5), Martinique (2), Puerto Rico (16), Saint Kitts (1), Saint Martin (8), Saint Vincent (1), Trinidad and Tobago (12), Turks and Caicos (1).

# African casinos

THERE ARE 35 COUNTRIES in Africa with legal casino gambling. Many only have one casino in the whole country, usually located in an international hotel. Others have more, such as Egypt with ten casinos and Mauritius and Nigeria with eight each. The big tourist trade in these countries helps support the gambling enterprises. Even though some of the casinos in these African countries are small, they all offer the standard games like blackjack, roulette, baccarat, and slots.

South Africa has 12 full-service casinos and three slot casinos. The national government recently approved an expansion of gaming to 40 casinos located throughout its nine provinces.

# North American casinos

*MORE THAN 600 CASINOS can be found in Canada and the United States. You can literally visit a casino all the way from sea to shining sea. Starting on the Atlantic coast and going to the Pacific Ocean you will find casinos in almost all the states and provinces of North America.*

## Canada

Canada has about 60 casinos in eight of its ten provinces, and the gambling authorized is large and quite varied. They also have temporary casino sites, which operate during special events like the Calgary stampede in July. Authorized games include blackjack, roulette, Pai-Gow Poker, Let It Ride, Caribbean progressive stud, baccarat, Red Dog, Sic Bo, keno, video poker, and slot machines. Recent laws now allow craps, which is just being introduced to Canadian casinos. Since 1982 Canada has also had tax-free lotteries (for Canadian citizens only), as well as two national lotteries and many regional ones.

## United States

It's been said that the 25 years before the Civil War was the golden age of gambling in America. Gamblers on steamboats practiced their trade in great numbers on the Mississippi and other rivers. But it was in the 1820s when the first casino, as we know them today, was opened on Bourbon Street in New Orleans. A gambler named John Davis provided a casino with great magnificence, costly fixtures, and luxurious furniture. The best wines and food were also provided. Davis supplied the roulette wheels, poker, faro, and blackjack tables for the patrons on a 24-hour, 7-day-a-week schedule. It was a grand place and a very profitable one for Davis.

■ **Bourbon Street** *is as famous today as it was when the first US casino opened here in the early 19th century.*

As with many other adventures, all good things do come to an end. All the gambling houses in Louisiana were eventually closed by reformers, and it took almost 175 years before another casino opened in New Orleans. In 1995 a new casino opened only a short distance from where John Davis had operated his and reestablished gambling in the heart of New Orleans. Today there are 30 states in the United States that operate casinos.

*Trivia...*
*In Minnesota you can gamble at 18 years of age if no alcohol is served in the casino; if alcohol is served you must be 21.*

# US GAMBLING ACTIVITIES

Since the 1980s, gambling in the United States has seen a period of unprecedented growth. Though gambling policy is often controversial, and the activity is still considered a vice in the minds of some Americans, its legal status around the country has clearly moved from prohibition to restricted tolerance.

| State | Activities | State | Activities |
|---|---|---|---|
| **Alabama** | Dog racing, horse racing, Indian bingo | **Illinois** | Riverboat casinos, lottery, horse racing |
| **Alaska** | Bingo, Indian pull tabs | **Indiana** | Riverboat casinos, horse racing, lottery |
| **Arizona** | Indian casinos, dog racing, horse racing, lottery | **Iowa** | Riverboat casinos, Indian casinos, horse racing, dog racing, lottery |
| **Arkansas** | Dog racing, horse racing | | |
| **California** | Indian casinos, horse racing, card rooms, lottery | **Kansas** | Indian casinos, horse racing, dog racing, lottery |
| **Colorado** | Casinos, Indian casinos, horse racing, dog racing, card rooms, lottery | **Kentucky** | Horse racing, lottery |
| | | **Louisiana** | Casinos, Indian casinos, riverboat casinos, horse racing |
| **Connecticut** | Indian casinos, dog racing, lottery, jai-alai | | |
| **Delaware** | Horse racing, lottery, jai-alai, slots | **Maine** | Horse racing, lottery |
| | | **Maryland** | Horse racing, lottery |
| **Florida** | Indian casinos, horse racing, dog racing, cruise ships, card rooms, lottery, jai-alai | **Massachusetts** | Cruise ships, horse racing, dog racing, cruise ships, lottery |
| | | **Michigan** | Casinos, Indian casinos, horse racing, lottery |
| **Georgia** | Cruise ships, lottery | | |
| **Idaho** | Indian casinos, horse racing, lottery | **Minnesota** | Indian casino, horse racing, lottery |

The state of Nevada had a monopoly on casino gambling from 1931 until 1978. That was the year New Jersey approved casino gambling in Atlantic City. With a dozen casinos operating, Atlantic City held a type of monopoly on gambling on the East Coast for many years. In 1981, North Dakota legalized low-stakes blackjack games. As large numbers of non-residents crossed into North Dakota to gamble, officials in other states began to look at gambling in a new light. Starting in 1990, land and riverboat casinos began to open in many states all across the nation. Today, we find casinos operating from New England to Southern California and from the state of Washington to the Florida Keys. Las Vegas remains the number one destination for casino gambling, followed by the Mississippi Gulf Coast, then Atlantic City.

| State | Gambling |
|---|---|
| Mississippi | Riverboat casinos, Indian casinos |
| Missouri | Riverboat casinos, lottery |
| Montana | Indian casinos, horse racing, card rooms, lottery |
| Nebraska | Indian casinos, horse racing, lottery |
| Nevada | Casinos, Indian casinos, card rooms, horse racing |
| New Hampshire | Horse racing, dog racing, lottery |
| New Jersey | Casinos, horse racing, lottery |
| New Mexico | Indian casinos, horse racing |
| New York | Indian casinos, cruise ships, horse racing, lottery |
| North Carolina | Indian casinos |
| North Dakota | Indian casinos, card rooms, horse racing |
| Ohio | Horse racing, lottery |
| Oklahoma | Indian casinos, horse racing |
| Oregon | Indian casinos, horse racing, dog racing, card rooms, lottery |
| Pennsylvania | Horse racing, lottery |
| Rhode Island | Dog racing, lottery, jai-alai |
| South Carolina | Cruise ships |
| South Dakota | Indian casinos, casinos, horse racing, lottery |
| Texas | Indian casinos, horse racing, dog racing, lottery |
| Vermont | Lottery |
| Virginia | Horse racing, lottery |
| Washington | Indian casinos, horse racing, card rooms, lottery |
| Washington DC | Lottery |
| West Virginia | Horse racing, dog racing, lottery |
| Wisconsin | Indian casinos, dog racing, lottery |
| Wyoming | Horse racing |

**INTERNET**

www.americangaming.org

The home page for the American Gaming Association has a lot of industry data and fact sheets related to gambling throughout the United States.

# Big people's playgrounds

TODAY, MONTE CARLO, BADEN-BADEN, *Lake Tahoe, Atlantic City, Las Vegas, Mar del Plata, and Macao, just to name a few casino destinations, could all be considered as Disneylands for big people, a type of theme park for adults. Gambling is only one part of the Fantasyland. For example, a recent survey by the Las Vegas Convention and Visitors Authority found entertainment, shopping, and fine dining had replaced gambling as the top attraction for visitors at casino-resort areas.*

## Monte Carlo

In addition to the four casinos, film festivals, international auto racing, and an aggressive tourist program attract visitors from all over the world to Monte Carlo. It is the playground of the world's rich and famous.

## Baden-Baden

The gateway to the Black Forest, this city, with the oldest casino in Europe, has been a famous health-spa vacation destination for hundreds of years. Every year in August the casino stages the International Horse Races at the Iffezheim racetrack as part of the resort's social calendar. The town also has a big winter skiing program along with world-class mountain climbing.

## Lake Tahoe

Casinos abound around the largest alpine lake in the United States. This natural beauty on top of the Sierra Mountains offers an endless variety of year-round recreation. Skiers from all over the world come to this resort area for some of the best skiing in the country.

## Atlantic City

With 12 casino-hotels, Atlantic City offers plenty of gaming for most people. With 31 million visitors a year, this is a big resort town by any standard. Sixty percent of the overall casino revenue comes from ordinary people who visit by bus every day. Most are known as "small players." They play slot machines rather than the more sophisticated table games.

# Las Vegas

La Vegas is a one-of-a-kind destination. When you look at the recent casino expansion all across America, wouldn't you suppose it would rob Las Vegas of most if not all of its customers? How does this city, with 98 casinos, in the middle of a desert continue to grow? The answer is really very simple: There is only one Las Vegas. Nowhere else on earth will you find such pleasures, games, diversions, and out-of-this-world attractions: a half-size Eiffel Tower, a Sphinx twice as large as the real one, King Arthur's court, rare white tigers, a roller coaster on top of a 1,149-foot (350-meter) building, a Venice canal with gondolas floating on the second floor, just to name a few local attractions. If you want to gamble and see some modern wonders of the 21st century, Las Vegas is the place to go.

■ **A gambler's dream:** *Las Vegas attracts tourists from all over the world. They come to wager their money in the casinos and see with their own eyes the most outlandish entertainment in all America.*

# 10 *THINGS YOU GOTTA DO WHILE IN LAS VEGAS*

1. Visit the Stratosphere Tower Casino and see two roulette games side by side, one with a single zero and the other with both the single zero and double zero.

2. Visit downtown and see where the World Series of poker is played every year at Binion's Horseshoe Casino.

3. While downtown, see the world's largest gold nugget in the Golden Nugget Casino.

4. Visit the MGM Grand and see the largest casino in all of Nevada.

5. Visit "Bugsy" Siegel's shrine at the Flamingo Hilton.

6. Visit the Tropicana and go to the Casino Legends Hall of Fame.

BINION'S HORSESHOE CASINO

THE GOLDEN NUGGET CASINO

7. Visit the Monte Carlo Casino and view the outside, modeled after the casino in Monaco. (The casino also has single-zero roulette games.)

8. Bingo lovers should get over to Ellis Island Casino for their free daily bingo session from 9 to 10 a.m.

9. Take advantage of the free gaming lessons offered by many large casinos throughout Las Vegas.

10. Visit Caesars Sportsbook, one of the biggest and best in town.

## Mar del Plata, Argentina

This famous seaside resort with three casinos has been a haven for wealthy Argentines for almost 300 years. Besides gaming, it offers sunbathing, swimming, fishing, golf, polo, a yacht club for private boats, and a new 41,000-seat soccer stadium.

## Other destinations

Australia, France, Macao, the Caribbean, and dozens of other countries and areas around the world offer the international visitor fun, exciting places to gamble. The Old and New World have recognized that today's traveler wants to enjoy all the luxuries of the 21st century, and gambling in casinos is another activity to be enjoyed.

**INTERNET**

**www.lvol.com**

*Las Vegas Online Entertainment Guide contains over 1,000 pages of information. The site includes listings of hotels, casinos, nightlife, events, shows, transportation, wedding information, museums, sightseeing, and an RV directory. There is even a poker player's aptitude test listed.*

# A simple summary

✓ Whatever part of the world you want to visit, there is probably a casino waiting for you.

✓ Casinos have been around for almost 200 years, in both the Old World and the New World.

✓ Each region seems to view casinos somewhat differently. In Europe casino gambling is treated as a formal dress-up event. Asian casinos are in five-star hotels. Caribbean casinos make up a big part of its tourist program.

✓ Many of the famous and best-known casinos around the world are located in resort areas.

✓ Casinos have become known as "big people's playgrounds."

# Chapter 21

# Gambling in the Modern World

IF GAMBLING ON LAND ISN'T ENOUGH for you, plenty of cruise ships also offer casino gambling. In addition, there is a large gambling business in the United States that offers shipboard gaming on "cruises to nowhere." When it comes to the Internet, the world of gambling has changed a great deal in just the last few years. Looking up the word gambling on the Internet can lead to almost a million different results. On many of these sites you can either gamble for real money or play for fun. In addition, there are news, tutoring, and general information sites (see the Appendices for a listing of gambling sites). In the United States, Native American, or Indian, casinos have been introduced only in the last 10 years.

## In this chapter...

✓ Cruise ships

✓ Internet gambling

✓ American Indian gambling

# Cruise ships

*AT LAST COUNT* *there were at least 138 cruise ships around the world offering casino gambling. The cruise-ship industry uses casino gaming as an added amenity for their customers, therefore casinos are not designed as the primary reason for a cruise. Although shipboard casinos are similar to land-based ones, there are differences. In Las Vegas or Atlantic City the hotels, restaurants, and shops are all there to serve the casino customer. On cruise ships just the opposite is true. The casinos on cruise ships are considered a bonus for customers rather than the main attraction.*

On the other hand, the so-called cruises-to-nowhere ships, whose primary purpose is gambling, offer little else except a couple of hours of sailing and lots of gambling. These boats simply go outside the territorial waters and cruise around for 6 hours while their passengers gamble, then return to port.

## Trivia...

*Gambling ships must be outside the 3-mile (5-km) limit along the Atlantic coast, but they must sail at least 9 miles (14 km) off shore in the Gulf of Mexico before gambling is legal.*

■ **Getting a sun tan** *and docking in exotic locations are why most people book themselves onto a cruise ship; gambling is simply an added extra.*

## Typical cruise-ship operation

On cruise ships the first thing you will notice is the casino hours of operation. They will vary somewhat, but while at sea they usually open around noon and continue to operate into the early morning. While in port, all countries require shipboard casinos to be closed. Many cruise lines are starting to offer players club programs similar to their land-based competitors. These programs include a cash-back system allowing for on-board purchases, points for future cruise discounts, and other special player incentives.

## Games and limits

The games, rules, and limits are similar to those found on land-based casinos. Blackjack, craps, Caribbean stud poker, American roulette, video poker, and slots are the standard games found on most ships. Poker is popular with many players, and sometimes you can even find a cruise that offers a large poker tournament program. Ship casinos are different from land-based ones: Cruise lines don't want you to experience big losses while on a cruise; therefore, they do enforce some restrictions. Betting limits ranging from $3 to $300 are common on most ships. Slots with denominations ranging from 5¢ to $5 can be found on all ships, with a few offering $25 slot machines. Free gaming lessons and lower minimums are commonly offered during the afternoon periods.

■ **Casino lovers** *can feel very much at home on a gambling cruise-to-nowhere ship where the casinos, though smaller, have all the popular table games and slots.*

## Gambling ships

Through the years Florida voters have consistently disapproved all ballot measures to allow land-based casinos to operate in their state. (There are three Native American casinos that offer slots and poker only.) This has led Florida to acquire the most cruises-to-nowhere ships (17) of any state in the US. New York, Georgia, Massachusetts, and South Carolina also have gambling cruises to nowhere, but with a very limited fleet. Most gambling ships are small in size by Las Vegas standards, but all offer the standard casino games such as blackjack, roulette, craps, Caribbean stud poker, video poker, and slot machines.

*Some ships that sail into the Atlantic can accommodate up to 1,800 players; however, most ships are designed to operate with 200 to 400 players a day.*

Cost for a cruise ranges from free to $30, and most include a buffet. (I've met some patrons who just enjoy the cruise and choose not to gamble at all while on board.)

■ **Elegant and sophisticated,** *the Mississippi's* Casino Queen *cruises daily through St. Louis.*

# Internet gambling

GAMBLING ON THE INTERNET is a new *phenomenon that is growing bigger every day. It's a type of gambling that no one really knows how to manage. Various government agencies all over the world are at a loss as to how to control it or what to do about it in general. The laws passed years ago about interstate gambling don't seem to apply to the Internet. Many Internet gambling companies are located in small Caribbean countries with liberal or nonexistent laws about gambling on the Internet. One example is the Central American country of Costa Rica, where 80 such companies have set up shop since 1995. Among the many reasons for this rapid expansion are cheap labor, very lax business regulations, and no licensing fees.*

**INTERNET**

**www.RGTonline.com**

*Rolling Good Times Online is a comprehensive gambling site. This is a good place to start using the Internet for wagering and obtaining gambling information of all types. With more than 1,000 links, you can find almost all the sites relating to gambling that are on the Internet at the present time.*

## Problems

The Internet does offer every type of casino game plus a large selection of sports betting and racing. However, one of the dilemmas with Internet gambling is how to deal with problems. Whether it's with a game play or a money situation, whom do you contact to resolve your particular problem? In most US states you can go to an outside agency like the state Gaming Commission for help. There is no comparable agency for the Internet.

**INTERNET**

**www.gamblerscorner.com.**

*Go to this site and click on "Online casinos." You'll find a listing of 563 individual online casinos that you can click onto directly. New sites are being added daily, while others have been online for many years.*

*I've been hesitant to engage in Internet gambling because I don't know who is providing the oversight to ensure that all that is being offered is fair and legitimate. I'm sure as regulations come to this industry it will become a safer and fairer gambling option. Until then? I'm not so sure.*

## Free gambling

Besides actually gambling, there are many sites on the World Wide Web that offer free tutorials on how to play and gamble. Name a game and you'll find it on the Internet. Anyone can look up and use the free news, advice, and reports about gambling. Trip reports about various gambling locations and specific casinos are always helpful to a gambler. You can also find basic information and tips on sports betting and horse and dog racing.

**INTERNET**

**www.jme.com**

*This is the author's own web site. You'll find various gaming products, services, free tips, plus a quiz on blackjack. If you have any questions or queries on gaming, go to this site and ask!*

*Nearly anything you can think of about gambling is available on the Internet. My advice is to look it up and use the information that's out there!*

■ **Internet gambling can provide a quiet alternative** *to the bright lights of the casino, but don't submit your credit card details if you have any doubts about the legitimacy of the web site.*

# American Indian gambling

INDIAN GAMBLING IS NOT *as new as some people think. Native American bingo halls have been operated on Indian reservations for many years, long before casinos were established. Today, Indian gaming has become an 8-billion-dollar-a-year business in the United States, but it still represents only 5 percent of the entire gaming industry. Some Native American casinos have the look and feel of a typical Las Vegas casino, others remain as simply large bingo halls.*

### Trivia...

*During the 1990s, Indian gambling was rated as the fastest-growing industry in the world. Today there are more than 150 Native American casinos in the United States.*

## WHERE ARE THE INDIAN CASINOS?

Today there are 26 states that have Native American gambling facilities. Some only have bingo halls, but many others have fully-fledged Las Vegas-style casinos. Both Michigan and Wisconsin have large numbers of Indian casinos throughout the state. Connecticut has the nation's largest Indian casino, Foxwoods. It should be noted that Indian casinos have no government oversight; what that means is that the tribe itself does all the reviews and makes the final decisions. If a patron has a problem there is no outside analysis, the tribe itself settles any disputes. The states that have Native American (Indian) casinos are:

| | |
|---|---|
| Alabama (bingo) | Montana |
| Arizona | Nebraska |
| California | Nevada |
| Colorado | New Mexico |
| Connecticut | New York |
| Florida | North Carolina |
| Idaho | North Dakota |
| Iowa | Oklahoma |
| Kansas | Oregon |
| Louisiana | South Dakota |
| Michigan | Texas |
| Minnesota | Washington |
| Mississippi | Wisconsin |

## A little history

In 1988 the Indian Gaming Regulatory Act was passed, which recognized the right of Native Indian tribes to set up casinos on their reservations in states that already had some form of legalized gambling. Each Indian tribe is required to negotiate a compact with the state agreeing on which games can be offered.

■ **The Casino Sandia** *on the Sandia reservation in Albuquerque, New Mexico, helps generate essential revenue for the local Indian government.*

## A simple summary

✓ Casinos on cruise ships are treated as only one small part of cruising amenities and not as an end in themselves as land-based casinos are.

✓ There are also many cruises-to-nowhere ships in at least five American states. Florida has the most gambling ships, with 17 presently operating.

✓ Internet gambling is very new and becoming more popular each day. This is an area that governments really don't know how to control. Players need to tread carefully when it comes to wagering on the Internet.

✓ Besides the casino and wagering sites on the Internet, there are plenty of sites that offer news, instructions, and information about casinos, games, and gambling in general.

✓ Many Native American casinos have developed in the United States since the lifting of restrictions in 1988.

✓ Today there are 26 states that allow American Indian casinos.

# Card-counting systems

VARIOUS AUTHORS HAVE DEVELOPED *counting systems which they declare are more powerful, more reliable, and more effective than any other count in use against today's modern casinos. I've collected more than 55 different card-counting systems that are known to have been used in actual play in casinos. Some authors claim that their count is more effective when it comes to betting, whereas others claim their count will be more powerful in playing strategies, and still others claim they work very well against insurance. My advice is to pick one that is easy to learn and, more importantly, one you can use successfully in any casino.*

## Reading the chart

Each author has established a specific value for each card. Using the Canfield Expert count as an example: it rates the low cards (3 through 7) as plus-type cards while the high cards (9 and 10 or X), are rated as minus cards, and the 2, 8, and Ace are zero-rated or neutral cards. In card counting, as the little cards are played, the big cards (9's and 10's), still in the deck, can be expected to appear next. The opposite will happen if the big cards appear before the small cards. Remember, little cards help the dealer and big cards help the player. (See "System Selection" in Chapter 6, "Advanced Blackjack").

| Author | Playing card | | | | | | | | | |
|---|---|---|---|---|---|---|---|---|---|---|
| | 2 | 3 | 4 | 5 | 6 | 7 | 8 | 9 | X | A |
| A.W.K. | 1 | 1 | 1 | 2 | 1 | 0 | 0 | 0 | -1 | -2 |
| Andersen/Reppert Pro Research | 1 | 1 | 1 | 2 | 1 | 1 | 0 | -1 | -1 | -2 |
| Braun/Dubner/Wong/Thorp/ Rouge et Noir/Ortiz/Revere/Hi-Lo | 1 | 1 | 1 | 1 | 1 | 0 | 0 | 0 | -1 | -1 |
| Canfield Expert | 0 | 1 | 1 | 1 | 1 | 1 | 0 | -1 | -1 | 0 |
| Canfield Master/Griffin 2/ Omega II | 1 | 1 | 2 | 2 | 2 | 1 | 0 | -1 | -2 | 0 |
| Chambliss-Roginski | .5 | 1 | 1 | 1 | 1 | .5 | 0 | 0 | -1 | -1 |
| Goldberg | 0 | 0 | 0 | 0 | 0 | 0 | 0 | 0 | 1 | 0 |
| Gordon/DHM/Revere advanced | 1 | 1 | 1 | 1 | 0 | 0 | 0 | 0 | -1 | 0 |
| Graham 2/ Ionescu/Tulcea | 1 | 1 | 1 | 1 | 1 | 1 | 0 | 0 | -1 | -2 |
| Graham 7 | 4 | 4 | 5 | 7 | 4 | 3 | 0 | -1 | -1 | -1 |
| Graham advanced/Tulcea | 2 | 2 | 2.5 | 3.5 | 2 | 1.5 | 0 | -.5 | -2.5 | -3 |
| Green Fountain/Koko Ita/Sys Research | 1 | 1 | 1 | 1 | 1 | 1 | 0 | -1 | -5 | -6 |
| Griffin 1 | 0 | 0 | 1 | 1 | 1 | 1 | 0 | 0 | -1 | 0 |
| Griffin 4 | 1 | 2 | 3 | 4 | 3 | 3 | 1 | -1 | -4 | 0 |

| Author | Playing card | | | | | | | | | |
|---|---|---|---|---|---|---|---|---|---|---|
| | 2 | 3 | 4 | 5 | 6 | 7 | 8 | 9 | X | A |
| Griffin 5 | 2 | 2 | 4 | 5 | 4 | 3 | 1 | -1 | -5 | 0 |
| Griffin 7 | 4 | 4 | 5 | 7 | 5 | 3 | 0 | -2 | -5 | -6 |
| Griffin Ultimate | 37 | 45 | 52 | 70 | 46 | 27 | 0 | -17 | -50 | -60 |
| Hi-opt I/Playboy/Austin Einstein/ Silberstaing | 0 | 1 | 1 | 1 | 1 | 0 | 0 | 0 | -1 | 0 |
| Hi-opt II/Accu-count/Steppine | 1 | 1 | 2 | 2 | 1 | 1 | 0 | 0 | -2 | 0 |
| Jacques Noir | 1 | 1 | 1 | 1 | 1 | 1 | 1 | 1 | -2 | -2 |
| Jacques Noir/Archer | 1 | 1 | 1 | 1 | 1 | 1 | 1 | 1 | -2 | 1 |
| Hecher/Goldberg/Casino Holiday/ Roberts KO | 1 | 1 | 1 | 1 | 1 | 1 | 0 | 0 | -1 | -1 |
| McGhee plus–minus | 1 | 1 | 1 | 1 | 1 | 0 | -1 | -1 | -1 | 1 |
| Olsen | 1 | 1 | 1 | 2 | 1 | 1 | 0 | -1 | -1 | -1 |
| Over-under 13 | 1 | 1 | 1 | 0 | 0 | 0 | 0 | 0 | -1 | 1 |
| Precision/Cant-Keen | 1 | 2 | 2 | 2 | 2 | 1 | 0 | -1 | -2 | -1 |
| Qwik | .6 | .6 | .6 | .6 | .6 | .6 | .6 | .6 | -1 | -1 |
| R & T | 1 | 1 | 2 | 2 | 2 | 0 | 0 | 0 | -2 | 0 |
| Revere 5 | 0 | 0 | 0 | 1 | 0 | 0 | 0 | 0 | 0 | 0 |
| Revere 71 | 1 | 2 | 2 | 2 | 2 | 1 | 0 | 0 | -2 | -2 |
| Revere APC | 2 | 3 | 3 | 4 | 3 | 2 | 0 | -1 | -3 | -4 |
| Revere plus–minus | 1 | 1 | 1 | 1 | 1 | 0 | 0 | -1 | -1 | 0 |
| Seri 1 | 1 | 1 | 2 | 3 | 2 | 1 | 0 | 0 | -2 | -2 |
| Seri 2/Wong halves | 1 | 2 | 2 | 3 | 2 | 1 | 0 | -1 | -2 | -2 |
| Seri 3 | 1 | 1 | 2 | 3 | 2 | 1 | 0 | -1 | -2 | -1 |
| Seri 5 | 3 | 3 | 4 | 5 | 4 | 2 | 0 | -1 | -4 | -4 |
| Silver Fox | 1 | 1 | 1 | 1 | 1 | 1 | 0 | -1 | -1 | -1 |
| Skovand | 1 | 1 | 1 | 1 | 1 | 1 | 1 | 0 | 100 | 0 |
| Snyder red-seven | 1 | 1 | 1 | 1 | 1 | .5 | 0 | 0 | -1 | -1 |
| T-Hop 1 | 0 | 1 | 1 | 1 | 1 | 1 | 0 | 0 | -1 | 0 |
| T-Hop 2 | 1 | 1 | 2 | 2 | 2 | 1 | 0 | 0 | -2 | 0 |
| Tekavec | -1 | -1 | -1 | -1 | -1 | -1 | 0 | 1 | 1 | 1 |
| Thorp 10 point/Roberts | 4 | 4 | 4 | 4 | 4 | 4 | 4 | 4 | -9 | 4 |
| Thorp Ultimate | 5 | 6 | 8 | 11 | 6 | 4 | 0 | -3 | -7 | -9 |
| Triple | 1 | 1 | 1 | 2 | 1 | 1 | 0 | -1 | -3 | -2 |
| Uston ace–five | 0 | 0 | 0 | 1 | 0 | 0 | 0 | 0 | 0 | -1 |
| Uston APC/Griffin3 | 1 | 2 | 2 | 3 | 2 | 2 | 1 | -1 | -3 | 0 |
| Uston plus–minus | 0 | 1 | 1 | 1 | 1 | 1 | 0 | 0 | -1 | -1 |
| Uston SS | 2 | 2 | 2 | 3 | 2 | 1 | 0 | -1 | -2 | -2 |
| Uston/Revere APC 73 | 2 | 2 | 3 | 4 | 2 | 1 | 0 | -2 | -3 | 0 |
| Wilson | -1 | -1 | -1 | -1 | -1 | -1 | -1 | -1 | 1 | 4 |
| Wong halves | .5 | 1 | 1 | 1.5 | 1 | .5 | 0 | -.5 | -1 | -1 |
| Zamecnik | 1 | 1 | 1 | 1 | 1 | 1 | 1 | 1 | 2 | 0 |
| Zen | 1 | 1 | 2 | 2 | 2 | 1 | 0 | 0 | -2 | -1 |
| Zen II | 1 | 2 | 2 | 2 | 2 | 1 | 0 | 0 | -2 | -1 |

# Books on Gambling

*THIS LIST CONTAINS 30 how-to-play titles that are recommended by Howard Schwartz, the marketing director of Gambler's Book Club/Shop in Las Vegas. Mr. Schwartz is a recognized authority on popular gaming literature, and his selections are considered the best-selling and most authoritative works of their kind. In this appendix, they are arranged, at his suggestion, by subject.*

## Baccarat

Hebert, Byron. *Power Baccarat 2.*
*Hebert and Associates, revised 2000*

> This book covers the basic rules, explains how the game is played, lists card values and totals, explains the 5-percent commission, and covers mini-baccarat. It's perfect for beginners or experienced players.

May, John. *Baccarat for the Clueless.*
*Carol Publishing, 1998*

> This book is excellent for the beginner or somewhat experienced player. It contains a history of the game, compares mini-baccarat to the "big baccarat," and offers ideas and strategies. It also contains sections on card counting and how to analyze the shuffle.

Vernon, David. *Baccarat Made Simple.*
*Self-published, 1994*

> This one's written for the absolute novice. It shows you the table layout, compares the mini-baccarat table to the traditional big game table, explains table etiquette and how to keep records of your play. It also discusses streaks.

## Bingo

Wyrick, John (Dee). *Complete Authoritative Guide to Bingo. Self-published, 1975*

> This book is a nice package of information for beginners, or for anyone who wants to know more about the game than the basics. It includes ways to play various types of games; a computerized coverall odds table; and, for those who are interested, advice on how to start and conduct a bingo game properly.

## Blackjack

Revere, Lawrence. *Playing Blackjack as a Business.*
*Carol Publishing, 1969*

> The strategies and color charts in this book will help anyone master everything from the basics of blackjack to four-deck games. It also offers several counting techniques. This is a must-read for intelligent players.

Uston, Ken. *Million Dollar Blackjack.*
*Carol Publishing, 1981*

> This book was written by the most flamboyant and charismatic player ever. It covers single- and multiple-deck play, includes flashcards, and is ideal for beginners as well as the more advanced players.

Wong, Stanford. *Professional Blackjack.*
*Pi Yee Press, 1994*

This remarkable classic is geared to the player who wants to move from beginner to a more serious level. This work comes from one of the most respected players of all time.

## Caribbean stud, Let It Ride, three-card poker

Ko, Stanley. *Mastering the Game of Caribbean Stud.*
*Gambology, 1998*

This book explains the rules and playing strategies of the game, as well as covering the progressive jackpot. It also contains charts on dealer qualifying frequency, player bluffing, and casino advantages.

Ko, Stanley. *Mastering the Game of Let It Ride.*
*Gambology, 1997*

This book explores the rules of play, including the side bet and the video versions of the game. It presents the basic strategies, and shows expected values of suited and unsuited three- and four-card hands.

Ko, Stanley. *Mastering the Game of Three-card Poker. Gambology, 1999*

This one presents the rules of play; discusses the bonuses; offers an optimal strategy; explores the impact of seeing additional cards; and shows hand rankings.

Scoblete, Frank. *Bold Card Play! Best Strategies for Caribbean Stud, Let It Ride and Three-Card Poker. Bonus Books, 1998*

This one-volume compendium of all three games presents a strategy for playing each of them. Also, the author compares the games, showing you the house edge for each strategy.

## Craps

Grafstein, Sam. *The Dice Doctor.*
*GBC Press, 1981*

This is a must-read book for those who are looking to "grind" a small profit from the tables and who need money-management ideas. It's packed with angles and system ideas from a 50-year veteran of the tables.

Patrick, John. *Craps for the Clueless.*
*Carol Publishing, 1998*

This beginner's guide to craps explains the odds, offers playing strategies and money-management advice, and will help the novice player become more confident.

Tamburin, Henry. *Craps: Take the Money and Run.*
*Research Services Unlimited Publishing, 1995*

This book explains the various bets, discusses gaming etiquette, and identifies the best bets (ten systems are included).

## Keno/video keno

Cowles, David. *Complete Guide to Winning Keno.*
*Cardoza Publishing, 1996*

This is a fine reference guidebook for a beginner or a somewhat experienced player, as it covers every aspect of the game (including progressive jackpots; combination, way, and king tickets; multigame tickets; odds; video keno; tournaments; and reporting winnings to the IRS).

Davis, M.G. *Beating Video Keno. Self-published, 2000*

This is geared for beginners – it includes information on how to pick numbers; the value of a four-spot; playing five-, six-, and seven-spots (or higher); scattering; applying money management; and the ESP factor.

# Poker

*Percy, George. Seven-Card Stud: The Waiting Game.*
*Self-published, 1979*

> After more than 20 years in print, this is still one of the best books for the low-limit seven-card stud player who must show patience and play conservatively to survive. It emphasizes the importance of knowing the odds; discusses timing in bluffing; promotes self-discipline; and explains when to call on the first round.

*Sklansky, David. Hold 'em Poker.*
*Two Plus Two Publishing, 1976 (revised 1996)*

> This is one of the most important beginner's books ($1-$4-$8 level) for a limit player to read on the hottest version of poker of our time. This book should get most beginners started correctly, with explanations of the importance and rankings of your first two cards; the correct interpretation of the flop; bluffing; raising; reading hands; and reading opponents.

# Roulette

*Jensen, Marten. Secrets of Winning Roulette.*
*Cardoza Publishing, 1998*

> This book begins with the basics and moves up to advanced techniques for beating the game. It includes the "biased wheel" approach to winning, and discusses classic systems.

*Miller, J.R. Roulette for the Weekend Gambler.*
*Flying M Publishing, 1995*

> This book explains the basics, illustrates virtually every type of bet, and discusses betting systems. It's educational and entertaining – for the recreational player.

# Slot machines

*Grochowski, John. The Slot Machine Answer Book.*
*Bonus Books, 1999*

> This book focuses on answering the most commonly asked questions about slots – how they work, how they've changed, and how to find an edge (if one exists). It also explains how machines differ, discusses myths and misconceptions, and offers some history of the machines.

*Scoblete, Frank. Break the One-Armed Bandits.*
*Bonus Books, 1994*

> This makes for fascinating reading for someone who's never played the machines. It covers payback percentages, playing techniques, and strategies for avoiding scams and rip-offs in a casino.

# Sports betting

*Lang, Arne. Sports Betting 101.*
*Gambler's Book Club Press, 1992*

> Subtitled "Making Sense of the Bookie Business and the Business of Beating the Bookie," this book answers basic questions about betting football, basketball, hockey, and boxing. It includes a history of bookmaking and handicapping, and explains the terminology used by bookies and bettors.

*Mendelsohn, Marty. The Theory and Practice of Las Vegas-Style Sports Betting. GBC Press, 2000*

> The author actually taught a class on the topic at the University of Nevada Las Vegas. Here he describes the components for a winning sports handicapper to master, including selection and getting value – especially for those who "shop" for key numbers on which to wager.

# Thoroughbred racing/ greyhound racing

Hamilton, Ross. *Greyhound Racing for Profit.*
*Gambler's Book Club Press, 1981*
  This one explains the basics of
  handicapping, with specific emphasis on
  betting the quinella (picking dogs that
  come in first and second). It discusses
  early speed, position, and consistency,
  along with other important factors.

Smith, Sharon. *The Complete Idiot's Guide to*
*Betting on Horses. Macmillan Publishing, 1998*
  This is an easy guidebook to the
  fundamentals of thoroughbred
  handicapping. It explains everything
  from how to read the *Daily Racing Form*
  to the importance of jockeys and the role
  of trainers.

# Video poker

Dancer, Bob. *10-7 Double Bonus Video Poker.*
*Privately published, 1996*
  This book contains various charts and
  strategies for playing this very popular
  machine, coming from one of the most
  respected experts in the industry.

Dancer, Bob. *9-6 Jacks or Better Video Poker.*
*Privately published, 1996*
  This book presents a direct approach to
  beating the basic video-poker game, telling
  you what cards to keep, what strategies will
  keep your bankroll intact longer, and so
  on. It also includes practice hands.

Paymar, Dan. *Video Poker – Optimum Play.*
*ConJelCo, 1998*
  This book is a virtual encyclopedia of
  material on the game, including ideas and
  strategies for Jacks or Better; Deuces Wild;
  Joker Wild; and dozens of other variations of
  video poker. It includes information on slot
  clubs, probabilities, and random numbers.

Scoblete, Frank. *Victory at Video Poker.*
*Bonus Books, 1995*
  This book provides a nice introduction to
  Jacks or Better; Joker Poker; Deuces Wild
  Video Poker; and other novelty games. It
  also contains material on video blackjack,
  video craps, and video keno.

*If you can't find these books in your local*
*bookstore, contact Gambler's Book Shop, 630*
*South 11th Street, Las Vegas, NV 89101 to place*
*an order. They may be contacted toll-free at*
*1-800-522-1777, or via their web site at*
**www.gamblersbook.com**.

**Author footnote:**
One general book that Howard didn't list is
*101 Casino Gambling Tips* by John Marchel
(Four Suits Publishing, 1998). As you
might have noticed, this is a book written
by the author of this book. It covers tips
on blackjack, craps, roulette, baccarat, slots,
keno, and even bingo. Whether you go to
the casino once a year or weekly, this book
is for you. It contains the tips, tricks, and
strategies for getting the upper hand.

# Gambling magazines

GAMBLING MAGAZINES AND NEWSLETTERS *can be an important part of staying current about the world of gambling. New ideas, upcoming tournaments, advanced playing instructions, and new places to play are all reported in these publications by leading experts in their fields. I believe that every little bit of information and advice can help you play better. The following is a list of worldwide magazines and newsletters that specialize in gambling. Some concentrate on casino gambling, while others focus on horse racing or sporting events. Write or call about subscription rates, and ask for a complimentary copy before you decide to subscribe.*

Atlantic City Insider
8025 Black Horse Pike, Suite 470
West Atlantic City, NJ 08232
(609) 641-3200

Baccarat Quarterly Newsletter
309 Orizaba Avenue
Long Beach, CA 90814
(562) 434-7348

Bingo Bugle Newspaper Group
(bingo/keno)
PO Box 527,
17205 Vashon Highway Southwest,
Building D1
Vashon, WA, 98070
(206) 463-5656
Toll free: 800-327-6437

Bingo Caller Gaming Guide
19607 88th Avenue
Langley, BC V3A 6Y3
Canada
604-888-7477

Bingo Manager
PO Box 720
Wayzata, MN 55391-9966
(612) 473-5088

Blackjack Confidential
513 Salisbury Road
Cherry Hill, NJ 08034
(609) 667-2122

Blackjack Forum
414 Santa Clara Avenue
Oakland, CA 94610
(510) 465-6452

Blackjack Monthly
PO Box 2830
Escondido, CA 92033
(619) 480-8405

Blackjack Review
PO Box 541967
Merritt Island, FL 32954
(407) 452-2957

Canadian Casino News
2100 Hartington Court
Mississauga, ON L5J 2G9
(905) 855-1869

Card Player Magazine
3140 South Polaris, Suite 8
Las Vegas, NV 89102
(702) 871-1720

Casino Boat News & Gaming Report
14 Carteret Street
Staten Island, NY 10307
(718) 984-8710

Casino Chronicle
10880 Crescendo Circle
Boca Raton, FL 33498-4873
(407) 477-3082

Casino Executive
50 South Ninth Street, Suite 200
Minneapolis, MN 55402-3118
(612) 338-1578

Casino Journal
8025 Black Horse Pike, Suite 470
West Atlantic City, NJ 08232
(609) 484-8866

Casino Magazine (Italian and English
language sections)
Via Porro Lambertenghi 28
20159 Milano
Italy
+39 (02) 607-2850

Casino Player
8025 Black Horse Pike, Suite 470
West Atlantic City, NJ 08232
(609) 641-3200

Casino Resort Business
1771 East Flamingo, 208A
Las Vegas, NV 89119
(702) 794-0718
(888) 794-0718

Casino World
The Maltings
50 Bath Street
Gravesend, Kent, DA11 0DF
United Kingdom
+44 (0) 1474 335-087

Chance
125 East 12th Street, Suite 2C
New York, NY 10003
(212) 505-9854

Fortuna Magazine (Gaming in Hungary)
PO Box 1536
Budapest, 114 PF.,356
Hungary
+36 (1) 2016-777 (fax)

Fun & Gaming
PO Box 6448
Reno, NV 89503
(702) 786-3594

Fun 'n' Games
1075 North Albany Ave
Atlantic City, NJ 08401
(609) 345-6623

Gaming for Africa (bi-monthly)
PO Box 2561
North Riding, Johannesburg 2162
South Africa
+27 (11) 704 3147 / 462 7047

Gaming Journal
PO Box 480
Sutherland, NSW 2232
Australia
+61(2) 9521 1437

Gaming Law Review
2 Madison Avenue
Larchmont, NY 10538-1962
(914) 843-3100
Toll free: 800-654-3237

Gaming South Magazine
371 Summit Boulevard, Suite 2
Birmingham, AL 35243
(205) 967-0100

Gaming Times
4089 Spring Mountain Road
Las Vegas, NV 89102
(702) 876-6020

Gaming Today
PO Box 93116
Las Vegas, NV 89193
(702) 798-2069 (FAX)

Grandes Casinos de España
Hermosilla 8
Madrid, 28001
Spain
+34 (1) 431-8422

Grogan Gaming Report
PO Box 359
2620 South Maryland Parkway
Las Vegas, NV 89109
(702) 737-7005

Indian Gaming (quarterly)
125 Maiden Lane
New York, NY 10038
(646) 458-6300
(800) 223-9638

Indian Gaming Magazine
4020 Lake Washington Boulevard
Northeast, Suite 10
Kirkland, WA 98033
(425) 803-2900

Indian Gaming News
Seven Penn Plaza
New York, NY 10001-3900
(212) 594-4120

InterGaming
4 Southlink Business Park, Hamilton Street
Oldham, Lancashire, OL4 1DE
United Kingdom
+44 (0) 161 633 0100

International Gaming & Wagering Business
Seven Penn Plaza
New York, NY 10001
(212) 594-4120

Las Vegas Informer
3540 West Sahara, Suite 164
Las Vegas, NV 89102
(702) 648-7709

Las Vegas Insider
PO Box 1144
Buffalo, NY 14220
(520) 636-1649

Las Vegas Sporting News
850 3rd Street
Whitehall, PA 18052
(800) 325-8259

Laughlin, Nevada Entertainer
2075 Miracle Mile, PO Box 1209
Bullhead City, AZ 86442
(602) 763-2505

Lottery & Casino News
321 New Albany Road
Moorestown, NJ 08057
(609) 778-8900
(800) 367-9681

Lottery Business
125 Maiden Lane
New York, NY 10038
(646) 458-6300
(800) 223-9638

Midwest Gaming & Travel
409 Tenth Street Southeast
Waseca, MN 56093
(507) 835-1662

Midwest Players
2233 University Ave. West, Suite 410
St. Paul, MN 55114
(651) 523-0666

National Gaming Summary,
8025 Black Horse Pike, Suite 470
West Atlantic City, NJ 08232
(800) 486-7529

Nevada Gaming News
Seven Penn Plaza
New York, NY 10001-3900
(212) 594-4120

Passenger Vessel News
PO Box 8662
Metairie, LA 70011
(504) 455-9758

Poker Digest
1255 East Tropicana, Suite 300
Las Vegas, NV 89119
(702) 740-2273

Riverboat Gaming News
Seven Penn Plaza
New York, NY 10001-3900
(212) 594-4120

Slot Manager
125 Maiden Lane
New York, NY 10038
(646) 458-6300
(800) 223-9638

Strictly Slots
5240 S. Eastern Ave.
Las Vegas, NV 89119
(702) 736-8886
(800) 969-0711

Temples of Gambling
Via Villoresi 26
20143 Segrate
Milano
Italy

The Colorado Gambler
8933 East Union Avenue, #220
Greenwood Village, CO 80111
(303) 773-8313

The Crapshooter
PO Box 421440
San Diego, CA 92142-1440
(619) 571-1346

The Gambler Magazine
27013 Pacific Highway South, Suite 333
Kent, WA 98032
(206) 874-5600

The Gaming Industry Weekly Report
177 Main Street, Suite 312
Fort Lee, NJ 07024
(201) 947-4642

The Horseplayer Magazine
PO Box 5365
Beverly Hills, CA 90209-5365
(310) 789-4410
(800) 334-6560

The Nevada Gaming Newsletter
95 Wells Avenue, Suite 3
Newton Centre, MA 02159
(617) 964-6250

Vernat Services L.L.C. (lottery)
12461 Silent Wolf Drive
Manassas, VA 20112
(703) 791-2417

# Record keeping

KEEPING GOOD RECORDS is not only important to the taxman; it's also important from a player's viewpoint. How well you do at a specific casino or game will become obvious if you keep good records. In this appendix, I've provided some tables to help you keep track of your playing. Most games are listed; however, if your game is not listed, you can create your own record. Keeping a good history of where, when, and how much is really what's important. The more you play, the more data will be recorded. As your records grow, you should see some patterns start to develop. For example, you might think you have been doing well at one casino, but a review of the data might show otherwise. It's a good idea to review your records before going on any casino visit.

## BINGO

| Date | Casino | No. of cards | Cost of cards | Win/Lose | Remarks |
|------|--------|--------------|---------------|----------|---------|
|      |        |              |               |          |         |
|      |        |              |               |          |         |
|      |        |              |               |          |         |
|      |        |              |               |          |         |
|      |        |              |               |          |         |
|      |        |              |               |          |         |
|      |        |              |               |          |         |
|      |        |              |               |          |         |
|      |        |              |               |          |         |
|      |        |              |               |          |         |
|      |        |              |               |          |         |
|      |        |              |               |          |         |
|      |        |              |               |          |         |

## BLACKJACK

Shift:  **D** = Day   **S** = Swing   **G** = Grave

| Date | Casino | Shift | No. of decks/ No. of players | Playing time | Win/Loss | Remarks |
|------|--------|-------|------------------------------|--------------|----------|---------|
|      |        |       |                              |              |          |         |
|      |        |       |                              |              |          |         |
|      |        |       |                              |              |          |         |
|      |        |       |                              |              |          |         |
|      |        |       |                              |              |          |         |
|      |        |       |                              |              |          |         |
|      |        |       |                              |              |          |         |
|      |        |       |                              |              |          |         |
|      |        |       |                              |              |          |         |
|      |        |       |                              |              |          |         |
|      |        |       |                              |              |          |         |
|      |        |       |                              |              |          |         |

## CRAPS

Shift:  **D** = Day   **S** = Swing   **G** = Grave

| Date | Casino | Shift | Buy-in | Cash out (+ or −) | Remarks |
|------|--------|-------|--------|-------------------|---------|
|      |        |       |        |                   |         |
|      |        |       |        |                   |         |
|      |        |       |        |                   |         |
|      |        |       |        |                   |         |
|      |        |       |        |                   |         |
|      |        |       |        |                   |         |
|      |        |       |        |                   |         |
|      |        |       |        |                   |         |
|      |        |       |        |                   |         |
|      |        |       |        |                   |         |
|      |        |       |        |                   |         |
|      |        |       |        |                   |         |

## KENO

| Date | Casino | No. of numbers | Cost of game | Win/Lose | Remarks |
|------|--------|----------------|--------------|----------|---------|
|      |        |                |              |          |         |
|      |        |                |              |          |         |
|      |        |                |              |          |         |
|      |        |                |              |          |         |
|      |        |                |              |          |         |
|      |        |                |              |          |         |
|      |        |                |              |          |         |
|      |        |                |              |          |         |
|      |        |                |              |          |         |
|      |        |                |              |          |         |
|      |        |                |              |          |         |
|      |        |                |              |          |         |

## POKER

| Date | Casino | Game | Buy-in | Cash-out (+ or −) | Remarks |
|------|--------|------|--------|-------------------|---------|
|      |        |      |        |                   |         |
|      |        |      |        |                   |         |
|      |        |      |        |                   |         |
|      |        |      |        |                   |         |
|      |        |      |        |                   |         |
|      |        |      |        |                   |         |
|      |        |      |        |                   |         |
|      |        |      |        |                   |         |
|      |        |      |        |                   |         |
|      |        |      |        |                   |         |
|      |        |      |        |                   |         |
|      |        |      |        |                   |         |

## ROULETTE

| Date | Casino | Shift | Table no. | Win/Lose | Playing time | Remarks |
|------|--------|-------|-----------|----------|--------------|---------|
|      |        |       |           |          |              |         |
|      |        |       |           |          |              |         |
|      |        |       |           |          |              |         |
|      |        |       |           |          |              |         |
|      |        |       |           |          |              |         |
|      |        |       |           |          |              |         |
|      |        |       |           |          |              |         |
|      |        |       |           |          |              |         |
|      |        |       |           |          |              |         |
|      |        |       |           |          |              |         |
|      |        |       |           |          |              |         |
|      |        |       |           |          |              |         |

## SLOTS

| Date | Casino | Coins start/finish | Mach. no. | Hours | Win/Lose | Remarks |
|------|--------|--------------------|-----------|-------|----------|---------|
|      |        |                    |           |       |          |         |
|      |        |                    |           |       |          |         |
|      |        |                    |           |       |          |         |
|      |        |                    |           |       |          |         |
|      |        |                    |           |       |          |         |
|      |        |                    |           |       |          |         |
|      |        |                    |           |       |          |         |
|      |        |                    |           |       |          |         |
|      |        |                    |           |       |          |         |
|      |        |                    |           |       |          |         |
|      |        |                    |           |       |          |         |
|      |        |                    |           |       |          |         |
|      |        |                    |           |       |          |         |

# Gaming on the Web

THE WORLD WIDE WEB has become a very large library available right in your own home, with so much gambling information available that no one person can review it all. You can sign up for newsletters about the gaming industry, or you can participate in chat rooms. You can gamble for fun or even bet real money on the Net. You can find studies about all aspects of past and present gaming. There appears to be no limit to what is showing up on the Net even as you read this.

What I have listed here are web sites that I have found helpful in learning, studying, and playing casino games and betting on sporting events. I am not advocating sponsorship for any of them; I just think they can be useful to you in learning more about your game.

**www.americangaming.org**
The American Gaming Association site is the official web site for the US gaming industry. It has a lot of data about gambling throughout the US.

**www.audiovegas.com**
Las Vegas radio personality Larry Grossman offers a wealth of resources on gambling, with interviews from experts on betting, casino games, sports books, poker, and more.

**www.bclc.com**
The British Columbia Lottery Corporation site lists current lottery numbers, past draws, prize claims and winners.

**www.betonsports.com**
This sportsbook site prides itself on paying their winning customers faster than any other Internet sportsbook.

**www.betwwts.com**
The World Wide Telesports sportsbook, which is licensed in Antigua, offers its members an excellent referral bonus and along with a terrific comp program.

**www.bingocanada.com**
This Canadian site offers online bingo games, a bingo forum, and links to other bingo web sites.

**www.bingo-directory.com**
The Bingo Directory Yellow Pages of bingo halls is the most comprehensive and up-to-date listing of bingo halls in the US and Canada.

**www.bingoseek.com**
The Bingo Seek web site has more than over 1,000 links, all related to bingo.

**www.bjmath.com**
The heart of this web site is the mathematics of blackjack. The articles discuss mathematical proofs, explanations, and discussions with experts on various subjects of math and blackjack.

**www.BJRnet.com**
This gambling information site is for advanced players and card counters. There are more than 45 message boards, chat rooms, casino blackjack rules and conditions, and free links for serious players.

www.blackjack.com

You'll find blackjack charts, rules, and a lot more for blackjack players at this site.

www.blackjackinfo.com

Here you can learn the basic strategies for blackjack. The site also features casino rules and answers to frequently asked questions (FAQs), and you can receive a free custom strategy chart by inputting specific casino rules.

www.britishcasinos.co.uk

This site provides information about all the casinos located in the UK.

www.canadiancasinoguide.com

This online guideoffers reviews and information about casinos in Canada.

www.cardplayer.com

At the *Card Player* magazine web site, you'll find selections from the print magazine, as well as merchandise and listings of upcoming events.

www.casinocenter.com

The web site for Casino Journal Publishing Group, a publisher of leading magazines and reports about gambling, has lots of articles by industry experts.

www.casinocontrolnsw.gov.au

This site contains rules and regulations for gambling in Australia with links to each state.

www.casinocity.com

This directory of thousands of casinos worldwide includes games offered, restaurants, amenities, location maps, and news.

www.casinogaming.com

This good gaming information site has a schedule of upcoming Nevada casino tournaments.

www.conjelco.com/faq/craps.html

This site offers lots of answers to frequently asked questions (FAQs) about casino craps.

www.craps.casino.com

This good site about the basics of craps has lots of articles, strategies, and quizzes about playing this fun and exciting game.

www.cybersportsbook.com

This sportsbook has very low minimum bets and a low deposit requirement. You can make a lot of bets, starting at $10, while getting your feet wet betting on the Internet.

www.drf2000.com

The *Daily Racing Form* magazine site has loads of racing information.

www.ebay.com

This auction site is where you find all kinds of gambling paraphernalia. Every day new items are added. It's an interesting place to visit on the Internet.

www.european-poker.com

Here you'll find a comprehensive look at the poker scene in Europe, with player rankings, club information, player profiles, a photo gallery, and contacts.

www.gamble.co.uk

This busy English site provides news, articles, forum and tips.

www.gamblersanonymous.org

This is the official Gamblers Anonymous web site. Answer the 20 questions to make sure you don't have a gambling problem.

www.gamblersbook.com

This is the Internet site for the GamblersBook Store, the original 1960s book store for gambling books, videos, and software, located in Las Vegas. Every gambler needs to visit here in person or on the Net.

**www.gamblesearch.com/casino.html**
A Gamblesearch Edition claims to have the best sports and gambling links anywhere on the Net. Their motto is, "If it's gambling, it's here."

**www.gambleup.com**
This site is a large directory of casinos, lottery games and results, games, handicapping info, books, and even collectibles. This fun site has excellent lifelike graphics allowing you to practice and perfect your gaming skills.

**www.gambling.jaxworld.com**
Lots of slot and video-poker information plus some good playing tips can be found on this web site.

**www.gamblinglinks.com**
Here you'll find a very large directory of gambling links that includes reviews, articles, books, and forums.

**www.gambling4dummies.ocm**
At this source for tips and instruction on baccarat, blackjack, craps, and roulette, you can also get tips on advanced topics such as money management.

**www.gamblingmagazine.com**
This online gambling magazine has over 150 casino and gambling links. It's a good place to visit any time.

**www.gamemasteronline.com**
The Game Master arcade has online casino gaming at no cost. It offers casino games including blackjack, Spanish 21, video poker, slots, roulette, craps, and more.

**www.interexna.com/freebj.html**
This good site helps you practice your blackjack skills over and over again.

**www.iplayslots.com**
This site contains loads of slot machine information, as well as offering a free e-mail newsletter. Check out the tips, strategies, online play, information on where to buy a vintage slot machine, and lots more.

**www.jme.com**
Go to this site for some gambling tips. Take a blackjack quiz, and see lots of products for winning at blackjack. It's also this author's own web site.

**www.kanzen.com/roulette.html**
Here you'll find Kanzen's roulette strategies. Pick up some free tips and learn how to succeed at roulette. You'll also find related gambling links.

**www.lasvegas.com**
This is a must-see web site before going taking a trip to Las Vegas.

**www.lottery.com**
All US lottery results, past and current, can be found at this site. Even a video is available to watch the weekly Powerball drawing.

**www.lvol.com**
This Las Vegas Online Entertainment Guide has more than 1,000 pages of Las Vegas information.

**www.playersedge.com**
This online gambling magazine has articles by experts in their fields. It also has an interactive question-and- answer column for players.

**www.pokerdigest.com**
At the *Poker Digest* magazine web site, you'll find a summary of the monthly issue with a few articles available on the site, plus a small list of links.

**www.rbstaxes.com**

This is the web site of R.B.S. Tax Services, known for their book *The Tax Guide for Gamblers*, a comprehensive book on the subject. The site has links to other pages dealing with gambling and taxes.

**www.slot-secrets.com**

You'll find everything you wanted to know about slots at this site. It explains in detail machine externals, internals, slot math, advanced math and much more.

**www.slots.casino.com**

This is a very big slot web site with lots of information, many articles, and free online newsletters. This is a great web site for slot players.

**www.sports.com**

A good Internet site about European sports, this is also a multilanguage web site.

**www.sportselect.com**

This Canadian site for Proline explains how to play and provides point spreads on hockey, football, baseball, and soccer games.

**www.stretchcall.com**

Click on "Site Search" and type in the word "bets." A list of relevant options will appear. Select "The Starting Gate" for an excellent betting tutorial, descriptions of payoffs, and info on reading the daily racing program.

**www.suntimes.com/index/grochowski.html**

Go here for author and *Chicago Sun-Times* gambling columnist John Grochowski's current gaming articles, which should be helpful to all players.

**www.tabracing.com.au**

This informative site provides information and form guides for betting on the horses, greyhounds, and harness racing in Australia.

**www.thegamblersedge.com**

Lots of different games, plus tips, strategies, glossaries, and even some history about specific games are included on this large web site.

**www.thehouseofcards.com**

The House of Cards site features all the traditional and family card games. You can learn the rules to new games, download software, and play games online. There is also information about playing cards themselves, from history to collecting. Use the directory to find what you're looking for.

**www.thewizardofodds.com**

The Wizard of Odds is a large site to help you gain an understanding of casino games. It has a very good section on gaming probabilities.

**www.vegasinsider.com**

This sportsbook has lots of articles and up-to-date information on handicapping major sporting events.

# A simple glossary

**Ace adjustment** Adjusting for the number of aces. remaining to be played in order to determine bet size in blackjack.

**Ace-poor** Having a lower-than-average number of aces remaining to be played; favors the house.

**Ace-rich** Having a higher-than-average number of aces remaining to be played; favors the player.

**Act** Action adapted by card counters in blackjack to give the impression that they are not skilled players.

**Action** The total dollar amount bet by a player on all hands played over a given period of time.

**Aggregate limit** The maximum amount paid out at a keno game regardless of the number of winners.

**All-in** To run out of chips while betting or calling. In table stakes games, a player may not go into his pocket for more money during a hand. If he runs out, a side pot is created that he no longer can participate in, though he can still win the pot he has put chips into.

**Also-ran** A horse that does not finish among the first three.

**American wheel** A roulette wheel with both a single "0" and double "0."

**Anchor man** The last player seated at a blackjack table; also called "third baseman."

**Ante** A small portion of a bet contributed by each player to start the pot at the beginning of a poker hand.

**Any craps** A wager that the shooter will next roll a 2, 3, or 12.

**Back-counting** Counting down a deck or shoe, but not playing at the table; usually standing behind the players.

**Back-line odds** A don't-come wager on a craps layout betting that the shooter will lose.

**Backstretch** The straightway on the far side of the racetrack.

**Bank** The playing stake of a player or team.

**Bankroll** The amount of money a player brings to the casino or track to gamble.

**Bar** To exclude a player from a casino or prevent him or her from playing; barring.

**Barrier** The starting gate.

**Basic strategy** In blackjack, the mathematically optimum way for players to play their hands for a given set of house rules.

**Betting ratio** The mathematical ratio between the highest and the lowest bets placed by a player.

**Betting the true count** A blackjack player's bet that matches the true count.

**Biased wheel** A roulette wheel that has an imperfection allowing numbers to appear out of proportion to their probability.

**Black** $100 chip, normally black in color.

**Black book** A list of excluded players, normally containing photos and data relating to cheats and card counters.

**Blackjack** An ace and ten-count card on the first two cards dealt.

**Blind** A forced bet or ante in poker put in by one or more players before any cards are dealt. Typically, blinds are put in by the first and second players immediately to the left of the dealer button.

**Blind bet** To bet without seeing one's cards.

**Blower** The air machine used to select keno numbers.

**Bluff** In poker, attempting to win the round with an inferior hand.

**Board** All the community cards in view in a Texas hold 'em poker game – the flop, turn, and river cards together form the "board."

**Break the deck** To shuffle up the cards or decks.

**Burn** To discard the top card from the deck, face down. This is done at the beginning of a new deal or between each betting round in poker before putting out the next community card. It is security against any player recognizing the next card to be used or dealt.

**Burn card** The card that is burned, or discarded, from the top of the deck. *See also* Burn.

**Bust** In blackjack, to exceed or go over a playing-hand total of 21.

**Button** A white, acrylic disk to indicate who is the designated dealer in poker.

**Buy-in** The original amount of money exchanged for chips by a player.

**Cage** A casino's cashier area.

**Caller** In bingo or keno, the individual running the game and calling out the numbers; in baccarat, the dealer in charge of the game.

**Capping** Adding more chips to a bet after the round has started; in roulette, adding chips after the ball has landed on a number; also known as "past posting."

**Casino host** A casino employee responsible for seeing that players receive comps and other casino amenities.

**Card eat** To spread to multiple hands in order to cause more cards to be dealt in blackjack.

**Carousel** A slot area that includes several machines grouped together.

**Center pot** The first pot created during a poker hand, as opposed to side pots that are created if one or more players goes all-in.

**Check** In poker, not to bet, passing on the option of betting in a specific round.

**Check-raise** To check and then raise later in the same round, an important poker-playing tactic, which is not permitted in some games or venues.

**Checks** Another name for casino chips.

**Chunk** To bet large or to over-bet.

**Clubhouse turn** The turn to the right of the grandstand, so called because the clubhouse is usually to the right of the stands.

**Cold deck** A deck unfavorable to the player. A deck secretly arranged in a special order and intended to replace the deck in play.

**Color up** To exchange smaller denomination chips for larger denomination ones.

**Community cards** In poker, cards placed face up in the center of the table used by all the players along with the cards in their hand. Used in games like Texas hold 'em and Omaha.

**Comp** Short for complimentary, the privilege of using casino-hotel services free of charge; to give a player complimentary services like room, food, and beverage (RFB).

**Conversion factor** The number by which the running count in blackjack is divided or multiplied to find the true count. It is generally equal to the number of full or half decks that have not been put into play.

**Counter** A player who uses a counting system to keep track of cards played to determine whether the deck is favorable or unfavorable.

**Cover** Actions used by counters to disguise that they are skilled players. *See* Act.

**Craps** The numbers totaling 2, 3, or 12 in casino craps.

**Croupier** The French word for casino dealer.

**Cut card** A solid-color plastic card inserted into the deck(s) to cut the deck before play or to determine when the deck will be shuffled.

**C & E** The abbreviation for craps-eleven; a bet that the next throw of the dice will be 2, 3, 11, or 12.

**Dead heat** A photo finish in which two horses are even at the finish line; the race is declared a "dead heat," or tie.

**Dealer** A casino employee who deals the cards, changes chips, makes pay-offs, and plays the house hands according to a fixed set of rules.

**Designated dealer** In poker, when a resident or house dealer does all the dealing, a rotating system is used to define which player is the "official" dealer for each hand.

**Dime** Sometimes known as a $100 bet.

**Double deck** A blackjack game played with two decks of cards.

**Double down** A blackjack option that allows the player to double the value of his or her wager; however, the player is then dealt only one down card.

**Double exposure** A game in which both dealer cards are dealt face up.

**Driving** When a horse is running under extreme pressure, he is said to be driving.

**Drop** The total amount of money and markers wagered at a gaming table.

**Dwelt** A horse that is slow in breaking from the starting gate is said to have "dwelt."

**Early surrender** A player's option of giving up half the wager before the dealer checks the down-card to determine whether he or she has a blackjack.

**Eighth pole** The pole situated 1 furlong (200 meters) before the finish line of a racetrack.

**Entry** Two or more horses in a race, owned by the same stable or trained by the same trainer are termed an "entry" and coupled as a single betting unit, a bet on one being a bet on both.

**Excused** To be withdrawn from a race after the regular time for scratches, a horse must be "excused" by the stewards.

**Expected value** The dollar amount that the player would win or lose in exact accordance with the statistical advantage or disadvantage to the house.

**Extended** A horse running at top speed under extreme pressure by the rider.

**Eye-in-the-sky** TV cameras mounted in the casino ceiling monitoring all action within the casino.

**Face card** Jack, queen, or king in a deck of cards.

**Far turn** The turn off the backstretch of a racetrack.

**Fast** A racetrack at its best condition is said to be fast.

**Field** The entire group of starters in a race.

**First base** The first player to receive cards.

**Five-card Charlie** A bonus popular in home blackjack where a five-card hand totaling 21 or less pays a bonus of 2 to 1 to the player; not found in a casino.

**Flat bet** To bet the same amount on each hand played.

**Floorman** The lowest echelon of pit personnel supervising a casino table game.

**Flop** The first three poker community cards, put out face up, all together, in Texas hold 'em.

**Foul hand** A poker hand that may not be played for one reason or another. A player with a foul hand (for example, too many cards) may not make any claim on any portion of the pot.

**Fractional time** The running time at various points between the start and finish of a race.

**French wheel** A roulette wheel with only a single "0."

**Front loader** A careless dealer who exposes the hole card in the process of dealing.

**Fun book** A coupon book used by casinos to encourage play. Usually contains discounts on food and drink and will sometimes contain 2-for-1 bet coupons.

**Furlong** One-eighth of a mile (220 yd/200 m); originally a "furrow long," or the length of a plowed field.

**Gorilla player** A noncounting player who receives signals from a counter and bets very high stakes in blackjack.

**Green** $25 chip, usually green in color.

**Griffin agent** An employee of the Griffin Detective Agency who is hired by casinos to detect cheats, dishonest employees, and card counters.

**Handicapper** An expert who studies, ranks, and/or wagers on sporting events or races.

**Hard hand** A hand without an ace that cannot be changed.

**Head-on** Playing alone with the dealer; one-on-one with the dealer; the only player.

**Heat** Actions by casino personnel when they suspect a card counter or cheater, normally leading to barring.

**High-end player** A player wagering $25 to $499 per hand.

**High roller** Big bettor ($500 to $19,999 per hand).

**Hit** To request another card from the dealer.

**Hole card** A card dealt face down and not exposed until needed for play.

**Hold** The amount of money retained by the casino after all bets have been paid.

**Homestretch** The straightway leading to the finish line.

**Hot deck** A deck or shoe favorable to the player.

**House** The establishment or owners running the casino, card room, or game.

**In the money** A horse finishing first, second, or third is "in the money."

**Index** The number in the upper left-hand and lower right-hand corners of a playing card that designates its denomination; also referred to as pips.

**Infield** The area within the inner rail of a racetrack.

**Insurance** A side bet when the dealer has an ace up-card that requires the player to wager up to half of the original bet. If the dealer has blackjack, the house pays 2 to 1; if the dealer does not have blackjack, the player loses his/her "insurance" bet and the hands are then played out normally.

**Junket** A trip arranged and subsidized by a casino to bring gamblers to their casino.

**Kicker** An unpaired poker card used to determine the better of two near-equivalent hands; usually a high card like an ace or king.

**King number** A single number circled on a keno ticket that is played in conjunction with other numbers.

**Lay off** When a sportsbook finds that too much money has been bet on one outcome in an event, some of the wagers are passed to another sportsbook.

**Length** The measurement corresponding to the average length of a horse and used to describe winning, or losing, distances. A horse can win, or be beaten, by a length or more, or by fractions thereof: three-quarters of a length, a length, a quarter of a length, a neck, a head, or a nose.

**Low-end player** A player betting less than $25 per hand.

**Maiden race** A race run by horses that have never won a race.

**Mare** A female horse, 5 years or older.

**Marker** An IOU given for chips instead of cash.

**Mechanic** A cheating dealer, one who deals seconds or from the bottom of the deck.

**Minus count** A cumulative negative count of cards in play which is a disadvantage for the player.

**Muck** The pile of playing cards that have been folded or discarded in front of the poker dealer.

**Multiple deck** A game played using two or more decks of cards, usually four, six, or eight decks.

**Money wheel** Another name for the Big Six Wheel.

**Natural** A blackjack or "snapper"; an ace and a ten-valued card on the first two original cards.

**Nickel** $5 chip, normally red in color.

**No-limit** A version of poker in which a player may bet any amount of chips whenever it is his or her turn to bet.

**On the rail** Observing a gambling game but not playing in it.

**Paddock** The area at the racetrack where the horses are saddled and viewed prior to a race. A fenced-off field on a farm.

**Paint** A face card; in blackjack, also a ten spot.

**Pair splitting** In blackjack, dividing cards of identical value into two separate hands, betting an equal amount of the original wager on the second hand.

**Pari-mutuel** A system of betting; normally, all wagers are pooled and winners receive equal amounts according to the number of winners, minus the standard operating deductions.

**Pat hand** A poker hand that a player does not try to improve by drawing additional cards.

**Payback** The long-term expected return of a video or slot machine.

**Payout** The actual receipt of units or the dropping of coins by a machine.

**Penetration** In blackjack, the depth a dealer goes into a deck before reshuffling.

**Pit** One area in a casino that encompasses a group of games. A group of pits makes up the entire gaming area in a casino.

**Pit boss** The casino official who supervises play at a group of games, often supervising the activities of several floormen.

**Plus count** A count in blackjack that favors the player, a positive count.

**Pocket** The face-down cards that only the poker player can see in his or her hand. "He had pocket aces."

**Post** In poker, to put in a blind-bet ante, required when you first sit down in a poker card room game. A player may also be required to post a blind when changing seats at the table moving away from the ante blinds. In horse racing, the starting gate, and also, the finish line.

**Post position** A horse's position in the starting gate from the inner rail outward, which is determined by a drawing at the close of entries prior to the race.

**Post time** The time at which all horses are required to be at the post ready to start.

**Pot** The total amount wagered in a single round or hand.

**Pot limit** A version of poker in which a player can bet up to the amount of money that is in the pot.

**Preferential shuffling** The actions by the dealer of intentionally shuffling decks positive or negative to the player.

**Premium player** One betting $20,000 to $499,999 per hand.

**Press** To increase or double the size of a bet after a win.

**Progressive slots** A machine or group of machines that have no set maximum jackpot but one that increases each time a player inserts a coin.

**Puck** A white-and-black disk used in craps to mark the shooter's point.

**Push** A tie in which the player neither wins nor loses.

**Quads** In poker, four of a kind.

**Quarter pole** On a 1-mile (1.6-km) track, the pole at the turn into the stretch a quarter of a mile (400 m) before the finish.

**Quarter** $25 dollar chip, usually green in color.

**Rainbow** In poker, a flop that contains three different suits, allowing no flush.

**Rake** The commission a card room takes out of a pot as a charge for using the facility.

**Rank** In poker, the numerical value of a specific card.

**Rated** Getting evaluated (getting rated) by the casino on how big a gambler one is; this helps management determine how much comp to grant the player.

**Readable dealer** A blackjack dealer whose hole card can be seen by a player.

**Red** $5 chip, usually red in color.

**Reel** One to five wheels inside a slot machine with symbols printed on each one that can be seen through a glass window.

**Resident dealer** A casino poker dealer, also known as a house dealer, who does all the dealing in a game, but does not play.

**RFB** The abbreviation for room, food, and beverage, the basic comps in a casino.

**Right bettor** In craps, a player who bets the shooter will win.

**River** In poker, the fifth (and final) community card, put face up in the center of the table; also called "fifth street."

**Running count** In blackjack, the cumulative value of all cards played at any given time.

**Scratch** To remove a horse from a race before it starts. Trainers/owners may scratch a horse because the track conditions are not favorable for their horse or because the horse is ill.

**Seconds** Dealing the second card from the deck while appearing to deal the top card; a form of cheating.

**Session** A period of time designated for gambling.

**Shill** A casino employee who plays to generate business for a casino game; in baccarat, he or she is called a starter.

**Shoe** A container or box used to hold undealt playing cards.

**Short shoe** A dealing shoe from which some cards have been removed to benefit the house.

**Showdown** In poker, the point at which all players remaining in the hand turn their cards over to determine who has the best hand.

**Side pot** A pot created in which a poker player has no interest because he or she has run out of chips and was not able to add any chips into this new one. However, this player can still win the chips in the original or center pot.

**Silver** $1 chip, usually silver casino dollars.

**Soft hand** A blackjack hand with an ace, which can be valued as 1 or 11, as the player chooses.

**Split** A player option in blackjack to make two hands from two cards of the same value; e.g., two 10s.

**Split pot** A pot in poker that is shared by two or more players because they had equivalent winning hands.

**Spooking** Spotting the blackjack dealer's hole card from the rear, when the dealer checks to see if he/she has a blackjack, then signaling that information to a player at the dealer's table.

**Spread** To bet or play more than one hand; to spread out.

**Stacked deck** A prearranged deck of cards.

**Stand** A player's decision not to draw additional cards in blackjack.

**Steaming** Playing badly or out-of-control and losing.

**Stiff** A hand that has a small chance of winning; a hand totaling 12 through 16 in blackjack.

**Straddle** In Texas hold 'em poker, an optional extra blind bet, made by the player one to the left of the big blind, equal to twice the big blind bet. This is effectively a raise and forces any player who wants to stay in the round to make two bets even before the cards are dealt.

**String bet** In poker, a bet in which a player fails to get all the chips required for a raise into the pot in one motion. Unless he verbally declares a raise, the player must withdraw the raise and just call.

**Suited** A starting hand in poker in which the first two cards are of the same suit.

**Surrender** A blackjack option allowing the player to give up a hand and forfeit half of the wager for that specific round.

**Table stakes** A rule in poker stipulating that players may not go into their pockets for additional money during a hand but may only use the money or chips in front of them to participate in the current pot. If one player runs out of chips during the hand, a side pot is then created in which that player has no financial interest. All casino poker games are normally played with table stakes.

**Tell** A clue that a player unknowingly reveals about the strength of his or her hand.

**Tap out** To bet the last of your money.

**Third base** In blackjack, the last player or seat before the dealer, the "anchor man" position.

**Time** A request by a poker player to suspend play while deciding what to do. An amount of money collected every half hour by the poker room as payment for use of the facilities. *See also* rake.

**Toke** A tip given to a casino employee by a player.

**Totalizator** A machine for recording bets and computing payouts in pari-mutuel betting.

**Totalizator board** The display board in the infield on which is posted electronically data essential to the race visitor such as approximate odds, total amount bet in each pool, track condition, post time, time of day, result of race, official sign or inquiry or objection sign if a foul is claimed, running time- and pay-off prices after the race is declared official.

**Trips** Three of a kind in poker.

**True count** The running count adjusted for the number of cards or decks remaining to be played in blackjack.

**Turn** The fourth community card in poker. Placed face up on the board, by itself. Also known as "fourth street."

**Twenty-one** Another name for blackjack.

**Under the gun** The position of the player who acts first in a betting round.

**Underdog** A person or team not favored to win a sporting event.

**Unit** A measurement in place of dollars; if a player's basic minimum bet is $5 that would represent one unit, three units would be $15. A basic $25 player betting three units would represent $75.

**Up-card** In blackjack, the dealer's card that is exposed to the players.

**Vigorish** The actual percent commission that a casino charges for various bets, also known as the vig.

**Whale** A casino player wagering $50,000 or more per hand.

**Win rate** How much a player wins, normally expressed as dollars per hour.

**Wired** To have a good blackjack hand, usually a 20.

**Wrong better** In craps, a bettor who wagers against the shooter.

# Index

# Acknowledgments

## Author's acknowledgments

I want to thank Beth Adelman and LaVonne Carlson-Finnerty at DK for selecting me to write this fun and challenging book. I need to give a special thanks to Jennifer Williams for maintaining her patience and providing encouragement throughout the entire project, which I greatly appreciated. I can't forget Matthew X. Kiernan, my editor, who kept me on the straight and narrow. Other thanks goes to Howard Schwartz, marketing director, Gamblers Book Club/Shop who knows more about gambling that anyone. Ron Ohlhausen of Instructional Services, of Henderson, Nevada. Through the years, Ron has developed the best strategy cards on casino gambling. I also need to thank a good friend and follow player Steve Bursey. Steve knows more about craps and plays it better than anyone I've ever seen. A special thanks goes to William Powell of Sacramento who kept my computer in tip top shape in spite of my long hours of abusing it.

## Publisher's Acknowledgments

Dorling Kindersley would like to thank Carta Mundi UK Ltd for the loan of their playing card illustrations, Anthony Pitt, Parade Bookmakers, Hereford, Ron Walton, Neal Cobourne for jacket design, Beth Apple for jacket text, Melanie Simmonds for picture research, Barbara Hogan Galvin for consultancy work, Sue Lightfoot for the index, and Jenny Lane and Jane Sarluis for editorial assistance.

## Picture Credits